Cat Hunters

by

P. Clauss

"Cat Hunters"
P. Clauss

Published by P. Clauss Scriptor
ISBN 979-8-9853413-2-4

This is a work of fiction. Unless otherwise indicated, all the names, characters,
businesses, places, events, and incidents in this book are either the product of the
author's imagination or used in a fictitious manner. Any resemblance to actual
persons, living or dead, or actual events is purely coincidental.

Due to the dynamic nature of the Internet, any site addresses or links included in
this book may have changed or become invalid since publication.

Cover Art and Design Mitch Foust

Dedication

To everyone in my cat loving family…
You understand…

Acknowledgement

My deepest gratitude to Kathy Locatelli for her editorial work and kind words!

To my supportive husband and children, I couldn't do this without you!

To those who have read my books and have given positive reviews, you help to fire up my creative engines!! Thank you for your encouragement and support!

To Mr. Joseph Tate at Tate & Co Licensing, thank you for your help in connecting me with a marvelous artist!

To Mitch Foust, thank you so much for not only agreeing to do the cover art for this book, but doing it with great energy, interest, and an amazing expression of your wonderful talent!

Table of Contents

Dedication 3
Acknowledgement 3
Prologue 7
Chapter 1 14
Chapter Two 20
Chapter 3 28
Chapter Four 33
Chapter 5 41
Chapter Six 46
Chapter 7 55
Chapter Eight 63
Chapter 9 70
Chapter Ten 74
Chapter 11 82
Chapter Twelve 89
Chapter 13 96
Chapter Fourteen 105
Chapter 15 108
Chapter Sixteen 114
Chapter 17 121
Chapter Eighteen 128
Chapter 19 133
Chapter Twenty 141
Chapter 21 153
Chapter Twenty-two 160
Chapter 23 170
Chapter Twenty-four 174
Chapter 25 179
Chapter Twenty-six 191
Chapter 27 194
Chapter Twenty-eight 199
Chapter 29 207
Chapter Thirty 216
Chapter 31 226
Chapter Thirty-two 228
Chapter 33 237
Chapter Thirty-four 245
Chapter 35 250

Chapter Thirty-six 252
Chapter 37 262
Chapter Thirty-eight 268
Chapter 39 274
Chapter Forty 280
Chapter 41 286
Chapter Forty-two 293
Chapter 43 299
Chapter Forty-four 306
Epilogue 318
BOOKS BY P. CLAUSS 329
AUTHOR BIO 331

Prologue

A woman ran frantically through the forest. Her disheveled, blonde curls caught on grasping tree branches, cruelly jerking her head back then violently forward as her hair was torn out of her scalp. She showed no sign of feeling the pain as she fought her way through the thick mist that curled heavily around the closely grown trees and tore through the stringy moss that hung down like curtains in her path. Her earth-toned long skirts and long-sleeved shirt, both made of sturdy, homespun fabric, were torn and bloodied. Her bloodless face was wet with tears and the cold sweat of pure terror. Her forest home was no longer a peaceful sanctuary but a living nightmare.

As she ran, she tried to avoid thinking about what she had witnessed minutes ago, the recent images burned painfully in her mind. She tried not to replay the gruesome death of her husband and his hunting cat by dog packs. She knew the larger cat was more than capable of fending off dogs, but he couldn't against so many. Since their hut was deep in the forest, she had to run to warn the others and to get help from the village. But when she got there, it was too late. Everyone had already been killed. As far as she knew, she was the only survivor. And she was being hunted.

The last words her husband had yelled to her, before he was pulled under the mass of dogs, were for her to go home. She knew he meant her birth home and not their home because it was now no more. His words echoed and reechoed through her mind as a prod to keep on going no matter what. She ran frantically and clumsily as she tried to breathe deeply but couldn't manage more than short, sobbing gasps. She tried not to cry, knowing she needed to conserve her strength for her escape. She must escape. She had to get to the next village.

Her endurance and agility were seriously hampered by her bulky body. Her huge belly made her slow and ungainly as it dragged her down and made her lungs labor harder along with her panic and exertion. She had to make it to the next village. She had to get her unborn babe to safety.

Suddenly, her water broke as the unexpected onset of heavy labor caused her to double over. She could go no farther; the pains felt like waves of tearing flames from her body's core to the outside. "Oh, no! Oh, no! Oh, Spirit not now! Cannot it wait until safety?!" she sobbed quietly into the misty night. She had no break, no reprieve, as another debilitating wave of pain tore through her as she heard the howling dogs closing in on her.

She fought through the pain as she crawled into a nearby stand of thorny bushes. She forced her way in, her face, hands, and arms punctured and torn as she pushed aside and broke branches until she was into the dense center and was hidden from sight. As she lay down, surrendering to the pain, she knew that the dogs would smell her, but she had a flimsy hope the bushes would give her some protection as she rested, hoping the pains would cease and she could continue her flight. She knew she was not completely safe and neither was her babe if she gave birth now.

"Oh, Spirit! Please, let help come! Please, soon!" she grunted, trying not to scream in agony as the contractions intensified even more. She tried to telepathically contact her house cat kitten that she had sent ahead. She couldn't concentrate enough to make a connection. "Oh, I hope you made it, Anong," she groaned in distress. Her favorite house cat, who had been one of her mother's house cat kittens given to her on her joining day, was now dead. The little cat had fought the attacking dogs ferociously, helping her mistress and her kitten escape. Once the pair had made it into the deep forest, out of sight of the attackers, the terrified woman had sent the kitten ahead for help. "Oh, I hope you made it home. Tell Mamm where I am!"

As she felt darkness flicker around her conscious mind, she became hyperaware of her surroundings. She heard the dogs sniffing for her scent, whining when they locked onto it and trying to push through the thorny branches. Suddenly, she sensed a large, powerful presence near her. She heard a guttural growl then scuffling of the forest floor litter followed by snapping bones and screeches of pain. Then, abruptly, it was all quiet.

In the sudden silence, she muffled a scream as a wave of pain more intense than the others hit. As it suddenly stopped, she felt the babe slip out of her womb. With a determined will and waning strength, she heaved up on her elbows then sat up to lean forward. She wrapped the shivering newborn in her shawl. She was thankful that even in her dazed and exhausted state, the years of medicine woman training took over. She tied off the umbilical cord and used a nearby thorny branch to sever it. She cleared the babe's mouth and nose and sighed thankfully as the babe started to cry. Using the last of her strength, she clutched the tiny life to her bosom and with weary effort, rolled to lie on her side. After curling her body protectively around her child, she looked up through the branches to see the dark blue eyes of a white tiger watching her.

"Oh, please," she cried. "Don't hurt the babe! Take me instead!" She sobbed as she threw her arm out to ward off the animal.

The big cat pushed his face carefully through the branches to sniff her hand and licked it. After nudging her arm back over the babe, the tiger trampled down the surrounding bushes as he circled to curl up around both of them to provide warmth and protection with his huge body.

The woman was too weak to be scared any longer. She felt as if she was starting to float. She could see herself curled around the babe and the big cat around both of them. Suddenly, other great cats surrounded them while an ethereal presence floated over them. It was a woman with bright silver hair and ocean blue eyes who seemed as real as the mist that lay between the trees. The figure had bent down to look closer at the babe. After her scrutiny, she beamed a huge smile, her eyes shining brightly with unshed tears. "You have arrived at last," she whispered, her voice hoarse with deep emotion. She placed her hand on the babe's head as a single silver tear fell from her eye onto the babe's forehead.

The new mother continued to feel disconnected as she looked on the scene with an out-of-body sensation. The apparition looked from the babe to her and smiled sadly. "I am sorry, my dear. Very soon it will be time for you to move to the next life. Your babe will be safe." She gestured with a glowing arm to show her an old woman with a torch stumbling through the trees following a small cat.

The young woman sighed in great relief that she had been found. She looked back to find the apparition had disappeared. She also saw that the other great cats had melted into the darkness to wait. Seeing that the old woman had stopped to assess the situation with wonderment and fear, she forcefully snapped back into her body and opened her eyes. The pain and profound weakness hit her with brutal force, but she hung on because she must, at least for a while. She had to say her goodbyes. Gratefully, she reached out a shaking hand to gently stroke the thick, striped pelt of the white tiger who had stayed curled around her and her baby. She wanted to thank him but could only manage to barely move her lips in silence.

The old woman shook her head and blinked when the misty, silver-haired figure that floated over a white tiger lying on a clump of trampled-down thorn bushes disappeared. She was in shock at what she had witnessed and wasn't sure what to think. Her mind barely registered that she had also seen a large group of great cats that had suddenly vanished. She remained rooted to the spot as she stared at the white tiger who had turned his massive head to look over his shoulder at her with eyes filled with sadness. She was unsure what was going on and didn't know what to do.

When the big cat stood up to reveal a woman lying on her side, the old woman cried out and ran to her. She had instantly recognized her daughter and was overcome with fearful despair. When she reached her side, she cried louder when she saw the blood rushing from the woman's womb and saw that she was dying. It was beyond what the old woman could heal.

She gathered her daughter in her arms as best she was able to do with her holding her baby. As she quietly sang to her, she rocked her gently, taking care with the infant between them. Her daughter's eyes flickered open for a few minutes and the old woman could see that she tried to smile at her. The old woman smiled back as best she could, comforted that her daughter knew she was there. She continued to sing the lullabies of their peoples until her daughter's spirit passed into the world beyond.

As tears streamed freely down her face, she laid her daughter's body gently down onto the ground. For the first time, she looked at the babe, her granddaughter. She marveled how beautiful she was and sorrowed for the loss of her mother. She was grateful that the babe had only known comfort as she had fallen asleep while being held by her mother and grandmother as they rocked and lullabies had been sung.

The howling of dogs close by startled her, snapping her temporarily out of her grief-ridden thoughts. She knew she had to act quickly. She scooped up the newborn and expertly tucked the loose ends of the shawl around her. Clutching the child to her bosom, she started to rise as the dogs howled again. She looked around but couldn't see anything out in the dark mists of the forest. Even though she was afraid of the dogs being so near, she was reluctant to leave her daughter. She stared down at her lifeless form with great sadness. She was conflicted. She didn't want to leave her daughter's body to be mauled by the dogs, but she had to get the babe to safety. She looked at the white tiger standing patiently nearby. Her indecision had frozen her ability to think and act.

The great cat padded over to her and nudged her to go. He turned to start digging a hole near the woman's body. Seeing this, the old woman understood that he would not leave her daughter's body to the dogs. He would bury her deep in the ground.

Tears falling like rain, the old woman nodded her thanks to the white tiger and called the house kitten to her. The small cat had curled up on top of the dead woman, grieving that her companion was no more. The big cat, seeing that the young cat did not want to leave, gently picked her up as if she were a newborn kitten. He set her down on the ground outside the trampled thorn bushes, licked her with his great tongue, and nudged her toward the old woman as if to say she had a babe to look after. The house cat licked the great cat's nose and slowly slunk to the old woman's feet as she kept looking back at her friend's dead body. The old woman stooped down to pet the kitten to reassure her. After they met eyes and nodded to each other, they turned to run through the forest to the old woman's hut. The howling of the dogs grew ever louder and nearer.

Bushes barely rustled around the area as the other great cats started to fan out into the forest. They were in place to make sure the old woman and babe made it to safety.

<u>*Chapter 1*</u>

"What happened, Mamm?" a woman's weak voice came from a straw pallet near the fireplace. "The house cat's yowling awoke me."

Mamm had just stumbled through her hut's door. Her gray hair had tangled in her face, sticking to the tears that still wetted her cheeks. She gently laid the bundle she carried onto her pallet and placed a hand on her lower back. She tried to stretch her crooked frame to stop the muscle spasms from spreading across her lower back and down her legs. "A tragedy. A horror." The old woman's voice cracked with unshed sorrow. She hastily wiped a sleeve across her face to clear the tears.

The young tortoiseshell cat who had arrived with her jumped onto the pallet to sniff at the bundle. She started purring and licking at it as she gently tugged at the wrapped shawl. Mamm knew she wanted to check on the babe.

"What happened?" asked the young woman as she propped herself up on one arm to talk to the woman. "What is that?" she asked as a small cry came from the bundle.

Mamm turned to look sadly at the weak woman in her care. She stood for a few minutes quietly taking measure of the person with her. *How much should I tell her?* she thought as she wondered what to do. The baby started crying louder. She scooped up the bundle to cradle her, trying to soothe the crying child. She made a decision. "It is a babe," she said quietly. "I found her in the forest. She is newborn, and the mother died."

The young woman immediately cried out, clutching the coarse, thickly woven blanket to her breast.

"I believe," the old woman continued, "that she was from the neighbor village, and they were attacked by Dog Hunters tonight."

The younger woman moaned and rocked as she pulled the blankets up higher and held them against her chin. "Should we call the men?" she asked tensely. Her voice trembled in fear even though she stared at the bundle hungrily.

"I will," Mamm answered quickly. She knew she had to settle something else first. "Sylvia, I know you lost your newborn babe a few hours ago. I know your heart aches to hold a babe and you are able to nurse her. Will your husband accept it as your own?"

Sylvia drew back and averted her eyes. "I would hope so," she whispered, "but I do not know."

Mamm, still holding the bundled babe who was quiet at the moment, sat down next to the younger woman as she patted her arm in comfort. She had to remind herself that to give comfort when she needed it herself was the call of the healer woman. She had decided not to tell anyone all the details of the night's events or that the child was her granddaughter. She hoped that this young couple, who had just lost their first child, could take the babe and raise her as their own. She knew the birthing problems that had taken their own child's life would likely keep this young woman from conceiving again. This was their chance to have a child. "I will summon him," she said quietly.

The young woman nodded as she looked down at the blankets that were now gripped in tight folds on her lap. Mamm could see that she dare not hope too much on the outcome as unshed tears shone in her eyes.

Mamm called one of her house cats to her. After linking with her mind, she gave her a message to take to

Sylvia's husband and sent her out into the night. She also summoned the grandmother to her late daughter's house cat. The young cat needed comfort as well. The older cat soon hobbled in and called to the young cat. Her grand-kitten ran to her and accepted her grooming and purring as if she were a nursing kitten again. Watching the pair for a while, the old woman said, "If you take the child, the house cat must go with her."

The young woman was also watching the young cat and nodded in agreement. "If we can take the babe, we will," she promised. Her voice was laden with reluctant hope and fear of disappointment.

They didn't have to wait long as they heard running footsteps stop at the door and an impatient tapping on the wood. Mamm stood stiffly and shuffled to open it. The young man on the other side was pale from worry and breathing hard from his run.

"Is she okay? The cat you sent didn't tell me anything!" he spoke breathlessly as he stepped in. When he saw his wife sitting up, he exclaimed, "Oh, thank the Spirit, she looks better!" He hastened to her, carefully sat on the edge of her pallet, and wrapped his arms around her. As he tenderly embraced her, he looked up at Mamm. "Why did you summon me in the dead of night? I feared the worst!"

"I am sorry, Stel," Mamm started. "The matter is of great urgency." The bundle in her arms started to cry loudly.

Stel stared at the bundle. "That's a babe!" he exclaimed as he looked at his wife and then at the old woman. "But our babe died! I buried him!" He stared hard and long at the bundle, his expression showing how confused he felt.

Mamm rocked the babe as she walked toward them. But the babe continued to cry and became louder as she insisted on being fed. When Mamm stopped to stand in front of the couple, the old woman clutched the newborn to her bosom protectively. "I was summoned into the forest tonight," she started simply. Stel nodded; he understood a healer woman was summoned out all the time. Mamm continued, "There I found a woman who had died in childbirth. The babe was still alive."

"Who was the woman?" Stel asked softly after he respectfully bowed his head briefly.

"I believe from a nearby village. I heard dogs howling in the distance. Her village may have been attacked, and she was running from it."

Suddenly, Stel let his wife go and stood up. "Dog Hunters!" he exclaimed as he paced around in the small hut. "They must be close! I must tell the others!"

Mamm held out a hand. "Yes, Stel. That is important and you can attend to it soon enough. However, the babe needs to be nursed."

Stel stopped suddenly and stared at her. Mamm could see that he understood what she was asking. "You want to know if we will take it as our own," he stated, asking for confirmation.

"Yes."

He looked at his wife. He didn't have to ask. The look of hope and longing on her face told him what she wanted. He sighed heavily and held out his arms. "Has she seen the child?"

Mamm shook her head. "No."

He carefully took the squirming and crying bundle from Mamm. Once he got the babe settled securely in the crook of one arm, he used fingertips from his free hand to move the corner of the shawl that was covering the babe's face. As he gazed at the newborn girl, his face began to radiate joy, his mouth splitting into a wide grin. "She is beautiful! She has my wife's looks and my coloring! She could be our own!" He carefully bent down to gently lay the babe in his wife's arms. "Look upon her, my dearest, and the decision is yours."

Sylvia looked upon the babe. Tears of joy flowed down her face as she smiled brightly. Then she quickly opened her robe and placed the babe to her breast to nurse.

Stel turned to Mamm. "I take that as a 'yes.' We have a daughter!" he exclaimed joyously. After a moment, he sobered suddenly. "How will we explain this to the rest of the village? Everyone already knows our babe died as he entered into this world."

Mamm thought a moment. She knew it was not an unreasonable concern as their people were very suspicious and superstitious. "We could say that there was a girl twin who survived when the boy did not. We could say she was born much later and unexpectedly since we thought there was only one."

"No one would know," Sylvia said quietly. "I've been in here since the labor started. I have seen no one else but Mamm. No one would know whether I had a second child or not."

Stel nodded once as his decision was made, then walked toward the door. "Then it is settled. No one needs to know anything but that she is ours."

Mamm nodded in agreement. She stifled a sigh of relief as she silently thanked the Spirit of the Cat Hunters that everything was working out.

Stel opened the door. "I need to tell the others about the dogs being heard close by." Both women nodded to him as he stepped out into the night, leaving the door ajar in his haste.

Sylvia sat back against the hut wall. Sighing, she relaxed as the babe nursed hungrily. "She is a lusty nurser," she commented as she stroked the soft blonde curls lovingly. "A good thing; I was going to burst!"

"It is a hard thing for a woman to lose a child when the body is ready to take care of one," Mamm said gently.

"Aye," Sylvia murmured. "It is a good thing another babe was there."

Mamm looked sharply at the woman. *Had she already taken the deception in so completely?* she wondered. She watched the woman handle the babe like she was her own and relaxed. *It is better that way for all concerned,* she thought as she stepped toward the door. Before she closed it, she glanced outside. Her gaze fell on the great cat that had been with her daughter. He stood near the forest edge that was adjacent to her hut. The white tiger met her eyes and nodded its massive head as if agreeing with her thoughts. After he dipped his black-and-white-striped head in farewell, he padded silently into the dark and misty forest.

The old woman clutched her shawl around her tightly as a shiver ran up her crooked spine. *Strange events this night,* she thought. *Strange events.* She stepped back into the hut and shut the door.

<u>*Chapter Two*</u>

She grew as other children grew, by leaps and bounds. She played like the others, learned like the others, and seemed to be exactly like the others. The old medicine woman kept watching and waiting. She knew what she had seen at the girl's birth was neither a dream nor her imagination. She knew at some point, the little girl with bouncing blonde curls, named Kilala by her adopted parents, would not be like the others.

"Good day, Mamm," the old woman greeted her. "You are joining the young ones again today?"

This was not the first time the grandmother who taught the small children their basics noticed Mamm sitting close by while she taught.

"It is a fine day, Atun," Mamm replied. "No one else demands my skills today, so I decided to enjoy the sun and watch the young ones."

The other older woman pursed her lips then smiled knowingly. "Ah, I think I understand." She waved her arm over the group of small children sitting in a circle at her feet. "You are looking for an apprentice."

Mamm smiled and nodded. "I think it is time to start considering who it might be."

"I should say so," the other huffed. "We were thinking you were going to leave us without a healer!"

Mamm bit her tongue and let the retort that came quickly die on her lips. She knew Atun was taking a jab at her age. She smiled pleasantly and dropped her gaze to admire all the children. "They are a fine bunch."

Atun smiled and placed her hand on a dark-haired girl. "They are. And this one shows much promise. She is a very quick learner!"

Mamm watched as the girl reached over and pinched a nearby boy on his arm. When the boy yipped in hurt surprise, his reaction was rewarded by a stern rebuke by the teacher who hadn't seen what the girl had done.

"I assume she is one of your grandchildren?" Mamm asked sweetly.

Atun looked away from the boy who was still rubbing his arm. Standing upright with hands on hips, she declared, "Yes, that is true. But that does not change the fact that she is bright!"

Mamm smiled at her knowingly. She knew the grandmother was angling to get a get word in for her descendent. The position of healer woman ranked high in Cat Hunter society and was aggressively pursued by families for their young girls. She knew that when word got around that she was starting to look for an apprentice, all the women who had daughters or granddaughters would want her to notice their kin. "We shall see," she remarked easily to Atun. "There are a few more years until they are old enough for their apprenticeship."

When the other woman looked away to start another lesson, Mamm allowed her eyes to seek out a tousled blonde head. When she spotted her granddaughter, she smiled slightly. Kilala had been watching the interaction between her elders with open curiosity. When the lesson started, she smiled at Mamm then watched her teacher with unusual focus and intensity. She only looked away when an orange tabby kitten brought her a flower. Mamm sat up and watched more closely. She knew that the kitten was not part of the household where the girl lived.

After she observed the girl gently take the flower from the kitten and then rub his whiskers and head in thanks, Mamm sat back against a tree and let her mind drift. She had never seen a break in the social structure. Ever since the Cat Hunter tribe came into existence, there were firm rules that dictated the human and cat roles. Every family had their house cats that helped with household chores, gardening, and rearing of children. They were only sent as messengers to a medicine woman who could have limited communication with them. The other group of cats, the hunter cats, also stayed with one family group. These larger versions of the house cats helped the men hunt as well as acted as protector of the family.

As she thought of the most powerful group of cats of the Cat Hunter tribe, the Sentinels, her mind drifted back to the night of her granddaughter's birth. They only served the Spirit of the Cat Hunters, the leader that was gifted special powers and responsibilities. She had seen the Sentinel of her village that night not too many years past.

She looked back at her granddaughter to see another kitten bring her a flower. Following the black and white kitten's path back, she noticed mother cats sitting in the shadows of the forest. *They are sending her gifts,* Mamm marveled. *This is unheard of.* When another kitten was sent with a flower, Mamm held her breath when the child whose family the grey kitten was bonded to turned and saw him give the flower to Kilala. The other little girl, ginger-haired with a spread of freckles across her face, grabbed the flower away from her granddaughter. This caused the kitten to react by arching his back and spitting at her. The mother cat raced out of the shadows to nab the kitten by the scruff and ran with him back into the forest.

At first, the ginger-haired girl was shocked into silence by the kitten's reaction but then quickly burst into tears. She acted like her hand had been scratched.

"What happened?" the teacher asked sternly. Her lesson had been rudely interrupted. She had been unaware of all the activity going on while she taught.

"My kitten had brought her a flower," she sobbed and pointed at Kilala. "When I took it, because it should be mine, she made it scratch me."

The teacher stood in shock at the story and accusation. She shook herself and declared, "That is ridiculous. Let me see your hand."

Mamm could see the ginger-haired girl's eyes rounded in fear as she faced her teacher. The medicine woman knew she had no injury to show the older woman. The girl kept her other hand over the pretend injury as she made tears flow down her cheeks. "It hurts too much to show," she muttered as an excuse not to reveal her wounds.

"Then you need to go over to the healer woman," Atun said sternly. She dismissed the girl and went back to her lesson.

Mamm sat up and beckoned the girl to her. "Let me see." When she looked at the hand, she noted wide surface scratches. She pursed her lips and inspected the fingernails on the girl's other hand. She nodded to herself as she found what she expected. "I see," she said quietly. "Apparently, that little girl made you scratch yourself?"

The little girl looked up into the older woman's eyes in bleak terror. Then anger clouded them. "No!" She stamped her foot. "The nasty little kitten did it!"

"I will make sure to tell your mother of what you went through today," Mamm said evenly. When she looked up, she saw her granddaughter watching them intently, studying every movement and interaction. Mamm smiled at her in reassurance, then stood up to walk the little girl to her family's hut to make sure the proper story was told.

Mamm continued to keep an eye on her granddaughter and the group of children her age as they grew. As time went by, she watched as Kilala was becoming more excluded from the cliques that children form. The medicine woman knew the other children were jealous of her easy bonding with all of the cats from the village. Some of the parents, hearing stories from their children, also started to notice the strange things surrounding this quiet child.

One day, the medicine woman noticed that the previously hidden patch of black hair at the edge of Kilala's hairline just off the center of her forehead started to grow. By the time of the girl's ninth summer, it had grown out to the length of her hair, a thick black stripe in the middle of her blonde waist-length hair.

"What does it mean?" the mother asked Mamm one day as they sat in the medicine woman's hut. "Where did she come from?" Sylvia added fearfully as she started to remember that Kilala was not her natural child.

"It means," the old woman said softly as she poured a cup of herbal tea that was blended and brewed to relax the worried mother, "that Kilala is destined for greatness."

The other woman's eyes widened in surprise and awe as the tea she drank soothed her worried heart and mind. "She is my only," Sylvia continued softly in reflection. Mamm nodded as she sat across the small table and held the mother's hand. "I couldn't have any others after…" her eyes welled with tears as she cleared her throat several times.

"I understand," the medicine woman murmured as she patted her hand. She had released the other woman from having to finish her sentence about the death of her newborn son.

The other woman smiled gratefully at her through her tears.

"Is there anything the child does to worry you?" the medicine woman asked quietly as she fished for more information.

Sylvia shook her head as she used the edge of her long sleeve to wipe tears from her eyes. "Kilala is a very good girl. Obedient. Trustworthy. Well liked." She stopped as she had a thought. Her eyes widened again as she sat up straighter. "She seems to have a very close relationship with all the cats in the village. You know how the cats of the different ranks bond usually to one person or family. And with that bond, they can communicate the best."

Mamm nodded silently as she waited for more. She had wondered if Kilala's ability had been noticed by her adopted parents.

"She talks with all the cats without problems. They tell her things they wouldn't tell their own people!" She fixed the old woman with a stare. "Only medicine women can do that and only with household cats, right?"

The old woman nodded. "We need limited communications with the cats closest to the family so when they are used as messengers, they can let us know what is wrong," she answered quietly. She gently stirred her tea around in the cup as she thought. She wondered what else the mother had noticed. She didn't have to wait too long.

Sylvia sat back in the wooden chair and looked out of the small window facing the forest. "There have been strange things lately," she muttered as she turned her head to meet the older woman's eyes. "The house cats in the village bring her things. Nothing big – flowers, leaves, nuts, and such." She looked away as she thought further. "We have been having extra game dropped on our doorstep. It's not from our hunter cat. Usually small game, like a bird or rabbit and such."

Mamm nodded to herself. This news further confirmed her suspicions. She sipped her tea as she thought. After a while she looked into the other woman's eyes to ask, "Are these events causing difficulties with the other villagers?"

Sylvia shook her head. "Not for the most part." She thought for a few moments then added, "There may be some jealousy but nothing more."

Mamm sat back in her chair. Even though this news slightly disturbed her, Sylvia's attitude seemed dismissive toward the reactions of the other villagers. The older woman knew jealousy could be a driving force toward evil. She patted the woman's hand once more, then released it. "Let me know if you notice anything further in the child or in the other villagers."

The woman nodded as she stood to leave. She turned back to the seated older woman before she left the hut. "You truly think she is destined for greatness?"

The medicine woman smiled in assurance. "I am sure of it," she stated firmly. She was glad to see the look of a mother's pride back on the woman's face.

∾∾∾∾∾

Soon it was time for the group of children her granddaughter grew up with to start their apprenticeships. As dictated by tradition, the village gathered for the ceremony at which the children chose their trade and were chosen by their mentors. This was true with every occupation except for the position of medicine woman's apprentice. With this one, the medicine woman would select who she wanted as an apprentice and the one chosen could accept or refuse. On this night, Mamm announced her choice. When she spoke Kilala's name, the other villagers gasped in surprise and then muttered angrily. Each of the families that had female offspring had wanted their own to be the choice for the prestigious role of medicine woman's apprentice.

"Kilala," Mamm repeated her name to the restless group. "The position is yours, if you choose."

The pre-teenager gazed at the older woman with unreadable blue eyes as she thought. She glanced at her parents then studied the rest of the villagers as she observed their reactions. She stepped forward into the space between the villagers and the mentors, then hesitated. In moments, the cats of the village gathered around her feet. This show of support from cat-kind for the girl distracted the villagers into a shocked silence. The resultant stretch of absolute quiet allowed Kilala time to fully decide. As she stepped forward toward Mamm, the gathered cats scattered to join their families.

"Thank you." The girl bowed to the medicine woman. "I am here to learn and serve." Her soft voice stated the expected response to a mentor.

As the choosing ceremony continued, Mamm stood with her apprentice. Outwardly, she was calm and respectful to the other mentors and apprentices. Inwardly, she was torn whether this would be the time to reveal her connections to the girl. She looked over at Sylvia and Stel standing across the clearing. They stood proud but were also worried. They seemed to know what she was thinking as their eyes pleaded for her to keep their secret. Even though she knew they had no idea of the extent of the secret, Mamm nodded slightly in their direction, silently agreeing to their wishes.

Chapter 3

Days, months, and years quickly flowed by as Kilala reached eighteen summers, the time of adulthood. She had spent the time since her eleventh summer apprenticing with the medicine woman, who never revealed their relationship or the circumstances of her birth.

During this passing of time, Mamm could tell that Kilala had come to realize that she was different from the others. Her wisdom, knowledge, and abilities far exceeded anyone in the area, including the medicine women from the nearby villages. Many young and old villagers feared her because she was different. With most, the fear was tempered with respect. With some, it was laden with suspicion.

The medicine women from the nearby Cat Hunter villages would gather every month to exchange herbs and medicines as well as knowledge of illness and their remedies. During these meetings, they all started to take notice of the young woman and, without her mentor telling them anything, they started to suspect who walked with them. They didn't have to say a word or ask any questions to confirm their suspicions; the Spirit of the Cat Hunters had appeared to each of them in their dreams. They had also seen the Sentinels, the great cats that served the Spirit of the Cat Hunters and protected their villages. Since they had not seen them in an age, the sightings were considered to be a sign of good things to come.

Mamm knew that they knew what she had suspected by their knowing nods and glances. They all were glad and relieved. It had been too long....

Kilala had noticed everyone around her had changed their attitude toward her. At the meetings, she wondered at the deference given to her by the medicine women when she talked. Her girlhood friends treated her with stiff politeness as if she were a stranger rather than with warm friendship to a person with whom they had grown up. She was mystified by why the villagers, especially the young men, seemed afraid of her. She wondered what was so wrong with her that she was treated so strangely.

Even with the changes in the people around her, she knew she wasn't completely alone. Her mother and father were still warm and supportive, and she had the old medicine woman who kept her busy and treated her like family and never changed her attitude toward her. Life had settled into a predictable pattern that Kilala grew used to and was able to tolerate until one day when everything changed.

Early one morning, before the mists cleared, she was gathering medicinal herbs in the forest when Kilala felt a powerful presence and the sensation of being watched. She slowly stood up from the bush she had been bending over gathering leaves and carefully turned to look around her.

She met the blue eyes of a white tiger sitting calmly between two ancient trees. Immediately, panic threatened to take over. Her heart raced. She broke out in a sweat as her breath came in heavy gasps. She had never seen one of the Sentinels before. Although she had heard the medicine women talk about how glad they were that they saw them again, there was always an undertone of fear. It had been said in tales of the past that the appearance of one could mean judgment and death.

The white tiger seemed to read her thoughts as he gently shook his head. He remained seated, partially closing his eyes while a loud purr reverberated in his broad chest. It was loud enough that she could hear it over the soft sounds of the forest.

With a lifetime of living with cats, she immediately knew she was not in danger. She closed her eyes and allowed the vibration to calm her heart and slow her breathing. Once she was fully relaxed, her fear transformed into curiosity. She wondered why this big cat had appeared to her.

When he sensed that she was at ease, he slowly stood up and padded with stately strides to her side. She resisted the temptation to fondle the great cat's ears. *One didn't do that with a Sentinel, did they?* she thought as she watched as the white tiger sat by her feet then started to purr again as he rubbed her dangling hand with his face. Tentatively, she started petting the broad head and rubbing the ears. She smiled then laughed as the big cat acted like one of the household cats, walking around her with lowered head and rubbing her legs with his face. She felt completely at ease. Her buried feelings of being an outcast disappeared and her loneliness dissipated like the forest mists with the heat of the sunshine. She didn't know why, but she felt that her place was wherever this cat was from.

Both the white tiger and the woman looked up at the sound of rustling leaves. The old medicine woman stood nearby holding onto a sapling branch. She smiled broadly at the pair, then turned to make her slow way back to the village. Her retreating footsteps were as silent as they had been on her approach.

After Kilala made it back to the medicine hut when the white tiger had gone his way, she sat with the medicine woman at the table. "You did that on purpose," she accused Mamm as they sipped herbal tea.

The old woman nodded. "I wanted you to know I was there as a witness. He already knew I was there."

"Who is the white tiger?"

"He is our village's Sentinel."

"If he is to protect our village, why have I not seen him before?"

Mamm took a slow sip from her tea. After she was done, she slowly set the cup on the table, then loosely clasped her hands and rested them next to the cup. Then she looked up at Kilala and said, "There are many of the Cat Hunters who live out their lives without ever seeing their guardian."

"Oh…" Kilala blushed. The encounter had been a rare privilege and she had frolicked with the powerful beast as if he were a household cat. "I wonder what he thinks of me," she muttered.

The old woman laughed quietly and patted the younger woman's hand. "He holds you in high esteem for who you shall be."

To Kilala, Mamm's words had an ominous ring. "What do you mean?" she asked timidly. She had finally adjusted to the fact that she was different than the other villagers and would always be an outsider. The sudden uncertainty of what the future might hold unsettled her.

The medicine woman shook her head. "You must make your choice. You must not know anything else before the time of choosing."

"What is this choosing?" she asked with a tremor in her voice. She was becoming scared. She was worried that she would do the wrong thing. "When will it be?"

Mamm studied her granddaughter closely. She saw how scared she was of the unknown. She decided a little information was allowed. "The Council of Sentinels will choose the time. The medicine women will be told where and when to gather."

"Is this a rite of passage for medicine women?" Kilala asked hopefully. She offered a trembling smile.

"No, my dear. Although, there is a rite for every level of society for the young to step into adulthood, this is different than anything else."

"What am I to choose?"

The old woman looked down at the ancient wooden table, its surface smoothed and oiled by many generations of hands. She couldn't meet the other woman's eyes. She had to swallow a hard lump in her throat before she could whisper hoarsely, "It is whether you will follow your destiny or not." She looked up to gaze in the young woman's eyes. "At the foundation, it can be considered a choice between good and evil."

Chapter Four

Kilala's jaw dropped as she grew cold and numb, a visceral reaction to the old woman's words. Her thoughts became a sudden maelstrom. *Isn't training as a medicine woman my destiny? What else could be my destiny? What am I supposed to do?* She was suddenly terrified that she would choose wrong and somehow unintentionally choose evil. *Am I not good? Why is everything so mysterious? Why does it sound like all the Cat Hunter villages are involved? Why do I feel like I am in the center of everyone's attention?*

After she heard the old woman's words, she left the medicine hut, making an excuse that she had an errand to run. Once she was out of the door, she dashed out into the forest. She wanted to be soothed by the whispering of the wind through the leaves and hear the song of the birds. She wanted to inhale the earthy fragrances and feel the mist caress her cheeks. Tears blurred her vision as her feet flew over leaf-littered paths.

Finally, she had to stop. She was out of breath and soul weary. She sat on a massive stump, a remnant of an ancient tree, to rest and catch her breath. As she looked around the clearing, she suddenly became aware that she had no memory of that part of the forest. She had never needed to venture that far into the ancient trees. As she thought about the direction she had run from the medicine woman's hut, she realized she had headed toward the village that was no more.

All her life, she had heard stories about the destruction of the nearby village by the Dog Hunters. She had heard the whispered questions about why the Sentinels were not able to stop it. She had wondered, along with the elders, what could have happened. But all through her young years, she had never thought to travel through the forest to see the ruined village for herself.

She stood up as she tried to peer through the ancient forest growth to see the destroyed village. When she couldn't see it, she debated about visiting the site she had heard so much about. With the logic that she should see it since she was so close, she started to make her way through the forest toward it. Suddenly, a movement caught her eye. She turned to face a figure wrapped in a filthy and tattered black cloak. A long, wispy, greasy grey beard escaped from the dingy black hood that hid his head and face. A thick, twisted, ebony black staff propped up his hunched form.

"You have come to learn the truth?" the deep grating voice asked, the stringy beard wobbling with each word.

As comical as the movement of the sad excuse for a beard looked, this person frightened her. Kilala knew to the core of her being there was a wrongness about him. She cleared her throat several times to talk, but the words still came out as a frightened croak. "What truth?"

The hunched figure cackled loudly, sending chills up her spine. "They all have lied to you!" the old man's painfully gravelly voice announced gleefully.

"Who?" She was still scared, but her fear was quickly being replaced by anger. "About what?" she asked suspiciously.

The old man lifted his staff to point into the forest. She looked in the direction he indicated and saw a woman running through the forest from the direction of the destroyed village. The fleeing figure was obviously terrified and gasping for breath.

Kilala ran to catch the woman as she fell, but she slipped through her arms like vapor. She jumped back in fright. "She is a phantom," she gasped as a horrified shiver ran through her body.

"The ghost of your mother," the old man croaked loudly.

Kilala glared at him in angry surprise. "My mother is back in the village."

"The one you call mother is not your mother," he stated firmly.

She looked down at the phantom and saw the woman was pregnant and having labor pains. She watched as the babe was delivered and the woman lay dying with the babe in her arms. "She was alone and no one helped her?" Kilala was suddenly angry and distraught. "What was she running from? Alone and she was pregnant, why was there no one with her?" Waves of indignant anger and a profound sense of injustice swept over her. Attracted and fed by these intense emotions, a darkness pressed in on the edges of her mind. It wanted her thoughts and to have control over her.

"I have shown you the truth of your birth!" the old man stated triumphantly.

Kilala looked down where the phantom had lain and knew the woman's body was buried under the soil of the clearing. The darkness pressed in further, wanting her to accept it, to embrace it. It seethed of anger, hatred, unforgiveness, all of which masked a heart of evil. "They lied to me! My mother died alone! Alone and scared!" She clenched her fists and screamed with fury into the forest. "That was wrong! That is injustice." She felt like running back to her adopted village and tearing it down with her bare hands.

The very thought of the years of her being kept in the dark about her real parents and the circumstances of her birth slapped her with feelings of betrayal, adding fuel to her raging anger. The darkness insistently pressed in on her with its deceptive influence as it used the rage and hurt to slowly seep into her soul. When she sensed it, she almost welcomed it as she began to feel stronger than she ever had before. She started to like the sensation of the dark power, ignoring how it made her feel soiled and that she was losing her self-control to its seduction.

As the evil power roared through her, it filled her mind and thoughts. She felt disconnected from her surroundings, and she was on the verge of being completely possessed when she heard a soft, gravelly meow. The familiar sound caused her to put in the effort to hold back the dark advancement as she looked down at her feet.

There sat her companion house cat, Anong, calmly looking up at her. This cat, ancient and gaunt now, had been a young cat when Kilala was born. The old cat meowed again; she insisted that her mistress give her full attention. She had memories she needed to share with her. Kilala fought back against the dark power to regain enough control so she could lock gazes with the brilliant green eyes of her tortoiseshell cat and establish a mental link to see her memories.

Suddenly, out of the mists, she saw Anong as a young kitten running with her mother through the forest. She was linked with their thoughts and saw what they had seen. The village had been caught by surprise in the deep of night. Her father and the rest of the villagers had been slaughtered by the Dog Hunters. The hunter cats had all died while trying to protect their people. The village behind the fleeing pair was engulfed with fire. There was no one to help her mother except for a young cat whose own mother died trying to protect them while they escaped.

Kilala sobbed at the horror of the memory as she realized that there couldn't be anyone with her mother. The village had no time to send word to the other villages for help.

She watched as the woman fell to her knees and then picked up the frightened kitten. Dogs bayed in the forest, the sounds becoming louder as they grew closer. Her mother whispered in Anong's ear to get her mother from a nearby village. The young cat ran as fast as she could, terror adding speed to her paws. She burst into a hut and desperately meowed at the woman who quickly gathered herself to follow the kitten.

Kilala realized she recognized the woman. It was the old medicine woman. *Mamm is my grandmother?* she thought in shock.

The memories continued. As dogs barked and howled all around them, the old woman and kitten traveled as quickly as they could through the dark and misty forest. When they broke through the thick trees into a clearing, they saw a white tiger lying in a clump of bushes. Anong ran up to the white tiger, grateful that he was there. But when he stood up to reveal a woman lying curled up on her side, Anong was horrified. Her mistress's tangled blonde hair was darkened with sweat and plastered to her head. Her skin was pale and shone with a sickly sheen in the torch light. Her eyes were closed, and she was not moving.

The medicine woman rushed toward the woman, then cried with distress when she saw the woman's face. Anong watched fearfully as Mamm quickly examined her daughter, her face twisting in distress when she found the pool of blood underneath her skirts. She desperately tried to stop the gushing blood from the womb, but it wouldn't stop. Anong saw as her mistress moaned softly and stirred. She feebly hugged and then kissed the baby wrapped in her shawl. Her eyes fluttered open long enough to smile up at Mamm before she slipped again into unconsciousness.

Kilala continued in the memories as she saw all the Sentinels gathering in the clearing. They stood around the trampled thorn bushes respectfully as they kept watch on the forest around them. As they sensed that death drew near for the young woman, they bowed their heads and purred softly as Mamm gathered her daughter into her arms. While the old woman gently rocked her and sang softly to her, the new mother slipped into eternal sleep. Anong had been distracted and looked away when she and the Sentinels heard dogs howling nearby. She had seen them looking around with ears swiveling to locate where the sound came from. After they had looked at each other, they moved silently into the forest. It was obvious that they knew the dogs were getting closer.

When Anong had turned back, she was overcome with great sorrow as she watched the medicine woman gently lay her daughter's body on the ground. After the old woman stood up, she looked toward the forest as worry etched her face, causing her wrinkles to deepen. She kept looking at her daughter, the babe, and the great cat, the white tiger, who had remained after the other Sentinels had left. When the black-and-white-striped big cat started to claw at the earth near the woman's body, then stopped to meet the old woman's eyes, a look of understanding passed between them. Anong had watched as the woman bowed to the big cat, gently removed the babe from her daughter's arms, tucked her securely into her own arms, and bent down again to kiss her daughter's forehead. She hastily wiped tears from her eyes and cheeks as she walked quickly into the forest toward her village.

When she had turned to go, Anong was overtaken by grief and gently settled herself onto her mistress's chest. She didn't know what to do or where to go. She had been awash with sorrow and guilt that she hadn't saved her mistress. The white tiger continued to dig a deep a hole near her mistress's body. When he stopped to look at her, he knew she was despondent. When Anong had felt the eyes of the Sentinel on her, she looked up to meet his gaze. He gently told her that she was not at fault and that her path had changed to go with the babe and to help care for her. Anong had been given a clear order and purpose. She had stood up immediately and obeyed. After she nuzzled her dead mistress's face once more, Anong bowed to the great cat, then ran after the medicine woman.

The memories stopped. Kilala became aware of the meadow and the sunshine of a bright day. The dark forest, burning village, and the baying of dogs were lost in the distant past. She could clearly see that the old man had revealed truth, but not all of it. He had purposely geared this encounter to open her up for the darkness to take her over. With these revelations, the full truth had been told, the darkness had been driven back. She knew when the old man realized that he had lost control. But she didn't care or fear his maniacal raging as she gently picked up her ancient cat.

As she hugged the tortoiseshell, she rubbed her face in Anong's soft fur, drying her tears. The old cat's gravelly purr soothed her thoughts. As she held her ear to the old cat's chest, she felt the vibration of her purr pulse through her body. The medicine women knew the vibration of a cat's purr linked perfectly with the rhythms of the human body and soul. As she soaked in the relaxing rhythm of vibrations, she turned her back to the old man.

She knew he was trying to tell her more things. She also knew that what he had to say would have some truth, but with enough left out to twist reality into darkness. She chose to ignore him. The darkness had completely receded from her soul and could leave no scar. She also sensed in her innermost being that not only had the truth driven the darkness out of her mind and soul, but also had made her immune to it to protect her against its influence.

When she turned toward her home village, she met the blue eyes of the white tiger. She stopped and waited. The Sentinel seemed to smile at her as he nodded his head in approval. She curtsied slightly then slipped past him to leave the clearing and find her way back through the forest to her village. She had questions for the medicine woman. *My grandmother*, she reminded herself.

As she walked through the brush and around trees, she heard sounds of a battle behind her in the clearing. She stopped as the roars and screams reached a fever pitch as the crashing through brush and branches intensified. She was tempted to look back as curiosity flared. She was turning her head to look when her cat gently patted her face with a soft paw, her nails carefully pulled back. Kilala looked down to lock eyes with Anong and saw worry and warning in her eyes. "You seem to know more of what is going on than I do," she whispered in the cat's ear as she quickly walked away from the noise.

Chapter 5

They were seated again at the small table with fresh tea. Mamm slowly sipped her tea as she watched her granddaughter stare into her cup. She was waiting patiently for her to speak. Kilala hadn't said a word since coming back to the medicine woman's hut looking extremely tired and pale. The old woman didn't know exactly what happened out in the forest but she knew the young woman was different. Her heart was heavy as she saw how her granddaughter cuddled her ancient house cat as if she were her lifeline. She also could hear the old cat's gravelly purr and saw the arthritic paws kneading the woman's arm as she comforted her human.

Earlier, she had seen the ancient cat come into her hut looking for the young woman. She was going to ask her why she was there when the house cat had pricked up her ears, as if she had been called, and ran as fast as her arthritic joints could move to leave the hut and speed into the forest. The old woman was tempted to follow but decided to boil more water for tea. If she had been needed, she would have been summoned.

৵৵৵৵৵৵

Kilala was exhausted to the core of her being. When she returned to the medicine woman's hut, she simply sat down in the chair across from Mamm. She didn't even look at the older woman while she carefully settled the old cat in her lap. After a deep, shaky breath, she had wordlessly taken the cup offered with a trembling hand. Her thoughts were spinning wildly as if caught in a mighty whirlwind. She needed to be quiet to try to sort out her thoughts and feelings about what she had learned. She sipped her tea slowly and was at the bottom of the cup when she recognized the calming blend of herbs. She sighed heavily as the tea helped to settle the upheaval in her soul.

She didn't know how to start the conversation with the older woman. The rage was gone. The darkness was abolished. But the truth of her origins had its own weight and needed to be sorted. She simply felt weary and a deep loss. Finally, she decided what to say. She looked up and met the old woman's gaze and simply asked, "So, do I call you grandmother?"

Mamm sighed deeply as she smiled gratefully. Tears came to her eyes as she looked at the young woman fondly. "I would be proud to claim you as my kin. Unfortunately, because of the way things are, it would cause complications."

Kilala had a sudden intense desire to know more about her parents. She leaned forward to touch the older woman's hand. "What was my mother's name?"

"Her name was Adara," the old woman whispered as she looked down at her tea. Her tears splashed small rings on the dark surface.

"She was very beautiful," Kilala whispered as she thought back to the vision she had seen in the forest.

"You look very much like her," her grandmother said quietly.

Kilala looked up at her with a slight smile. She had never considered herself beautiful, especially when the young men avoided her. "Was she a medicine woman?"

"Yes. I had taught her everything I knew until she was of age." Mamm took a slow sip of tea, then continued. "She married and moved to your father's village so she could help the people there. They had lost their medicine woman to old age." She lifted the teapot to see if her granddaughter wanted any more tea.

Kilala nodded and held out her cup to be filled. "Did you have any other children?'

"No. And you were her first." The old woman had anticipated the next question.

Kilala sighed. "I think I was secretly hoping for siblings," she said wistfully.

Mamm reached across the table and patted her hand. "You are not alone. Your adoptive parents love you very much. And you have me."

The younger woman nodded slightly as tears came to her eyes. When they spilled over onto her cheeks, she dashed them away with a hasty hand. She refused to think of how things could have been if her mother had lived. *Past is past,* she told herself. *I need to focus on the here and now.*
"How did they come to adopt me and convince everyone that I was their natural born?"

After a thoughtfully slow sip of tea, Mamm sat the cup down and leaned forward on the table. She told her what had happened on the night of her birth. She described the plight of her adoptive mother at the loss of her natural born child and the desire she had to nurture one not her own.

"What would've happened to me if she hadn't just lost a child?" Kilala asked curiously.

"I would've raised you as my own." The old woman gripped the younger hand as she locked gazes with her. "You were better in a family and not burdened by an old woman. Also, if I had raised you, the truth of where you came from would be known. The superstitions of the villagers would have considered you a danger to them because you were from the destroyed village."

The younger woman's eyes widened with the recognition of the truth in her grandmother's words. She nodded slightly to signal that she understood that the secret needed to remain a secret.

They continued to talk as the afternoon spent itself into evening. Kilala asked more questions about her father and the village that had been destroyed. Mamm told her everything she knew. When the younger fell silent in her thoughts, the old woman thought she had satisfied all her questions for the time being. Suddenly, Kilala looked up with an intense expression, more serious than with the previous questions. "Why did a Sentinel bury my mother?"

The medicine woman was taken aback for a moment as she thought, *They showed her that much?* She broke the connection with the younger eyes to look out the small window into the forest. She thought back to that night. She had wondered the same thing at the time but was prevented from dwelling on it with her daughter's death and a newborn granddaughter to care for. "My thoughts are that it was for respect." She looked back to meet the steady gaze of her granddaughter. "The Dog Hunters pack was closing in. I didn't have time to bury her myself and that added to my burden of grief. I didn't want her body to be mauled by dogs." Tears sprang to the old woman's eyes. "I was so relieved when he offered to do it." She dabbed them with the hem of her loose-fitting shirt. "It was an honor that he cared for her to do that." The emotions overwhelmed her as the memories flooded back. She silently sobbed into the rough fabric of the long sleeve of her shirt. Soon she felt young, strong arms gently encircle her shoulders as the younger woman shared in her grief.

As the sorrow that had been bottled up for so many years released, the old woman felt lighter. The time of mourning for both of them had passed and the medicine woman had to prepare for what was next. She knew she would lose her granddaughter to a higher calling and had to prepare the younger woman.

"Tell me what happened in the forest," Mamm urged as Kilala sat down again. "I need to know everything."

Kilala related the events in order as they happened from the point when she left the hut. The older woman listened attentively, only interrupting for more detail. When she was finished, the medicine woman sat back to think. She had noticed that not all of the details of her granddaughter's birth had been told. She reasoned the Spirit had a reason for the omissions and it was not her place to reveal anything else. "You have met the evil one," she stated instead. "He tempted you to walk the path of darkness, of evil." She looked at her granddaughter and smiled. "And you resisted it." She nodded her head slightly several times. "That is good. Very good," she muttered to herself. "Now we wait for the summons."

"From who?"

"The Spirit of the Cat Hunters."

"What will happen?"

The aged head shook slightly side to side. "This occasion has not been completed in many generations. All I know is that all the medicine women and Sentinels will be brought together."

"All in one place?" Kilala asked in amazement. She had never seen all the medicine women in one place and couldn't imagine seeing all of the Sentinels gathered together.

The old woman nodded solemnly. "All in one place."

Chapter Six

The summons came swiftly. That night, the medicine woman heard the low moan of a great cat under her window. With the wan light from a half greater moon and the lesser moons dark, she saw an eerie yellow-green reflection off the eyes of the white tiger when she peered out into the semi-gloomy night. She hastily dressed and grabbed her cloak. When she stepped out into the night, he was waiting by her door.

After they had quietly walked to the family hut of her granddaughter, Mamm tapped lightly on the mud and straw wall next to Kilala's bed. When there was no response, the medicine woman repeated the rhythmic sequence a few more times, then stopped. The great cat's ears swiveled forward as an answering tap was heard. Soon the young woman, fully dressed and cloaked, slipped out the door. She carefully closed and secured the door behind her before she moved toward them.

Without a word, they followed the white tiger through the forest where there were no paths. They walked through fallen foliage, broken twigs, and small branches of the various trees and bushes. They ducked under ancient, gnarled and thick, low-hanging branches and the curtains of moss that hung heavily from them as they wove around tangled, spiny vines. As they traveled deeper into the heart of the ancient forest, the mists that gathered around them thickened with each step. Soon all they could see of their Sentinel was the black tip of his tail. Time seemed to be frozen as they were cocooned in wet, wispy white.

Suddenly, as if they had stepped through an opaque divide from one room to another, they stepped out of the mist into a well-lit clearing that was thickly carpeted with vibrant green, short grass. It was an expansive forest room with large, gnarled tree trunks as walls; their long, spindly branches formed the ceiling, and their leaves created the roof. Huge stones were placed in a circle near the edges of the clearing, allowing for a large, open space of grass in the center. Each of the boulders was unique in texture and colors while all of them had a hollowed out area on the side facing the center of the circle to form a rough stone chair. The atmosphere of the meeting place was thickly silent with mystery and expectations.

"Why are there ten stones?" Kilala barely whispered, her instinctive reaction to the reverential atmosphere.

Mamm didn't seem to hear her as she followed her Sentinel to her place while she nodded to the other women who had already arrived. The white tiger nodded to his comrades: a panther, a lion, a cougar, and a lynx. When she reached a coarsely surfaced, black stone with white crystal delicately veined through it, she sat down in its hollow. The white tiger took a few paces in front of the boulder onto the grassy area and lay down. Wide-eyed as she tried to take in everything at once, Kilala remained standing beside her grandmother.

As they waited, Kilala watched the Sentinels, fascinated by having so many in one area. After a few minutes, she noted subtle shifts in body language that had her wondering if they communicated without sounds. She was soon absorbed in the study of the slight changes in facial features, narrowing of eyes, slight flick of an ear, twitch of whiskers, slight tremble of a tail. She jumped slightly when her grandmother whispered.

"There were ten medicine women. Ten Sentinels. Ten villages," the old woman said softly as she belatedly answered the younger woman's question. "At the last meet, there were seven."

"When was the last meet?"

"Twenty-five summers ago."

"Have all of them been destroyed by Dog Hunters?"

"We know of only one that was destroyed by Dog Hunters. It is not known what happened to the others."

"Are the other young women with those medicine women also in training?" Kilala asked as two medicine women came in with younger ones in tow. Their Sentinels, a puma and a leopard, didn't look pleased. "They are not happy," she added as she whispered to her grandmother.

"Which ones? The medicine women or the girls?"

"The Sentinels," Kilala said as she watched the body language of the new arrivals and the reactions of the ones present.

Mamm glanced at her in surprise then turned back to watch the big cats closely, trying to see what she saw. She was quickly distracted when she saw the newcomers were strangers. "I haven't met these medicine women before." She glanced back at the Sentinels to realize that Kilala was right, the great cats were upset with the women.

"They are from the far side of the forest, closer to Snake Hunters territory," the old woman whispered when she noted which stone seats they sat down in.

"They ..." her granddaughter hesitated as she tried to find the correct words, "don't seem trustworthy."

The old woman chuckled. "Very good try at diplomacy. They are downright unsavory," she muttered under her breath. "I am glad we don't meet often with them."

Kilala was about to ask more questions when a low tone, as if from a giant bell, resounded through the clearing. The deep bass vibration was felt as well as heard. As the reverberation faded, the clearing grew absolutely quiet. An expectant hush fell over everyone. As the seconds flowed into minutes, the silence was gently broken by a rumbling crescendo that grew to vibrate the air. The Sentinels were purring. At the height of the sound, they all stood in unison. Their ears pricked forward as they looked to the same spot in the mist-screened forest.

A figure seemed to materialize as it came through the mists. The bent, wizened woman tottered on feeble legs as she was supported on either side by a lioness and a white tigress. She sat down in the nearest stone chair made of smooth, dark red stone.

All the medicine women had stood up as she entered, then sat down after she had settled in her chair. The big cats lay down. All eyes were on the newcomer.

The ancient woman gazed around the circle with bright blue eyes not dimmed by age. Her thick, steel-gray hair was braided and pinned around her head like a crown. Her blouse and skirt fit loosely but were clean and whole. Her voice was aged but still strong as she addressed everyone in the clearing. "I have not appeared in this form in many years since my body started to enter into advanced age. I have decided to appear once more before my spirit is released to return no more." Her eyes moved over the clearing noting the women present. "What do we have here? Three replacements?" She looked at the big cats. The three Sentinels who had young women with them stood up and padded over to stand in front of her.

As all the medicine women in the circle silently looked uneasily at each other and the young women present, Kilala's attention focused on the ancient woman. She sensed an intense silent conversation between her and the three

Sentinels who were before her. The white tiger stood with confidence, his head held high, his ears forward, with the black tip of his tail slightly waving behind him. The others were crouched down looking downcast. She looked up to meet the bright blue eyes of the ancient woman. At first, she was startled and fearful, but as she continued to gaze into the mysterious woman's eyes, she felt a warmth blanket her then fill her. The ancient nodded slightly with a ghost of a smile on her lips, then she turned her gaze on the other two young women in their turn. As her face became stern, her mouth firming into a slight frown, the Sentinels went back to their positions.

"Why are there three replacements? Only one was chosen." The ancient woman demanded an answer from all those in the clearing.

The leopard village medicine woman stood up abruptly and grabbed the young woman with her by her arm. She dragged her forward to stand in front of the old woman. "She has the mark," she exclaimed as she pointed to a streak of bleached hair among the thick, raven black hair.

The medicine woman from the puma village hustled her charge to the front. "No! She does!" she exclaimed as she pointed to a silver streak behind the ear of a ginger haired girl. "Hers is natural," she spat at the other woman.

The ancient woman shook her head as she waved an arthritic, bony finger at them. "This is not a competition but a birthright." She glared at them fiercely. "Are you spending time with the Snake Hunters?"

Both medicine women were stricken silent as their eyes widened in fear, and they started to shake their heads vigorously. As they slowly retreated backward to their places, they found their voices to deny the accusation loudly and stridently. They finally grew silent as the ancient one stared at them long and hard; suspicion crackled from her like lightening.

After a long silence, the ancient one sighed heavily and sat back into her stone chair. The big cats flanking her relaxed as they sensed her mood shift and knew they wouldn't be needed to spring into action. Her piercing gaze jumped from woman to woman in the meadow. "Any others that would make a statement or a claim?"

No one dared to speak or move. They seemed to be holding their breath.

The ancient one's eyes softened when she gazed at the young woman with her grandmother. Holding out an arthritic hand, she beckoned her forward.

Kilala slowly stepped toward the ancient one. Outwardly, she appeared calm and confident. Inwardly, apprehension battled anticipation. Her soft leather shoes sank into the thick grass as her long skirt skimmed across the surface. She didn't look back but could sense that all the great cats followed her on silent paws. She stopped in front of the ancient and gently held the bony hands that were held out to her. She was afraid she would break the fragile bones.

"You have been chosen by right of birth to be the next Spirit of the Cat Hunter tribe. You have a choice to fulfill this, your destiny, or to decline it for all eternity. Know if you decline, there is a danger that the Cat Hunters will lose their Spirit and therefore lose their voice and protection amongst the tribes." Her eyes locked with Kilala while her voice could be heard by all.

Kilala swallowed hard as she moistened her lips. "Has anyone ever declined?" she asked softly.

The old woman dropped her gaze and answered softly, "Yes."

"What happened to her?"

The ancient woman let go of one of her hands to rub her face wearily. She sat back and stared at the surrounding trees. She looked so sad, Kilala wished she could unask the question. "She lived an unfulfilled life without purpose. She died unwedded and without a legacy or worthy memory."

Kilala nodded slowly. She understood that she was being warned about the consequences of missing her intended destiny. "What happened to the tribe when this happened?"

The Spirit of the Cat Hunters focused on her face again. "I continued as best as I could, far past the intended time. The result..." she raised a feeble arm to gesture toward the empty stone chairs, "I weakened to where I could not protect all the villages." Tears flowed gently over the finely wrinkled cheeks as she stroked the smooth surface of the stone chair where she sat. "Including my own." She wiped the tears from her face as the lioness sitting beside her purred and rubbed up against her to comfort her.

Suddenly, Kilala sensed a deep grief permeating the area. She looked around and saw the mists escape its boundary and start to seep into the clearing. Soon all the medicine women were looking around nervously as they noticed the change.

"I cannot go on," the ancient whispered huskily. Her head hung and body bent as if she had carried a great weight for a long time.

Kilala studied the frail form thoughtfully. She knew that following her destiny would take her away from all she ever knew. She felt something brush her side and looked into the blue eyes of her Sentinel. She looked about her and saw all the other Sentinels crowding around, their eyes seeking hers. They silently pleaded with her to be their leader, to give them structure and purpose. She could sense rather than know that they did not wish to go back to the mindless wildness of their ancestors.

Kilala looked around the area filling with the forest mists. Then she looked into the pleading eyes of her grandmother and the other medicine women she had known all her life. As she met the glares of the two renegade medicine women, she could see that they were troublesome and deceitful. She studied each one of the empty stone chairs, knowing that one of them represented her true village. She knew she had to protect her tribe from forces without and within. With that realization, a fierce instinct welled up inside her. Her destiny was no longer a duty but a desire.

She knelt in front of the ancient woman and reclaimed her other hand and bowed her head. "Go to your well-deserved rest," she said as she gently squeezed the dry, withered hands. "I wholeheartedly take on this position and responsibilities."

The ancient leaned forward to touch forehead to forehead. "It is not all responsibility, my child, but great blessings and power," she whispered so that only Kilala could hear. "Be sure to quickly learn the balance so that you are neither drunk with power nor unduly hampered with the burden of responsibility." She lifted the young woman's face to look into her eyes. "Be careful of affairs of the heart."

The Spirit of the Cat Hunters struggled to her feet as Kilala helped her. The old woman gently turned the younger to face the others. "I am no more. Look to her for strength and guidance. She is the Spirit of our tribe. Serve and obey her well, and she will serve and protect the tribe." Her voice became tight and urgent. "Beware, the days darken and the storm approaches. Be true to the call of the Cat Hunters and to each other."

The ancient woman turned Kilala around to face her. "I wish I could give you proper instruction but I no longer have any time. Trust the Sentinels. Listen to those you trust." As the last words left her mouth, the aged flesh dropped away like a well-worn garment to reveal a bright spirit that was young and virile. The flesh turned into a pile of sand while the spirit splintered into a thousand tiny stars that drifted into the mist and was seen no more.

What the others in the clearing could not see was the shimmering aura that floated where the ancient one had stood. As Kilala stepped into it to turn and face the others, she could feel power wrap around and flow into her like warm, thick honey. As her body hummed with the intensity of the energy, she realized that she could hear the thoughts of every human mind in the meadow.

Chapter 7

She ended the meeting soon after the transfer. All the jumbled thoughts in her mind made her dizzy and nauseated. With effort, she could briefly separate snippets of thoughts from the humans in the clearing. She felt her grandmother's concern and secret pride. She picked up the relief of the others who had seen her growing up. And she saw the lies of the renegades and fully understood the ancient one's reaction to them. The other young women, the supposed candidates, had thoughts of their boyfriends. She had quickly turned away from them, not wanting to risk knowing something she would rather not. She was relieved when the intensity of the mental voices faded into a low mental mutter, like indistinguishable whisperings far away. It was a wordless sound that she could easily disregard.

Before they left, each of the medicine women greeted her individually and bowed to her. Many gave her a small amulet depicting their Sentinel carved from the stone that represented their village. As she slipped the beautifully crafted pieces into her leather script, she wondered if she could fashion a bracelet out of them. The renegades had nothing to give her and simply murmured a few stiff words to her before they slipped into the mists with their charges in tow.

Mamm hung back, waiting for the others to leave. When the area was clear, she approached. After she gave her granddaughter a white tiger cleverly carved from the black stone streaked with white crystal, she started to bow.

Kilala caught her up in a tight hug. "Thank you," she said with tears in her voice. "I may not have known that you were my grandmother, but you have always been there for me."

Her grandmother kissed her on the cheek. "Even though I cannot claim you as kin, you are in my heart," she replied, her voice husky with deeply felt emotions.

"I have left you without an apprentice." She released the older woman as she smiled through her tears.

"We will choose another," Mamm said as she indicated the white tiger sitting nearby. "She will not compare to your talents and skills." She hugged her granddaughter tightly once more, then quickly let go and stepped away from her. "No one is capable of coming close to your abilities." She turned away from her to follow the white tiger into the forests. Before she stepped into the mists that had retreated behind their boundaries after the transfer of power, she turned back and smiled at her.

Kilala smiled back and watched her grandmother until she could no longer see her in the swirling shadows of the cloudy grey and white. She sighed heavily while she looked around the meadow. "Which one is the chair for my original village?"

The white tigress padded to a smooth-surfaced gray stone chair heavily veined with dark green and blue crystals. Kilala walked over to it and sat on the thick, mossy cushion that grew in the hollowed-out part of the boulder. As she stroked the rock on either side, she thought of her birth mother. She wondered if she had ever been able to sit in this chair. She quietly mulled over the idea that her parent's death seemed to be the direct result of the previous candidate's refusal to take over the care of the tribe. Sighing, she let her contemplations drift away from the unchangeable past. She sat back and cleared her mind of all thought.

Within moments, unbidden, wordless images of events swirled through her mind like the mists through the forest. As she slipped into a trance, she witnessed the destruction of a great society. The remnant of humanity that survived by partnering with hunters of the non-human kind. The growth of the resultant tribes leading to fights for territory and resources. The vision faded while showing the losses suffered in each of the tribes from warfare and disease. Once the trance lifted, the memory of what she had seen faded to the faintest impressions like a nearly remembered dream.

Becoming aware of her surroundings again, she shook her head and looked down to see that the lioness and white tigress, who had escorted the ancient woman into the meadow, had stayed with her. Sitting on either side of her feet, they had been patiently waiting and watching her. As she met their gazes, Kilala started to wonder what she was supposed to do next. She stood up and addressed the big cats. "What do I do now? Where do I go?"

Responding to her questions, both females stood and stepped a few feet away and stopped side by side with a small gap between them. Looking back over their shoulders, they met her eyes. As she looked into their gold and blue eyes, she knew she was to follow them. She walked up to stand behind them but they still waited and watched her. Unsure of what to do, she slowly moved forward step by step until she stood between their shoulders. As they gazed up at her with soft eyes, they started to purr. She felt that they wanted her to place her hands on their withers. When she touched them, she started to lightly stroke the lush, thick fur. With that contact, she felt the strong sensation that she was going home, to where she belonged. Along with that, like her first encounter with the white tiger, she felt complete acceptance; the lifetime of stares and whispers was past. With the newly acquired powers from her predecessor, her bond with cat-kind deepened and strengthened. Suddenly, she could hear her new companions' conversation.

"...could understand us then we can figure out what to do." The lioness was talking with the tigress. Kilala could tell that they didn't know she could hear them.

"From what I understand, these things take time," the white tigress said quietly as she looked toward the misted forest. "Look, it is time. We need to go," she said as she stepped forward. The lioness fell in pace with the other big cat.

Kilala walked with them, keeping her hands on their withers as she felt the power of their muscles moving beneath their pelts. She wondered if she should tell them she could hear them when they reached the mists. What she saw in the mist suddenly distracted and shocked her. It was as if her eyes had been opened and she saw wispy tendrils of grey and white move as if they were alive as they encompassed and flowed around all the trees. She was amazed to also see bright spots of flashing luminescence drifting randomly within the thick, foggy substance. She was on the verge of saying something about it when she felt both great cats bunch their muscles for a leap.

The powerful intensity that she felt as the two big cats jumped forward surprised and thrilled her. Their momentum pulled her with them into a glowing vortex that instantly formed by the quickly swirling mists. In a short time, no longer than exhaling a breath of air, she felt firm ground under her feet. They landed as softly as a feather drifting to the ground as the wind intensity settled into a sigh of a gentle breeze.

She used both hands to move her waist length blonde, black-striped hair out of her face where it had settled after the swirling winds had blown it into a messy mop. "Wow!" she reacted as she caught her breath. "That was exciting." Curious about her new surroundings, she simply knotted her hair at the nape of her neck as she looked around.

She stood in the middle of a bright glen facing a high grassy mound with a cave opening on the side nearest her.

Slowly turning around, she saw a clear, bubbling brook near the cave. Surrounding the grassy area were fruit trees and fruit-bearing vines of all types. Beyond them were patches of an assortment of grain-producing stalks waving gently in the slight breeze. As she looked past the grains, all she could see was a solid wall of grayish white.

Am I a prisoner or very protected? she wondered to herself.

The white tigress padded up to her, her huge paws silent in the lush grass. She looked up at the woman, her blue eyes soft but searching.

Suddenly, the new Spirit of the Cat Hunters felt uncertain and, out of that, a vague fear of not knowing what she had gotten herself into. She trembled slightly as she held out her open hand, palm up to the big cat.

The white tigress sniffed at the offered hand then rubbed her muzzle on it. Then she stepped closer to gently butt her head into Kilala's stomach. Purring loudly, she said, "It is for privacy and protection."

Kilala knelt down and hugged the huge white-and-black-striped neck. "Thank you," she said softly, her voice choked with emotion. She was glad to know she wasn't bound to this place without a choice. The area was beautiful but so quiet. Although she wasn't close to the others in the village, she was used to the sounds and sense of their presence.

"You do hear us!" the lioness exclaimed as she watched from a distance.

Kilala turned toward her as she petted the other big cat. "I do. It is clearer now," she said as she reached a hand out to the lioness to invite her forward for petting.

The lioness's golden eyes widened as if surprised, then narrowed as she glanced at the white tigress. Then she ducked her head in a bow as she slowly shook it. "Mistress, you will learn the way of things. I cannot receive such attentions for I am not the mate of your village's guardian."

Kilala looked at the lioness in surprise then turned to look at the white tigress.

The big black-and-white-striped cat calmly met her eyes through half-closed lids as she rolled onto her side and purred.

"Am I restricted in showing my affections?" Kilala asked the white tigress.

"There are expectations," she purred in response. She rolled to her other side to signal her to continue petting. "Certain ways have been adhered to over the centuries."

"And she doesn't want them changed now," the lioness muttered as she made a show of washing her face.

Kilala looked from the contented white tigress to the complaining lioness and sensed tension between the cats. Her thoughts were interrupted by a third voice.

"Don't mind them," commented a puma female, as black as a star-starved night, as she gracefully walked out of the cave. "They've been rivals since they were cubs."

Any further discussion was interrupted by a deep bell tone. They all turned toward the cave as the bass sound reverberated around them.

"What is that?" Kilala asked in a tense whisper, reminded of a similar sound that had announced the arrival of her predecessor.

The white tigress had rolled upright and was standing up when she said, "It is a summons. Follow me." She padded quietly ahead as she led Kilala into the dark cave.

The young woman followed with a nervous curiosity. As she stepped into the darkness, she felt a slight resistance as if she passed through a thin barrier. Once she was inside, she was greeted by a well-lit chamber decorated with bright colors on the walls and brilliant multi-hued fresh flowers of all kinds that filled vases scattered around the room. A simple wooden table and chair were set against the wall. Another more heavily built chair with thickly padded cushions sat near the center of the room. The large cavern was carpeted with separate lengths of thickly woven rugs, leaving none of the stone floor to be seen. Bookcases that hugged the walls were laden with books, carved cats, and various bric-a-brac. On the far wall, at the back of the cavern, hung a curtain that was partially drawn back to show a bed carved into the wall.

Although she took all this in at a glance, it left only a vague impression as she stared at four specters hovering by the chair placed in the middle of the cave. All the ghostly faces appeared relieved as they looked at her.

One of them, a bulky male, with wild, shaggy hair and beard and dressed in bearskin, heaved a loud sigh and muttered in a deep baritone voice, "Finally."

To the right of him was a thin, male figure with penetrating eyes, bald head, bushy eyebrows, and hooked nose and chin. He spoke next with an abrupt question that came across as a sharp command. "Is she gone?"

Kilala nodded mutely. She was stunned into speechlessness.

"She held on as long as she could," said a soft, sibilant voice from a female form to the left of the others who was wearing a hooded cloak covered in scales. Kilala couldn't see a face in the deep shadows of the hood but thought she saw the dim glow of dull green eyes.

The fourth figure hovering to the right of the cloaked female was another male. He wore a grey wolf skin cloak that was fastened with a dull bronze clasp adorned with an engraved wolf head. She could see, over the collar of his cloak, a thick braided collar that hugged his neck. He appeared younger than the other two males with dark mid-length hair and a shadow of a beard and mustache adorning his stern face. He remained silent as he watched her with unreadable, dark brown eyes.

As Kilala studied them, they studied her, giving her enough time to recover from her surprise. Thinking she should look official, she stood erect with her hands clasped loosely in front of her. "I assume you all are the guiding Spirits for the other Hunter tribes," she stated rather than asked. The hovering forms all nodded and remained silent. "I had no idea there was communication between the tribes."

Chapter Eight

Welcome to the Council of the Spirits," said the Spirit of the Eagles, the" bald, thin male. The others softly murmured their welcome except for the Spirit of the Dogs, the younger male. He continued to stare at her boldly and unashamedly.

Kilala gave a slight bow to the hovering specters as she met the gaze of each one, ending with the Spirit of the Dogs. With him, she continued to stare until he finally relented and looked away.

"Are you done with your dominance thing?" the Spirit of the Bears growled lowly at the Spirit of the Dogs.

The Spirit of the Dogs answered with a glare as he lifted a lip into a snarl.

"Stop it!" the Spirit of the Eagles shrieked.

In the following silence, the Spirit of the Snakes hovered closer to Kilala to whisper in a slightly sibilant tone, "Dog boy does that stare-down thing to everyone. All of the Dog Spirits have been like that."

As Kilala nodded that she understood, she was thinking how amazingly human the Spirits acted. Somehow she thought they would act differently, more like mystical and powerful beings.

The white tigress sitting at her feet yawned at her while she telepathically answered her thought. *You are still human but with special powers. There is a Greater Power that is pure that rules all.*

Kilala shot a surprised glance at the big cat. She had never heard of a higher power that was more powerful than the Spirits of the Hunter tribes. She immediately shoved the thought away as she concentrated on what was happening at the moment. She calmly nodded at the white tigress as she settled in the chair to contemplate the group. She decided to ask the uppermost question on her mind. "Why did the Dog Hunters destroy our villages and kill my people?"

They all looked to the Spirit of the Dogs. His downcast expression and lowered gaze spoke of his discomfort, but he didn't answer. She turned to the others. "There are other villages that have been destroyed that border the territories of the other tribes."

The other Spirits also appeared uncomfortable. Before she could speak further, a quiet hiss broke the silence.

"We have all suffered losses," the Spirit of the Snakes whispered loudly enough for all to hear.

Kilala looked sharply at the others. "Is this true?" She had been raised not to trust anyone of the Snake Hunter's tribe, even their Spirit.

The Spirit of the Eagles leveled a penetrating gaze at her. "It is as she has stated," he confirmed with solemn but imperious tones. He was silently supported by the other Spirits as they nodded sadly.

"Who is doing this then?" She looked to each one of them for an answer.

The Spirit of the Bears growled softly, "There is an unknown group hidden within all the tribes that are causing these problems. We have not found them or their leaders."

"We need to start this meeting again," announced the Spirit of the Eagles. "Your questions and concerns are just, but premature. We took the unprecedented tact to come to your haven with this meeting on an emergency basis. There are concerns amongst us due to the fact that you were not able to be mentored in the position you are now in."

"You need to be able to project as we are doing now," growled the Spirit of the Bears.

"We felt that ...," The Spirit of the Eagle Hunters gestured toward the Spirit of the Snakes, "would be the best to teach you." He then added, "If you can trust her."

She cringed at the thought of help from a Snake Hunter. The white tigress nudged her leg. "Our previous mistress considered her a friend."

"I will only be helping with projecting," Snake Hunter Spirit said. "I know many of my tribe are deceitful. I hope you believe that I have learned to admire the Cat Hunters and respect your ways." She nodded to the white tigress. "She will help you with the secrets of the Cat Hunters. Her mistress made sure she knew the ways of gaining those secrets."

Kilala nodded at the Spirit as she reached down to pet the large black-and-white-striped head. Suddenly, she felt bone weary and overwhelmed. She lifted her hand to press it to her brow as she closed her eyes.

"You are exhausted," Snake Hunter Spirit hissed with concern. "We must leave and let her rest," she said as she turned to the others. "I will return to start training when she is rested."

"How will you know?" The Spirit of the Dog Hunters finally spoke, his voice deep and soft.

"I have my ways," she hissed. She made shooing motions with her hands at the others. "Get along, boys. I'll let you know when we are ready." When the others hesitated, Spirit of the Snake Hunters shouted, "Go!"

Each of them bowed to Kilala, then flew out of her haven.

Snake Hunter Spirit shook her head at the space where the spectral images of the men had hovered. "Men!" She drew back her hood to reveal her face and uncover her head.

Kilala stared in surprise.

"Not what you expected, yes?" Snake Hunter Spirit said with a slight smile.

Kilala nodded slowly as she beheld not scaly skin, lipless mouth, nor eyes without lids. The woman's face before her would be regarded as beautiful in any of the tribes. Her pale, oval face, graced by almond eyes and slightly upturned nose, was framed by a head full of flaming red, thin, long dreads. Her full-lipped mouth was slightly distorted with her lower lip caught between small, white teeth as she thoughtfully studied her in return.

"Now," Snake Hunter Spirit continued, "with practice you can alter your spirit form to look like anything you want. Basically, this is me. The only thing different is my darker skin. Oh, and all the snake tattoos." She stopped to think, then added, "and the filed teeth to look like fangs." She hovered closer to Kilala and looked her up and down. "Your tribe doesn't do much as far as body art," she stated matter-of-factly.

Kilala nodded wearily, then opened her mouth to make the effort to speak.

Snake Hunter Spirit stopped her by putting a slender finger to her own lips as she shook her head. "No. Sleep. Under normal conditions the transfer of power is exhausting. And that is for someone prepared. It must be far worse for you," she said sympathetically. "All I ask is if I can leave a little friend who can be my liaison."

Kilala furrowed her brow and was about to ask who when the Spirit of the Snake Hunters stopped her again. "Normally our havens," she gestured around the room with her hands and ended by extending them palms up toward her, "are protected from intrusion from the others by a force fence we erect. You need to set up yours." She nodded toward the cave entrance. Kilala was too weary to turn her head and look. "When you do this, I will not be able to come in, but we will be able to communicate through our friend." When she gestured to the floor, Kilala looked down to see a small, green snake looking up at her with dark eyes filled with curiosity.

At the sight of the reptile, Kilala had the visceral reaction handed down from generations; she pulled up her feet and screamed.

The white tigress sat up, laid her head in her mistress's lap, and purred loudly. "This little one is known to us," she said quietly. Her purring and gentle words helped Kilala settle down her rapidly beating heart. "He came here to be trained by the old mistress to communicate with us and learn our ways."

The adrenaline shock left Kilala's weary body shaking even more. "I am sorry for my reaction," she said, her voice quavering.

Snake Hunter Spirit dismissed it with a careless wave of a hand. "No offense. We expect such. I am sorry to cause you distress, but it needed to be done."

Kilala heard a soft hiss from the floor. "To be truthful, my cat lady," the green snake said respectfully in the language of cats with a slightly hissing undertone, "We usssually take pride in causssing a reaction."

She looked down into the blue eyes of the white tigress. She could swear the big cat's eyes were twinkling in merriment. She lifted an eyebrow in a silent question.

"Our old mistress was amused by the little snake's nickname, cat lady," the tigress said as she rolled to her side and playfully batted at the slender reptile. The snake responded by coiling around one of her paws like an emerald bracelet. "He's fun, too!" she said as she gave the scaly skin a swipe with her rough tongue.

When the little snake let out a long hissing stream of sound, Kilala jumped back in horror until she realized that the creature was laughing! She shook her head slowly in disbelief. *A laughing snake. What next?* Rubbing her face wearily with her hands, she felt even more exhausted and overwhelmed. Everything was becoming cloudy and distant. Sounds and voices seemed to echo. She desperately needed sleep.

"Party's over," she heard someone say but was too out of it to tell who. "Get her to bed," the voice ordered.

She tried to stand but couldn't muster the strength. She vaguely registered a moving sensation and sluggishly worked out that she was being pushed toward the sleeping area. She looked on either side of the solid, dark wood and deeply cushioned chair to see that several male great cats were shouldering the chair to position it alongside her bed.

She crawled onto the comfortable mat with a sigh of relief, then snuggled down into its softness. After she pulled thickly woven blankets over herself, she reached over the side and found a big head to pat. "Thank you," she mumbled. As she drifted between awareness and somnolence, she felt a light thump on the bed and a small weight settled down to curl up on her stomach. At first, she was mildly alarmed that it might be the snake until she realized that the bundle was purring and her fingers brushed soft fur. Feeling secure, she allowed herself to slip into the fullness of a deep, dreamless sleep.

Chapter 9

Slowly, she drifted into consciousness. She rolled onto her side, snuggling into the bed, thinking how so much softer it was, and vaguely wondering what had changed. She felt a cat snuggled next to her, just like at home. Turning to her other side, she flung her arm over the side of her bed and hit something large, hard, furry, and warm.

Hey! a grumpy voice bounced into her sleepy thoughts.

She felt around and found two large, upright ears. "A Sentinel!" she gasped as she bolted upright and opened her eyes. All of a sudden, she started to tremble and her vision blurred as the previous day's events swarmed her memory. A huge muzzle nuzzled her leg as a small purring body sat in her lap and patted gently at her face.

Blinking her eyes rapidly, she came out of the maelstrom of memories and emotions to recall who she was now and where she called home. Her eyes focused on the small cat in her lap, who was trying hard to rub her face on her chin. "Anong!" she exclaimed "I thought I would never see you again!" She tenderly hugged the old, frail cat to her chest.

Looking into her eyes, the old cat spoke, "You have always underestimated me." She shook her head at her as the end of her tail flicked back and forth. "I have been granted longer life to aid you as you learn the role of Spirit of the Cat Hunters."

"Granted by whom?" she asked in confusion. As far as she knew, the Spirits of each Hunter tribe were the top authority of that group. With the revelation of the existence of the Counsel, she figured it existed to keep balance between the five tribes.

The old cat shared a glance with the white tiger sitting by the bed. Then she turned her head to look into Kilala's eyes and started to explain, "The truths have been watered down or forgotten. Cat-kind still teaches our young the whole truth." She gingerly laid down and tucked her front paws under her chest. Kilala waited patiently for her to continue. "There is a much higher authority. A being that existed before all this was created. That is who granted me longer life. That is who all people, no matter their tribe, should be seeking for guidance." She intensified her gaze as she stared into the woman's eyes. "That is who you need to seek. That is who has given the Spirits their power."

"Who is this being?" Kilala asked in an awed whisper. She remembered the white tigress saying something about a Greater Power and wondered if it was the same entity. *No one has ever mentioned such a being*, she thought, mystified by this new information. Looking from the small cat to the big cat, she sensed they had a reverential fear of whomever they were talking about. The concept of such a powerful being frightened her but also made her curious. She mutely nodded for her old cat to continue.

"This one has no name that we know or can understand," Anong bowed her head as she spoke. "Each individual has their own name for this being."

"But isss it a myth?" a sibilant whisper came from the nearby chair. In it was coiled the small snake, his head stretched up to look into the sleeping area. "It may be a lie perpetuated by wishers that want to give false hope."

The Sentinel stood up and stared at the reptile. He lifted a massive paw as if he was prepared to strike. "Your kind may not believe nor teach your young the truth, but we do."

The little snake stared at the tiger without backing down. After a moment, he hissed a response, "That may be true for you, but what about her?" He swiveled the upright part of his body to stare at her.

Kilala recoiled from the lidless stare. *How can I believe in something I just learned about?* she thought apprehensively.

The white tiger turned his head and looked at her in concern. He narrowed his eyes briefly then turned away. "I must check on the village," he announced as he padded out of the cave.

Confused, the young woman looked down at the old cat. "Did I do something wrong?"

Anong didn't answer immediately as she stared at the snake. When she saw the reptile had settled back down into the chair and wasn't planning on moving, she relaxed. "You did nothing wrong," she stated as she licked a paw. "You simply need to be taught about the Eternal One so you can make a choice." She set the paw down and looked up at Kilala. "The Sentinel has his duties. I have mine, and so do you." She glanced over at the snake again.

Kilala petted the old cat as she swung her legs around to hang over the side of the bed. "Eternal One? I thought there was no name."

"As I said, each one that knows of the entity has their own name. That is my name for the nameless one." The old cat jumped down to the floor. "I need to hunt." She looked back at Kilala before she left the cave. "I will be back soon to help the white tigress with your education."

She nodded at her old cat and then slipped out of bed. She was also hungry, and she needed to change. She looked around the cave and decided to see what was in the shelves and cupboards. She slipped around the large chair that was beside the sleeping area, trying not to disturb the snake still resting in it. As she passed by, she heard a hiss.

"Will you sssseek the truth," the snake whispered. "Or ssssimply believe what they tell you."

Clenching her fists at her side, she stopped to look down into the chair. Steeling herself to look directly into the lidless eyes, she locked stares with the snake. "I will learn all I can and make my own choice," she stated firmly. Without waiting for a response, she turned away to explore her new home. She determined that she was not going to trust this reptile, no matter how much of a friend he had been to her predecessor.

Chapter Ten

Eventually, Kilala found a stash of clean, linen, floor-length tunics of tans, greens, and browns. Some were sleeveless while others had long, loose sleeves. As she eyeballed them, she thought they looked about her size. After washing up with water from the brook and untangling her hair with a sturdy wood comb she found, she changed into a tan one without any sleeves. She was surprised when it fit perfectly. Although she wondered how that was possible, she dismissed it as she neatly braided her hair and tied the end with a bit of twine. Gathering up her old clothes, she decided to wash them. After scrubbing them in the stream, she hung the rough spun blouse and skirt on top of a hedge near the cave entrance to dry.

When she was done with that, she started to look around for food. On the table, she found a stack of handwritten notes from the previous occupant. One page told her about a storehouse of food and an inventory of what it contained and that it was part of the small group of caves that extended from the one she was currently in. With it was a map titled 'Haven' that showed what was in each small cave in the network, which included not only the storeroom but also one that had a hot spring for bathing and washing, one that was set up as a privy, and a deeper one that was cooler to store perishables. Several other pages had a sketch detailing all the types of trees, vines, and grains. It also specified when to expect the fruit to be ready from the fruit-bearing trees and vines, as well as when to plant and harvest each type of the grains. As she studied the sketch more closely, she saw that there was also a small garden in which an assortment of vegetables was planted. The last page was a note that detailed where to get the other supplies she would need. Glancing over all the pages, she thought, *Whatever else I would need is very limited with all that is here!*

She knew the pages were for her to keep for future reference, so she restacked the notes neatly together, set them on a bookshelf, and placed a stone cat statue the size of her hand on top of them for a paperweight. *Housekeeping things,* she thought as she made sure the pile was secure. *What about learning what I am supposed to do?*

Taking a stone plate and cup from one of the nearby shelves, she went to find the supply cavern. After admiring the variety and vast amounts of stored-up supplies, she gathered some bread, strips of dried meat, and apples. After she filled her cup with water from the brook, she set the filled plate and cup on the table and sat down in the single, simple, wooden, straight-backed chair facing toward the cave entrance. While she ate, she studied the cave to take in more details about her new home, glad that the little snake was out of sight. She found on the opposite wall a small hearth with a metal pot hanging over kindling that was ready to start a fire. Nearby was a modest supply of dry wood. Hanging on metal pegs drilled into the wall was a large metal pan and a skillet. Also on the wall was a wooden counter on which was a wooden bowl and metal baking pan.

Feeling like she knew where all the essentials were in her haven, she sat back and enjoyed the rest of her meal. As she chewed on the strips of well-spiced meat, she thought of the suspicions her predecessor had of the medicine women from the villages close to Snake Hunters territory. *Why then*, she thought, *did she seem to have an alliance with the Spirit of the Snake Hunters and allowed a spy to stay with her*? She had no answer for the conundrum, so her thoughts turned to the Eternal One. *Why had I never been taught of a higher being?* she wondered. *Neither my adopted parents nor my grandmother ever said anything,* she thought as she ate the bread and drank the cool, sweet water.

After she finished her meal, she sat at the table with her chin in her hands, elbows on the table, and stared off into space. Those thoughts and others tumbled through her mind. She didn't know how long she was trapped in her contemplations when she heard a sound.

"Ahmmm."

She snapped out of her thoughts and looked at the source. The white tigress sat close by, watching her. She turned in her chair so that she was fully facing the large cat.

"I am glad to see you up and looking well," the big cat purred.

"Thank you," Kilala replied quietly. "I hope you can help me. So much has happened so quickly that I don't know anyone's name."

The black and white head nodded once. "I am Teigra. My mate is Nemr. I am now the leader of the mates of the Sentinels, known as the Shoku. Nemr is now the leader of the Sentinels." She stopped to think for a few seconds then added, "The other Sentinels and their mates you will learn as you need to. But you may have some dealings with the previous Spirit's attendants."

"The lion and lioness?" Kilala asked curiously.

"Yes," the white tigress confirmed, looking pleased. "They were the previous leaders of the Sentinels and the Shoku."

"I see." Kilala nodded slightly as she more fully understood the interaction between the two female great cats when she had arrived at Haven. "And what are their names?"

"The female is Tiaret and her mate is Tau."

"Thank you," Kilala said as she smiled at Teigra. "Now what do I do?"

"Are you ready to begin learning the secrets of the Cat Hunters?"

"Yes, certainly," she said decisively. She wanted to add that she was more than ready since she had had no mentoring in the position she now held.

The big cat's head dropped in a small bow. "Good, I see you are eager." Teigra stood and padded silently over to the bookshelves that were near the table. Kilala watched her curiously and saw when the big cat looked at her and then cut her eyes to the shelves. "You need to read those."

Kilala responded to her direction and stood up so that she could see the contents of the bookcase more easily. Other than placing the housekeeping papers on a shelf, she hadn't paid much attention to them before. As her eyes skipped along the wood-planked shelving that was supported by iron spikes imbedded into the rough cave wall, she picked out several books lying about haphazardly. "Any particular order?" she asked as she leaned over to study the volumes more closely, then glanced back at the white tigress.

The big cat looked at the books, then turned away and shrugged. "We do not read the words of human-kind." She yawned widely. "I do remember the Companion mentioning something about the colors." She padded back to where she was before.

At first, Kilala was shocked that it looked like this was the only instruction she was going to get from the white tigress about her new position. Then her attention was caught by what Teigra had said. "Companion?" She was distracted by the term and looked to the white tigress for an explanation.

The big cat licked a paw before she answered. "The other tribes have either masters or mistresses that act as Spirits for their tribes. But we have Companions." She looked up at Kilala and locked eyes. "We are not bound to serve. We made a choice to serve."

She looked around and saw representatives of all the great cats entering the cave. The Sentinels and their mates, the Shoku, formed a semi-circle around her and sat. As their eyes of blue, brown, gold, and green bored into her, she slowly turned to meet the gazes of each one. The appearance of so many big cats in the same place made her nervous. She felt like something was expected of her, but she didn't know what.

A gravelly meow broke the silence. Her ancient cat had come into the cave and was running to her side. Kilala bent down to pick her up, glad for a familiar friend.

Anong purred as Kilala cuddled her close to her chest, and then the old cat turned to stare down the big cats. "What are you doing?" she growled with an intensity that made the mountain lion envious. She was fearless as she confronted the largest of her kind.

All the great cats seemed to smile as they licked a paw or flank or flicked an ear. "You are aware she was not properly instructed on how to proceed," the ancient tortoiseshell cat continued as if she was admonishing a group of rowdy kittens.

Teigra sat up on her haunches to look at the smaller cat. "That is understood. We simply need her to enter into a formal agreement with us."

"Agreement?" Kilala finally was able to speak in a small voice.

Nemr, the white tiger, spoke up. "When a new Companion is chosen, they must do this for the sake of the tribe."

"The previous Companion is usually the one to instruct on the oath and to administer it with all the Sentinels and the Shoku present," Tiaret, the lioness, added as she spoke up.

"She is not here," the puma pointed out. "So how do we proceed?"

"And will it be binding?" the leopard called out.

Tiaret spoke up again, "It is not the fault of our old Companion that she could not hold on long enough for this."

"Well, if that other human had taken over, we wouldn't be in this mess," a lynx blurted out.

"But that didn't happen," Nemr spoke calmly, the voice of reason.

"So, how can this be done? And be sure it is binding?" the cheetah chattered.

To stop all the speculation, Teigra roared suddenly and loudly. It shook the cave and caused Kilala to jump back into the shelves. In the silence after the roar, a small squeak and a slithering sound was heard leaving the cave.

Tau, the lion, looked at the entrance. "Well, you got our attention and got rid of that spy."

All the big cats nodded, then looked at the white tigress. "Our last Companion did instruct me on how to proceed," she said as she looked at Kilala then back at the group. "There is no doubt that she was chosen at birth to be our Companion."

"No one argues that," the cheetah commented.

"Have you ever thought about how the first Companion took the oath?" Teigra continued, ignoring the comment. The big cats looked thoughtful; several shook their heads.

"I didn't either," the white tigress spoke again. "It had happened so long ago." She padded past Kilala and nosed a book on the very bottom shelf. "She placed this here so it would be easy for me to point it out to you."

"What? Are you going to read it?" the puma yipped in surprise.

"No, are you stupid?" Tau growled.

Teigra bowed her head to him. "No, she will." She looked up at Kilala then at the book.

Kilala responded to the request as she bent down to pick up the book and opened it. She scanned through the pages of ancient parchment and squinted at the faded ink as she struggled to read the scrawling words. As she read, the words became clearer. She could see the first of the book was a summary recounting the early history of the tribes and the disaster that led to their formation. She quickly realized that the account was written by the first Spirit of the Cat Hunters, also regarded as the first Companion to the Sentinels and Shoku.

The writer detailed how the great cats had approached her, at that point for her to simply serve as a leader to the newly formed Cat Hunters. They had questioned her intently on her character and what she wanted for her tribe and the cats that would help them. It took time, but they had formed an alliance, a trust, to work together for as long as they lived to protect and aid their charges.

When she had reached the section relating how the alliance was built, Kilala started to read out loud to the gathered cats. Many of them seemed to know the history as they nodded their heads in agreement. She reached the point in the writings where the first Spirit had given an account of the oath that was to be taken by each of the Spirits/Companions that followed. She stopped and took a deep breath.

She looked to all the great cats in front of her. "It is my understanding from these writings that this is the oath that she gave to the Sentinels at that time to serve human-kind and cat-kind all her life. I am going to read this to you just as I would have recited it after the previous Companion if she were still with us." She met each of the Sentinels' and Shokus' eyes. "Is it agreed that this will be sufficient to satisfy tradition?"

The big cats looked at each other. Since she couldn't hear anything telepathically, she could tell they were discussing it in their mysterious language of body movements. She reached down to pick up her old cat who had curled up by her feet while she read the book. Stroking her gently, she watched and waited.

<u>*Chapter 11*</u>

She was startled by a slithering noise returning. "Hey, what'ssss going on?" Kilala looked around to see the small snake coiled at the cave entrance. All the Sentinels turned their heads toward him and snarled as Nemr stood up and stalked toward the little green snake. As the big cat advanced on him, the snake started to look nervous and quickly turned to slither back outside. The white tiger followed him.

"What will he do?" Kilala asked quietly.

"This is Cat Hunter business," Teigra said to her. "No one wants him here."

"He won't hurt him, will he?"

The white tigress regarded her with questioning blue eyes. "Do you care?"

"Um." She looked down at her old cat. "Well, if he is as important to his mistress as she is to me, I wouldn't want another tribes' Sentinel to hurt her."

Teigra glanced at the old cat then nodded as she understood. "No, he will not hurt him."

"The snake doesn't seem to be as well received here as you told me yesterday," Kilala observed.

Teigra glanced at the rest of the big cats before she answered, "Our Companion tolerated him and his mistress. She allowed a friendship to develop so that she had better insight into the Snake Hunters tribe than she would have had otherwise."

"She didn't trust her completely." Tiaret spoke up. "And she didn't allow the little snake to be around when serious discussions needed to be made." The lioness looked toward the cave opening to make sure it was still clear. "She would even let things slip out that weren't completely true when the snake was here."

Kilala nodded as she furrowed her brow. "I see. She kept her enemies close and slipped them misinformation."

Tiaret nodded and seemed relieved that she understood. "She did it all for the benefit of our tribe."

Kilala smiled at the big cat. "I understand." *Interesting*, she thought to herself. *I will need to keep these things in mind.* She noticed movement in the cave entrance. Nemr had come back alone.

"Our snake friend has decided to sun himself on a rock for the afternoon," the white tiger announced as he rejoined the group.

"Very good," Teigra purred at her mate. She looked up at Kilala. "You may proceed."

Kilala nodded, then gently set her cat on the floor. When she straightened up, she picked up the book. "It is agreed that this will fulfill all the requirements?"

Teigra looked at the group once more. She nodded and turned back to Kilala. "Yes, it is agreed."

Kilala took a deep breath and then let it out slowly. She found the passage again and solemnly read it aloud, inserting her name where indicated, as her finger traced under the words. At first, her voice was shaking slightly but then steadied as she recited the passage and meant it from the depths of her heart. "I, Kilala, solemnly swear to aid and protect all those in the Cat Hunter tribe, both human-kind and cat-kind alike. I will endeavor to provide in time of need. I will protect from and fight against destructive forces outside the tribe and purge any enemies found within. All this I will do to the best of my ability, with the power given to me, for the remainder of my life."

She read the next sentence silently before reading it out loud. "Oh, I need to do something to seal the bond with blood." She looked around on the shelf. "Here it is." She picked up an ancient tooth. "It is from an ancient great cat," she whispered as she admired the extra large and long fang tooth. "I am to leave some of my blood on this." She held it up for them to see. "How do I do that?"

When none of the big cats answered her, she looked back to the book. It didn't give details on how the oath would be sealed. She shifted the tooth to her other hand to turn the page when the razor-sharp point cut into her finger. "Ouch," she reacted as she saw the blood oozing from the wound. When it came into contact with the fang, the tooth began to glow. As the tooth absorbed the blood, the glow spread to envelop her entire body. Suddenly, she felt excruciating pain searing through her whole being. When it lifted, she found herself looking down at her body still standing by the shelves surrounded by the big cats. She looked up and saw that she was floating near the ceiling of the cave.

As one, the gathering of Sentinels and Shoku looked up at her and purred. "You are now our Companion," Teigra announced. "And Spirit of the Cat Hunters."

"All hail the Spirit of the Cat Hunters," roared all the great cats as they looked up at her floating image. "And Companion to all of cat-kind," they purred as all bowed to her. She noticed that her ancient cat also bowed and could swear she saw a smile of pride on her face.

While she bowed to each of them as they looked up to her, she sensed they expected something from her.

Uncertainly, she hovered quietly as she thought hard about what she should do next. She wound up saying the first thing that popped in her mind, "Any news from the villages?" She cringed inwardly as the words seemed inadequate for the occasion. She was glad when her Sentinel took it in stride.

"All is quiet," replied Nemr. "But we also watch the borders and our territory between the villages. And they are quiet as well."

She nodded at him, thankful for the information. When her head moved, locks of her long hair floated back and forth in front of her face. That was nothing new but she was suddenly distracted by the fact that they now were semi-transparent and had a silver glow to them. She looked down at her hands and body to see that they were also semi-transparent and glowing silver as well. She didn't know how long she hovered staring at them when she heard someone clear his throat, snapping her attention back to the big cats looking up at her. They seemed to be smiling, amused at her astonishment as they would be with a cub learning his world.

"Any orders, my lady?" the white tiger asked, giving her a way out of the awkward moment.

She pulled herself together. "Go back to your usual territories and continue your duties as directed by my predecessor. I will study more about my duties and contact you if there is anything else."

"Very well, Companion." Nemr said as he bowed. The others bowed one by one before they turned to leave the cave in their stately, unhurried pace. The white tiger hesitated then turned to talk to his mate who would be staying. Even though she couldn't understand their language of minute expressions and body movements, Kilala could tell when their conversation grew intense. Suddenly, Nemr turned to pad out of the cave. Teigra looked out after him then proceeded to lie down to lick her paw. To Kilala, the big cat seemed intensely thoughtful but felt that there something else she couldn't put her finger on.

After Kilala figured out how to hover closer to the ground, she moved in front of the white tigress. She watched her for a moment before the big cat's eyes focused on her and her ears swiveled forward. The surprised look was quickly replaced by a friendly, welcoming gaze. "May I assist you with anything?" Teigra asked.

Kilala shook her head. Her glowing locks still distracted her, but she quickly disregarded them. "Anything I should know about?"

Teigra shook her head and yawned. "We were discussing the antics of one of our cubs," she said in an off-handed fashion. But Kilala had a feeling that she was trying to keep something from her.

"Oh, how many?"

"Eight."

"How old?"

"They are entering into their third cycle of the great moon." The white tigress looked away, clearly not wanting to talk any further about her cubs. Kilala was surprised by a mother that didn't want to expound on the antics of her young. This made her wonder about what was going on but didn't feel that she should pry into family affairs.

"Um." Kilala glanced toward her body, looking rigid as it stood. "Am I going to be sore?"

"Possibly. Your predecessor always lay down," Teigra answered as she glanced from the floating image to the body of her new Companion.

Kilala studied her physical body thoughtfully, noting the open-eyed blank expression. She waved a hand in front of her physical face and didn't see any reaction. Then she started to move around the cavern to learn how to better control the floating state. When she mastered it enough to be comfortable with it, she didn't know what to do next. She looked back at her body, then at the white tigress who had been watching her. "Um, how do I get back in?"

Teigra stood up and walked up to her body. "You are not out." She licked her hand with a rough tongue. Kilala felt it as she hovered close. "Oh," she said in surprise. "I thought with the spirit thing, I had left my body."

The big cat shook her head then lay down. "If your spirit had truly left, you would be dead."

"Why did it hurt so much?"

Teigra shrugged. She lay her head down to watch her. "I do not know. Maybe it will explain in the books."

When Kilala went to pick one of the books up off the shelf, her hand passed through the book and shelf. Fascinated by the sensation of passing through matter with barely any resistance, she pushed in farther until her hand was deep into the stone of the cave. Slowly, she pulled it back and laughed. "Guess I need to use my body for that."

The white tigress yawned, then rolled to lie on her side.

She studied the big cat a bit. It seemed old to the white tigress, but to her it was new and exciting. "I think I will explore a bit," she said out loud to herself.

"You may want to read the books first." Teigra had opened an eye to watch her. "There are rules to learn. And things you must do."

Kilala looked at her body again. "If I wake up now, I may not be able to do this again. It hurt too much."

Teigra lifted her head to regard her with soft, blue eyes. "I truly don't think it will hurt again. I never saw pain in the one before you."

Kilala sighed heavily with relief; she never wanted to experience that excruciating pain again. She started to approach her body. "How…?"

The big cat shook her head and yawned. "I don't know the details but she didn't need to be here to touch her body. She would simply wake up."

Hmm, she thought, *wake up.* Suddenly, the floating sensation was gone and she was seeing out of her physical eyes. Every muscle in her body was cramped and painful. "Aargh," she groaned, gritting her teeth while she forcibly moved her limbs. "Definitely need to be lying down," she grumbled.

Teigra lay her head down and flicked an ear in response.

After Kilala marched around the cave, moving her arms in wide arcs to loosen up her muscles, she grabbed the book she had been reading and sat at the table. Starting after the oath, she read the experiences of the first Spirit. Soon she was immersed in the discovery and drama of the early days of the tribe.

Chapter Twelve

When the day started to darken into dusk, Kilala put the book down and started to rub her weary eyes. Reading the scrawling handwriting had given her a headache. She was contemplating making some medicinal tea when a voice startled her.

"Excussse me, cat lady." The little snake was coiled up on the floor by the white tigress. "My mistress would like to visit."

Teigra had her head up watching her. Kilala noted a subtle nod from the striped head as the big cat prompted her. "Oh, yes!" She acted enthusiastic. "She is more than welcome," she gushed.

The little snake looked at her strangely as he ducked his head once. "I will inform her." He ducked his head again, then slithered out the entrance.

She looked back at the big cat to see that the white tigress was shaking her head slowly. "Too much?" Kilala asked quietly, embarrassed by her act.

"A bit." Teigra yawned. "But they will think that you are acting that way because of being excited about your new position." She glanced toward the entrance. "Remember, we don't fully trust them. We tolerate them and are friendly within boundaries." She met her Companion's eyes. "Do not ever feel comfortable nor give any of the deep secrets away."

Kilala was about to ask about what she meant about deep secrets when they heard slithering at the entrance. The little snake reappeared. "She will be here shortly," he announced as he came into the cave to coil by the white tigress again.

Soon the floating apparition of the Spirit of the Snakes moved slowly through the cave entrance. "Hello!" she greeted in a friendly voice. She had her hood thrown back, showing her face and hair.

Kilala nodded in her direction as she studied the Spirit closely since the last time she had seen her, she had been extremely tired. She felt she needed to in case there was any deception she needed to see that gave her cause to completely distrust the Snake Spirit and sever any ties with her. She respected her predecessor's tact in dealing with her, but she wanted to assess for herself what relationship she wanted with the Snake Hunter tribe.

She relaxed a bit since she didn't notice anything different as the Spirit looked and acted the same as before. "Hello," Kilala replied as she dropped her hands to lay the book on her lap.

"How are you settling in?" As the ethereal figure drew closer, it was obvious that she was trying to see what Kilala was reading.

Seeing her interest, Kilala nonchalantly closed the book and tossed it onto the table. "I am doing as well as expected." She stood and shrugged. "It will take time to understand all that is expected of me."

The Snake Spirit suddenly exploded in raucous, humorless laughter. "Expected of you?!" she burst out as she sneered.

Kilala hid her shocked surprise at the other Spirit's reaction. She was confused. "Why do you say that?"

"Well." The Snake Spirit floated down to hover face to face with Kilala. "You are the most powerful force in your tribe. You should expect things from them!"

Kilala watched her thoughtfully. She was extremely uncomfortable with how near the Snake Spirit was to her and deeply disturbed by this explanation. Finally, she asked, "Do the Spirits of the other Hunter tribes feel that way?"

The floating figure drew away from her a bit, then replied, "Well, of course! That is the way it always was and will be."

Kilala chewed her lip in thought. She was sure this was not the case. She glanced over at the book she had been reading. So far, the writings had revealed the symbiotic relationship of each Hunter tribe and their Spirit. It was to be a cooperative and not a dictatorship. When she looked up at the apparition still floating near her, she decided she needed to change the subject. She did not want to get mired in a discussion about how leaders should act. "What did you want to show me?" she asked, mustering as much pleasantness as she could as she grew more uncomfortable with her guest.

"Oh, yes." The Snake Spirit floated even nearer to her. "You need to learn to project. That way you can patrol your territory and keep watch on your people. That is also how the Council of the Spirits communicates."

As Kilala nodded at her, she wondered what she was going to tell her. There was something about how the Spirit of the Snake Hunters was acting that added more to her feeling of unease. Deep down, she knew that she couldn't reveal to her that she could already project. With no other options, she decided to go along with her. "What do I do?"

The Snake Hunter Spirit moved to hover face to face with her. "You need to stand perfectly still." Kilala nodded as she pushed back from the table to stand up straight. "Good." The figure nodded in response. "Now, close your eyes." Kilala closed them down to slits so she could watch the Snake Spirit through her eyelashes. She had seen cats do this so they could appear to be sleeping but were actually watching and aware. In the corner of her eye, she saw the white tigress nod in approval, then turn away to lick her flank after she asked the little snake something that distracted him.

The Snake Spirit hadn't noticed the deception. "Very good." She licked her lips as her eyes started to become wider. Kilala tried not to recoil as the pupils of the specter's eyes became slits like a venomous snake and her skin started to pop up with scales. The tongue became forked as it continued to flicker in and out of the widening mouth that became lipless while it stretched. When Kilala took a deep, loud breath to calm herself, the Snake Spirit backed up. "What are you doing?"

"I thought I should relax," she said as innocently as she could. She was glad her voice didn't betray her nervousness. She looked toward Teigra through her eyelashes again. The big cat didn't show any signs that anything was amiss. *She must not be able to see what I am seeing,* she thought tensely.

The Snake Spirit nodded and laughed nervously. "Yes, that is good. That could help." She slowly glided closer to where she was almost touching noses with Kilala. "Now, imagine your mind tearing free from your body to float near me." The tongue flickered faster as the Snake Spirit's body elongated into a man-sized snake, coiled and posed to strike. It was obvious that she was waiting in hungry anticipation. "It will be like your soul is ripped away," the Snake Spirit whispered with a hollow echo, giving her voice a creepy sound.

Kilala was frightened to the core of her being, but steeled herself so as not to show any fear. She took another deep breath and forced herself to relax completely as she let it out slowly. Imagining a breeze flowing through her body, she let her thoughts drift away from her, and translated. As she floated near the Snake Spirit, she saw shocked surprise in her dull green eyes.

"It should have hurt!" the Snake Spirit exclaimed as she backed away from Kilala. In a blink of the eye, her features had snapped back into the image of a young woman without any snake features.

"Why," Kilala asked curiously as she glided closer to her. "Is it important that it should hurt?"

"You would have been incapacitated long enough…" the apparition stopped herself. She had been caught by surprise and almost admitted to something. She quickly regained command of herself before she said any more.

The Spirit of the Cat Hunters stared long and hard at the Spirit of the Snake Hunters. She knew that the other Spirit wouldn't admit to anything. It didn't matter; she knew what she had seen with her own eyes and could guess the rest. "You would've taken advantage of that incapacitated state. And, what? Devour me? Be able to set up control over me?"

The other Spirit had nothing to say as her mouth gaped open, then snapped shut. "You could know nothing about any such things," she finally gasped. "What are you?"

"I am the Spirit of the Cat Hunters," Kilala said calmly. The indecision of what to think of this leader of the Snake Hunters was firmly replaced by distrust. "And this meeting is at a close," she stated firmly.

The Snake Hunter Spirit started to sputter, "I-i-i c-c-can help you with other things!" She started to wave her hands around in agitation. "How will you know where to meet with the other Spirits?"

"I have no doubt that I will figure that out." When she looked down at the little green snake, she saw his confusion about what was going on. He didn't seem to be in league with his leader. "I suggest that you return to your mistress, little one. I need time to learn my new role. This is not a time for visitors." His bewilderment and obviously growing dismay brought out in Kilala a feeling of compassion for the little reptile, despite her deep-seated fear and distrust of snakes.

"Yessss, cat lady." The little snake bowed to her. "I will return home." He looked up to his mistress. "By your permission?"

"Yessss," the Snake Spirit replied irritably as she waved a dismissive hand. She glared hatefully at Kilala. "You better protect your borderssss!" she hissed, warning her spitefully.

The Spirit of the Cats smiled at her and nodded decisively. This seemed to infuriate the Snake Spirit, who turned and flew out of the cave. Soon the little snake reluctantly slithered after her.

When she was assured that the Spirit of the Snake Hunters and the little snake had truly left her haven, Kilala set out to patrol the territory of the Cat Hunters. From her readings in the book, she had found that the first Companion had erected a metaphysical fence that separated the territory of the Cat Hunters from the other Hunter tribes' territories. When she reached the border, she found the shattered remains of the fence and set about to repair them.

At first, her efforts were clumsy and resulted in a feeble structure. But with practice and care she became more sure-handed, and the repaired sections of fence were sturdy and impassable. After many days, she had it all completed.

As she expanded her mind, she was able to view the whole perimeter. After she studied it and tested it for weaknesses, she nodded happily. She felt that the territory of the Cat Hunters was more secure than it had been for centuries.

With her tribe safe, she turned her attention to her haven. She erected walls that were impassable by Spirits and physical beings except for her Sentinels, their mates, and any of cat-kind. She felt safe enough that she could concentrate on reading the books.

Chapter 13

Soon after she completed her security tasks and before she delved back into the books, she heard deep bell tones. It was the summons for the Council of the Spirits. She had already found in the writings where they met, so she set her book down and lay on her bed. With an escape of breath, she freed her thoughts, translated, and was soon gliding out of her territory. Before long, she joined the others in the heavens, completing the circle of the Council in the company of the stars.

"I am glad you could join us," the Eagle Hunter Spirit stated.

After she bowed to him, she looked over at the others. The Bear Hunter Spirit smiled at her, the Snake Hunter Spirit ignored her, while the Dog Hunter Spirit just stared at her as before.

"No longer best friends?" the Bear Spirit growled good-naturedly at the Snake Spirit.

She hissed at him, turned her back, and looked off into the distance. She was obviously not willing to look at any of them. "Why are we here?" she asked spitefully, throwing the words over her shoulder.

Eagle Spirit glared at her for a while, then shrugged. "Apparently, you have surprised some of those in this Council," he commented as he locked eyes with Kilala. In that amber-eyed piercing gaze, she could see the penetrating stare of the predator birds. She met his hard stare, keeping her own soft and fearless. She refused to challenge or fear him. As he broke eye contact, she thought she saw a slight smile on the thin, angular face.

He looked to the others. "When a new Spirit emerges, we call a council meeting to introduce the new one to our laws." He looked to the Spirit of the Dogs. "As you know, being the previous newest Spirit."

Kilala looked at the Spirit of the Dog Hunters in surprise. She had thought all of them had been present for decades if not a century. "You did not wonder at his youth?" the Bear Spirit asked her when he saw her surprise.

"I was under the assumption that the Spirits could change their image as they wish," Kilala commented curiously.

Eagle Spirit nodded. "True. We could if we wanted."

"Generally, we don't," the Bear Spirit muttered as he leaned toward her. "To us, it is deceptive." He cut his eyes toward the Snake Spirit and raised his eyebrows.

"Shut up, Bear," the Snake Spirit hissed. "How do you know I do not look like this?" She turned back to face the group but avoided looking at and even acknowledging Kilala's presence.

Kilala looked from the Snake Spirit to the other Spirits with great interest, wondering if they had ever seen her look like a man-sized snake.

Eagle Spirit raised a hand. He was clearly the leader of the council. "Chusi, we know you have been a Spirit for a long time. There is no way you could look that youthful."

Kilala thought about mentioning what she had seen but decided to keep quiet. *Maybe I was mistaken in what I saw?* she thought.

Snake Spirit hissed viscously at them. "Ssssso that'ss what thisss issss!!! To harasss me!!" Her apparition drew back, her human form taking the posture very much like a snake about to strike. "How dare you use my given name! That is against the rules of Council!" Kilala noticed the Spirit's speech slip in and out of the hissing snake accent and looked around again at the other Spirits. They didn't seem to have noticed it.

Eagle Spirit looked bored as he shook his head. "No, Chusi," he enunciated her name slowly to make his point. "There is no such rule. This meeting is to inform the newcomer. It is also to open a forum so that we can discuss any further incursions on each of our territories." The piercing eyes turned toward Kilala. "You are welcome to add anything to the report, if you are aware of any changes to the status of your territory."

Kilala nodded at him but stayed quiet. She wasn't going to reveal that she had repaired the ancient fences of the Cat Hunter territory.

"We will go into discussion," Eagle Spirit continued, gesturing toward the Bear Spirit while he looked at Kilala. "Bemot will fill you in on the laws after we are through here." She nodded again as she glanced at the Spirit of the Bear Hunters; he smiled at her and nodded. Apparently, he didn't have a problem with his name being used.

"Now." Eagle Spirit took over again. "Any reports?" He looked pointedly around the group.

The Spirit of the Bear Hunters spoke up, "Someone has been getting into our caves. Some young are missing without a trace." He looked down with fear in his eyes. "I cannot find them." He looked at the others. "I will not trespass onto your territories, as the rules state." He glared at The Spirit of the Snake Hunters. "Can each of you check your territories?"

Kilala readily joined the Eagle and Dog Hunter Spirits in promising to check their territories. They all stared at the Snake Hunter Spirit when she murmured something no one could make out, and she refused to repeat it.

Dog Spirit reported next. "There have been reports of big cats on our territory," he growled low and deep, staring at Kilala. Her eyes opened wide with honest surprise. "And our prey is disappearing. We are running out of food." He continued to stare at her as he challenged her.

"We are also experiencing prey shortage," Eagle Hunter Spirit said. "We have no explanation." He looked to the Snake Spirit. "Anything to report?"

She shrugged. "We, too, are experiencing food shortages." She looked around at the others. "I do not know why, either." She looked at the Bear Spirit. "Maybe your kind are hunting on our territories. I did not hear you report food shortages," she accused harshly.

The Spirit of the Bear Hunters shook his huge head, causing his glowing massive beard to swing gently. "We have noticed prey animals are fewer and farther between. My Sentinels, as well as all bear-kind, are omnivorous. We can deal with fewer prey animals by eating more berries and such." His eyes turned hard as he locked eyes with the Snake Spirit. "I noticed that you have not reported any missing young. Could it be your kind are stealing mine?"

Snake reared her head back and floated farther away from him. "Thatsssss ridicuoloussssss," she hissed nervously. "We do not eat cubsss!"

Bear Spirit turned away muttering, "I bet you would if your mouths were big enough."

"What about the big cats in our territory?" the Spirit of the Dog Hunters barked in frustration. He stared at Kilala.

She met his gaze without flinching. "I will look into it," she stated calmly. "There has been much upheaval in our territory as of late. I am in early days of re-establishing structure."

The Dog Spirit continued to growl at her. "Cut that out," the Bear Spirit growled back. "You know the law. You have informed her; now she has a full cycle of the greater moon to correct it and report back."

"Yeah," the Dog Spirit grumbled under his breath as he turned his head away from her. "Whatever."

"Any other new reports?" Eagle Spirit asked loudly to get everyone's attention. No one answered. "Meeting over," he announced, then turned and flew away from the group. The Snake and Dog Spirits soon followed suit, each heading off in different directions. The Bear Spirit looked over at Kilala. "Cat, you ready?"

She looked over at him blankly as she was still processing the sudden ending of the meeting. Bear Spirit grinned. "We are not a social club." He read her reaction correctly. "We get together because we have to. We do this to try to prevent a full-scale war between tribes."

She nodded slowly as she turned to him. "Apparently, there are many things I need to learn." She looked back to where the others had been hovering a few moments ago. "What are the names of the others?" she asked as she turned back to face the shaggy apparition.

He seemed to consider her question thoughtfully. Soon he shrugged, as if it didn't matter one way or the other if she had that knowledge. "We don't usually use our birth names after we become Spirits. We typically are known by our Hunter tribe's animal group." He looked away from her and seemed to study the stars around them. "However, after a while even we can form relationships, forged through common experiences in the roles we bear." He looked at her again. "With that and time, we have come to know some of the other Spirits' names."

She studied the sparkling, dark eyes under bushy eyebrows. "Are names to be kept a secret?" she asked as she wondered about the Snake Hunter Spirit's reaction to her name being used.

The shaggy head tilted to one side as he watched her. "No, there is no special power in knowing each other's name," he said as he flashed a wide, big-toothed grin at her.

She returned his smile. "I see."

The Bear Spirit studied her closely as his expression grew serious. "You are a quick learner. You have come a long way without a mentor." He smiled briefly before his expression became serious again as he got to the matter at hand. "The laws of the Council of the Spirits can be boiled down into one phrase, 'Do not step on our toes, and we won't step on yours.' There are many specifics to learn to fill this in. For example, the law about a tribe's Sentinels encroaching on another tribes' territories. Your predecessor has a copy of them around your haven somewhere. If you can't find it, let me know and I'll get you another one."

Puzzled, Kilala asked him, "Is that it? Why did the Eagle Spirit make it seem more intense?"

"I asked him to let me go over the rules with you since you weren't mentored. But I had a question to ask you." He glanced around. They were still alone floating in space. "Did Snake try anything with you when you first projected?"

"She tried," she answered slowly. "Why?"

"How did you repel her during the pain of the first time?" the Spirit of the Bear Hunters looked honestly surprised.

"Repel?" She was further confused. "I don't understand."

Bear Spirit licked his lips as he looked around again. "As I said, we are a council to aid in protecting our own territories. What happens with others is not our business or concern." He looked intensely in her eyes.

She felt as if he wanted her to understand what he was about to tell her. She nodded uncertainly but wanting him to continue.

"We have been aware that Snake has tried to exert her influence over some of the Spirits of the Hunters tribes. The most recent changeover was in the Spirit of the Dog Hunters. Snake acted strange and pushed to be present for his first projection. When it looked like she was going to harm him, she was blocked by his mentor who had not completely passed through death into the other life." He held up a finger for her to wait when he saw questions in her eyes. "That first projection with the pain is the most vulnerable time that any of us go through. Once that is over, we cannot be influenced or killed by any of the other Spirits."

Kilala nodded that she understood. She studied the Bear Spirit and felt she could trust him. "She was present for the second time that I projected."

The Bear Spirit looked at her closely as what she revealed sank in, his eyes and mouth opened wide. "Your first projection was by yourself?" he urgently whispered for verification.

She nodded. "Why? Is that strange?"

The Bear Spirit shook his shaggy head. "No one has been able to do that for centuries." He studied her intensely. "You are going to be one worth watching," he rumbled solemnly.

Kilala wasn't sure how to take his comment so she shrugged it aside. She had questions she needed answers to. "May I ask questions of you?"

After the Bear Spirit nodded slowly, she asked, "What is the Higher Power or Eternal Power?" She watched him closely as she awaited his answer.

He looked away to study distant stars while he pursed his lips. When she thought he wouldn't answer, his deep voice whispered with awe, "It is called many things: The Eternal Power, the Higher Power, the Greater Power, and more. It is a mystery to us. Even being Spirits, we recognize there is a Power beyond us. It is something that affects events, places, and all living things. Whoever it is, that is the one who enabled the Spirits to have certain abilities and powers."

She nodded as she looked around at the stars. "And the life beyond?" she whispered as she gestured around them, taking in the heavens with their multitude of stars.

The Bear Spirit shook his head. "This is not it," he said solemnly. "It is what we cross into once we leave this life."

She opened her mouth to ask another question when she saw a fleeting look of concern cross the shaggy, glowing face. She could see he needed to get back to his territory. She ducked her head in respect. "Thank you for this information."

He answered by bowing his head to her, smiling despite the lingering concern in his eyes. "We can talk more in the days ahead," he offered. Before he left, he met her eyes and winked. "You can use my name if you like. My name is Bemot."

"Thank you, Bemot. You may use mine as well." She smiled back. "I appreciate the offer." She bowed slightly to him. "I will look over my territory to see if your cubs are there."

"Thank you, Kilala." He smiled at her and nodded at her once. Then he turned to fly back to his territory.

Chapter Fourteen

As soon as he was gone, Kilala wondered if his missing cubs were of bear-kind or human-kind. *These Spirit beings seem to identify more with their Sentinels than the humans in their tribe.* Then she realized that with the flow of conversation, he hadn't shared the names of the other Spirits. Thinking of how the Snake Spirit had reacted to her name being used, she shook her head slowly in amazement. *But even with the powers and special abilities, they bait each other like any other human,* she thought, then heaved a great sigh. She had much to learn. She let the weightlessness of the heavens relax her consciousness as she floated in the space between the stars. *So many more mysteries*, she thought. *I thought the Spirits of the Hunter tribes knew it all.*

She sighed again and was about to go back to her body and the books when she saw a movement in the corner of her eye. At the same moment, she was suddenly filled with a smothering, fearful foreboding. She whipped her head around trying to catch sight of the black that stayed on the fringe of her peripheral vision. As she tried to see what was with her, she refused to succumb to the fear that was trying to overwhelm her. "What or who are you?!" she demanded; her voice steady as she replaced fear with anger.

"Who are you?" a chilling moan answered her, mocking her.

"I am the Spirit of the Cat Hunters," she answered back firmly, flatly refusing to give ground. She kept looking around, still unable to fully see the entity that was with her. Frustrated, she drew a deep breath and closed her eyes. Firmly concentrating on the waves of fear that were washing over her, she pinpointed the origin then abruptly turned to face it. She quickly opened her eyes, then froze in fright as she struggled not to scream at the sight.

Floating face to face with her was a skull wrapped in dark wispy shadows like tattered black rags. The eye sockets blazed blood red while the hands reaching to touch her were skeletal with decayed flesh hanging from the bones.

Kilala slowly floated away from the apparition, wanting to put distance between her and the foul being. With a great effort, she found her voice. "What are you?" she whispered hoarsely.

The skull head tilted as it studied her, "You are either naïve or stupid," the jaw clattered as it talked.

"I. Am. Neither." She bit off each word angrily.

"You should fear me." The skull waved back and forth, the hands stretched their reach to try to claw her.

Anger flared within her as Kilala quickly tired of the game. She put her head down to glare up at the entity. "Answer my question, you foul being." She turned her back to it, defying it to do something. "I do not answer to nameless fears." She glanced back over her shoulder to see it staring at her in confusion. "Name yourself or be gone!" She turned her head back and started floating away. "You disturbed my peaceful contemplation."

The entity floated around so she could see it. "I am the Spirit of the Death Hunters," it intoned in a hollow, echoing voice, then suddenly flew backward until it was out of sight in the blink of an eye.

Kilala floated in space staring at the spot where the apparition had been. Her mind was racing with this revelation. *Death Hunters?* she thought frantically. *Who are they? I have only known of the five tribes! Who and what are they?* A chill finger of fear stabbed her soul. *What can they do?* Feeling the fear that slipped past her defenses, she spun around to see if the Death Hunter Spirit had reappeared. *Did it touch me?* She felt around on her spirit-like body to see if there was any evidence of wounds. *Why did I turn my back to it?* she chided herself as she shivered. Clammy cold started to envelope her senses. "What is happening to my body?" she cried to the stars, then willed herself back into her physical body.

<u>*Chapter 15*</u>

Kilala popped open her eyes, expecting the apparition of the Death Hunter Spirit to be hovering over her body. As she frantically sat up and looked around, she saw that there was no one else in her haven except the white tigress and her old cat. She kept scanning the cavern and saw absolutely no hints of any problems. When she focused on Teigra and Anong and saw how soundly they were sleeping, she felt foolish. She knew they would not be so relaxed if there had been any recent intruders.

Trying not to disturb her ancient tortoiseshell cat who slept next to her, she slowly eased out of bed and stood up. To shake off the chill of fear, she closed her eyes and took slow and deep breaths to calm the frantic pace of her heart. She knew that once she was calm, she could think more clearly.

Feeling more in control, she made her way to the table, taking care not to wake the sleeping cats. Once she settled in the chair, she stared out of the cave entrance to think. As she dissected the encounter with the Spirit of the Death Hunters, she knew what happened to her. The Spirit exuded something that instilled fear in her. The fear she felt after the Spirit had left was not from the apparition but from within. She remembered her grandmother teaching her that fear from within was the hardest to control but that it could be mastered. She had also told her that this type of fear was easily aroused when a person was uncertain or faced with something they had never seen or done before. She nodded to herself. Not only was she in a position where she was unsure of what she was doing, but also she was faced with a dark truth that had never been revealed to her before.

After this point was clear in her mind, she knew there were other things to consider, but she felt the need to move and break away from her dark thoughts. Picking up the stone cup from the table, she went outside the cave to go to the brook. When she walked out into the late afternoon sun, she stopped to enjoy the warmth on her face and arms. Looking around, she watched bright colored butterflies of all kinds flit around the flowers and blooming trees and heard the droning buzz of bees. The breeze whispered through the garden, bringing her the sweet scents of the flowers along with the fresh smells of growing things. "This is beautiful," she whispered.

After she stooped down to fill her cup with cool, clear water, she took a long drink. After filling it again, she sipped it as she walked around the various fruit trees. As she felt the short, soft grass under her slippered feet, she realized that this was the first time that she had a chance to really look around the grounds outside the cave. Curious to see if any fruit was ready to eat, she looked up into the trees as she passed. Even though she made her way through her private orchard without seeing any ripened fruit, she was not disappointed. She was enjoying the simplicity of exploring her haven and temporarily pushing aside newly revealed dark problems and the feeling of foreboding that was growing within her.

As she approached one of the corners of the property, she saw a fig tree. Its low branches spread out leisurely from one misty boundary to the other to fully fill the angular space. As she looked into the mists that formed the barrier around her haven, she saw grayish-white ghostly fingers of mist reach toward her then deflect upward suddenly as if on some prearranged path. Suddenly, the bright sunshine struck the misty wisps at just the right angle to cause the light to refract into a vivid rainbow. Kilala smiled cheerfully at the ethereal beauty and watched it until the perfect juxtaposition shifted and the rainbow faded away.

When she turned away to look at the fig tree, her smile returned as she found figs that were soft and ready to eat. After picking a handful of them and washing them in the stream, she went back to the table, placed the cup on the table, figs in a bowl, and then sat down to consider what she needed to do next. The jaunt around her haven grounds helped her to relax and clear her mind.

After she ate a few figs, she remembered that the Spirit of the Bear Hunters requested his fellow Spirits to help look for the missing Bear Hunter cubs. Then she thought about the Dog Hunter Spirit accusing her Sentinels of encroaching on their territory. She chided herself in almost forgetting these essential tasks that had to take priority. As she thought about phrasing a message to the Sentinels that covered both areas, she realized she didn't know how she should accomplish the task.

"Teigra?" she called gently to the sleeping black-and-white-striped great cat. She saw a blue eye pop open to look at her. "How do I call the Sentinels? Do I contact Nemr and have him pass on the message? Or should I contact all of them at the same time?"

The white tigress sat up and yawned. "How important is the message? Do only a few need to hear it or all of them?"

"I need to get a message to all of them."

Teigra gave a quick lick to a paw before she answered. "As Companion you have a mental link to all the Sentinels. Concentrate on them as a group and send them your message."

"Ah," Kilala muttered as she thought, *That sounds easy.* She closed her eyes and tried to concentrate on contacting the Sentinels. As she felt a sudden connection to multiple minds, she was overwhelmed by an eerily expansive sensation. She quickly shook off the distracting feeling to instruct them to look for Bear Hunter young, animal and human. Then she asked if any of them had gone into Dog Hunter territory or had knowledge of any of their kind who had done so. Every one of them responded that they had not but they would check amongst their kin. She wished them well, then broke the connection. Taking a deep breath, she opened her eyes and glanced at Teigra. The big cat was watching, her whiskers twitching as if she was hiding a smile. "Did I do all right?" she asked.

"You did well, for the first time," the white tigress replied. "It was a bit loud and all of cat-kind heard it, not just the Sentinels."

Embarrassed, Kilala muttered softly, "Oh." She felt her cheeks burning as she ducked her head. "Sorry."

Teigra stood and stretched before she padded over to rub her face on Kilala's legs to comfort her. "With that message, it was better that it was broadcasted to all cat-kind. Now everyone knows to look for bear-kind." She looked up at Kilala with concern in her blue eyes. "Were they very young?"

"Their Spirit didn't say. But his level of concern for them gave the impression they were very young," she answered quietly.

"That is not good," the big cat muttered as she padded out of the cave.

"Where are you going?" Kilala called out to her before she was completely out of sight.

"To look around haven and the nearby territory for the little ones," she called back. "Anong is there with you. She can contact us if there is a problem here."

She looked over at her old cat. Anong was awake and staring at her. "Yes, it was loud. Woke me up out of a very pleasant dream," she meowed crankily.

"Sorry," Kilala apologized quietly.

Anong licked a paw, then rubbed it over her face as she washed. "Teigra is right; you are learning. No matter." She stopped to stare at her again. "This time," she warned.

Kilala nodded and smiled at her, then turned back and saw the book she had left on the table. Curious about what else could be in it, she scanned the rest of the volume. When she reached the end, she was a bit disappointed that it didn't mention anything about the Death Hunters. She sat back and looked at the other books on the shelf. *Teigra had said something about colors,* she thought as she stared at them, hoping for a revelation. After several minutes, she couldn't figure out what that could mean. When she looked around the cave, she saw that the white tigress hadn't returned so she could ask her for more information.

She knew she could contact her but decided not to. She wasn't sure if she could narrow down the communication so that only Teigra would hear it. Restless, she paced around the cave. When she passed the entrance, she saw that it was getting darker outside. She stopped to watch as the night took command of the sky, revealing the full and bright moons, the greater moon and its two lesser companions, and an expanse of a multitude of stars of various colors and intensities.

After several minutes, the mystery of the volumes, the meaning of the colors, and the mystery of the Death Hunters started to invade her peaceful contemplation. She sighed as she turned to go back into the cave to resume her pacing. Suddenly, something caught her eye as she turned back into the cave; she reversed the motion to look back outside.

She almost disregarded the mists that she had seen all her life that swirled throughout the forest starting at dusk and ending at dawn. But she noticed that it appeared to be different from the mists in the forests around her old village and looked similar to the mist that she had seen as she passed through to the meeting place with the boulder chairs. But now she could see tiny, twinkling energy bursts and hair-thin lines of light that swirled through the moisture-laden, cottony white. Again, she had the impression that the mist was alive. She stood in the entrance of the cave, watching it approach. It moved to within feet of the cave and then stopped. She was tempted to reach out to touch it but hesitated.

"What do you see?" She heard a gravelly meow behind her. She turned to see Anong sitting on her haunches on the floor with her tail coiled around her paws.

"The mist." Kilala felt foolish. "It appears to be alive."

The old cat padded to the entrance to sit by her feet as she also looked out into the night. "Cat-kind feels it is filled with a life-force," she said simply. "This mist we call the Kuatrukai."

"The Kuatrukai," Kilala repeated quietly, careful to say it as Anong did. Then she turned to look at the old cat. "Is it dangerous?"

Anong shook her head. "It seems not to be good or bad. It simply is."

"It's so mysterious," she observed. "It's different than the mists at home. Could the Death Hunters have anything to do with it?" Once the words were out of her mouth, she knew she leapt to conclusions because of her recent experience. She felt like she embarrassed herself again and was about to change the subject when she looked down at Anong.

Chapter Sixteen

The old cat's body had tensed as she stared long and hard at Kilala. After a few seconds, she asked, "Where did you hear of them?"

Kilala wondered why Anong did not seem surprised to hear them mentioned but decided not to ask since her old cat seemed very tense and almost angry. "After the meeting of the Council of Spirits, their Spirit appeared to me," she answered carefully.

The ancient cat's eyes grew large and round with surprise and concern. She turned to walk back into the cave. "Come. We must not talk of this out here."

Kilala looked again at the Kuatrukai that settled around the trees and crops, then turned into the cave. Her old cat had jumped up on the table and settled down with her front paws tucked under her chest, waiting for her. She walked around the table to sit in the chair.

"What did it say?" Anong asked urgently after Kilala had settled. "Did it touch you?"

Kilala related the experience she had with the Spirit of the Death Hunters. After she was done, she waited while the small cat considered what happened. After several minutes, she ventured to ask," What can you tell me about them? I have never heard of them before."

"They are not talked about," Anong stated firmly as she flicked an ear. "They live in the shadows."

"What makes up their Sentinels? Their humans?" She was curious to hear more about this hidden tribe, although she was repelled by the thought of them.

"They are a tribe of outcasts. When the tribes were formed, those not wanted by the others banded together to make their own way." Her eyes narrowed as her tail tip flicked back and forth in irritation. "They are made of corpse eaters."

Kilala was confused. "We eat meat that has been killed…"

"No!" the cat yowled suddenly. "Not fresh kill. They eat flesh that is rotted and decayed."

Kilala suddenly felt very sick at the thought. Then they were interrupted by a low growl. She jumped at the unexpected sound and turned to look into the narrowed blue eyes of the white tigress.

"What are you talking about?" Teigra was standing by the table looking from one to the other. Neither Anong nor Kilala had heard her come into the cave.

"I had asked about Death Hunters," she told the big cat.

Teigra growled at the little cat, "Why are you talking about that which cat-kind do not talk of?"

The little cat hissed at the larger one. "I did not bring it up! The Spirit of the Death Hunters appeared to her. She needs to know…"

The big cat's head swung around to stare at Kilala. "It appeared to you?" Deep concern clouded the blue eyes. "I wonder why?" Her expression showed concern and contemplation as she sat down facing them. The end of her tail twitched slowly behind her.

Suddenly, the Shoku filed into the cavern. Kilala looked at them in confusion as she wondered why they were there. "I summoned them," Teigra explained quietly. "We all need to hear what happened."

"Should the Sentinels hear it?" Kilala asked.

"We are to guard you. The males guard the villages and patrol the territory. We will report to our mates of what you tell us."

Kilala nodded to each one and then started to reveal to them what happened after the council meeting. When she was done, all the cats sat in perfect silence. As she waited, she suspected they were conversing amongst themselves in their secret language.

After a while, she interrupted the charged silence. "I need more information," she told them quietly. "Who makes up their tribe? Anong was telling me they were outcasts. What outcasts? Everyone is accepted into a tribe."

"The tribes have been established for centuries," Teigra started to answer. "When they were first formed out of need, there were several groups that were not accepted by the others. They were strange of tastes and dark of spirit."

Kilala nodded, indicating that she followed. "But who eats rotten flesh?"

"Hyenas, jackals, vultures and such are the animal-kind in that tribe," the white tigress said quickly. "They were created for such things. But the human-kind with them is not naturally so."

"Oh," was all she could say. She had not heard of these types of animal-kind before. "So there are also people in this tribe?" she asked to clarify. She was even more horrified and baffled by the thought of human-kind being involved in such things.

Teigra ducked her head. "Yes. They also have an alliance with insect-kind. They are said to command fly swarms and other bugs that eat rotted flesh and excrement."

Kilala shuddered as a chill crawled up her back. "How dangerous is the Death Hunter tribe?"

"For centuries they have been on the fringe of the tribes. They claim the dead that are not properly buried." The big cat locked gazes with her. "They should not have power over the living."

"Do they have their own territory?"

"No, they migrate throughout all the Hunter territories."

Kilala nodded as she thought. She was so new to her position of leader of her tribe that she had a sudden need to want the implications of what she heard to go away. "So, they have always been around." She nodded to herself again. She wanted to be comforted and to deny there was a problem. "So, there should be nothing to worry about. They haven't harmed us before, so why worry now?" She sighed deeply in relief. *The encounter with their Spirit was a fluke and really nothing to worry about,* she thought, wanting to convince herself. "Good. Now I need to study the other books." She stood up to get another volume but stopped as she looked around. All the great cats were still watching her. None of them had made a move to leave. She looked at them, meeting each pair of eyes. "Am I missing something?" Even as she asked, she knew that she wasn't missing anything but just wanted the problem to go away, and they weren't going to let it.

Teigra stood and waved a forepaw toward her chair, a motion that indicated she needed to sit down again. "We need to talk."

Kilala had a sinking feeling as she moved away from the bookshelves toward her chair. She knew that her wanting to deny there was a problem was wrong. To be a worthy leader, she had to face the facts head on. She slowly sat down as she watched the big cats watch her. "I am listening."

"We have been monitoring strange events that have happened for the last several seasons. At first, we thought it was because of our former Companion getting very old and weak." Teigra looked out of the cave where the Kuatrukai glowed faintly. "But now, we believe something else is happening that we have not seen before."

Suddenly, Kilala remembered what the previous Companion had said about a storm approaching. "What are the details?" she asked quietly. The uneasy feeling she felt before solidified into a premonition of dread that started to fill her innermost being.

"The latest event is that one of the Death Hunters appeared to one of the Spirits of the Hunter tribes. That event was their Spirit appearing to you." The big head shook back and forth. "That is unheard of in all of the tribes' history."

The lioness came forward to add more details to the report. "The prey animals are becoming fewer. There has been no explanation for this to be happening." Kilala nodded in response, remembering that the other Spirits had reported the same.

The puma came forward next. "Some of our mothers have lost cubs. They have not been found. Now we hear that the Bear Hunters are also experiencing this." Kilala's mouth dropped open at this news and wanted to ask for additional details when she was distracted by more of the Shoku relating other suspicious events.

"We now wonder if the destruction of the Cat Hunter villages was due to Dog Hunters or something else," the white tigress stated. Kilala was surprised and perplexed by this news but the conversation still flowed on, not giving her time to ask questions.

The bobcat stood up. "We also believe the life-force in the Kuatrukai is weakening."

The lioness shook her head at the smaller female. "We are not sure of that," she chided her.

The bobcat refused to back down. "We all have seen the energy is weakening! It is not as strong as it was when I was a kitten."

Teigra signaled both females to quiet down. When they saw her gesture, they immediately ducked their heads in apology then moved back to their places. She turned to Kilala. "There has been discussion amongst us about the Kuatrukai. Many of us feel that the power or life-force has diminished."

Kilala looked from one of the Shoku to the other. She was overwhelmed by all that had been revealed and didn't know where to start. "What could all this mean?" she said half to herself as she looked away. She rubbed her forehead as she tried to dispel a budding headache. "I must contemplate all I have learned today," she told the big cats. "I will keep it all in mind and see what we can do. I will contact you if I need more information. Let me know if you or your mates notice anything else." All the cats bowed, and most of them left until all that remained with her were Teigra and Anong.

As she wearily slumped into the straight-backed chair, she continued to rub her forehead. After a few moments, she sighed and closed the book that remained on the table. She turned to look at her bed and then looked back, peering outside the cave entrance. Trying to ignore her worsening headache, she stared at the whitish grey cottony shroud as she pondered on what she had learned about the Death Hunters. Then she started to wonder about what was in the Kuatrukai, what happened to the cubs, the question of who was responsible for destroying their villages, and what was happening to the prey animals. *And what did my predecessor mean about a storm approaching?* she thought glumly. *Are all these things happening now? Or is there more to come?* Her painful contemplations were interrupted when her stomach grumbled to remind her that it was past her meal time.

"You need to eat. That may help your headache," Teigra pointed out. "What would you like for me to hunt for you?"

When she heard the word 'hunt', she thought of meat. She gagged as she was suddenly assaulted by an image of rotting flesh. Kilala shook her head slightly. "I will eat light. I'll have some bread and fruit. I'll brew some medicinal tea as well," she muttered as she rubbed her head some more.

Teigra nodded once to her and to Anong. "That should help," she said over her shoulder as she turned to leave the cave. "I will return after my hunt."

Kilala has asked Anong if she needed to hunt. When the old cat shook her head and jumped down from the table to curl up on the bed, she quickly gathered her food and made her tea. After eating and sipping the hot tea, she was so weary that she had to sleep. As soon as she moved to her sleeping area and carefully lay down next to Anong, she fell fast asleep.

Chapter 17

With the dawn of a new day, Kilala felt much better. Her headache had dissipated, and her mind was clearer. The encounter with the Death Hunter Spirit was not forgotten, but the intensity of her reaction toward the event and knowledge of such a tribe had waned in the face of the jumble of all the news the Shoku had shared. She knew she had much to learn and adjust to in her position as the Spirit of her tribe. Sitting at the table, she broke her fast with freshly baked muffins and fruit along with a cup of steaming tea.

As she ate, she thought about how there were serious problems that could not be ignored, and she accepted the fact that she had to deal with them. She knew she couldn't thoroughly study everything she had learned at the same time and needed to prioritize things. She took a deep breath and allowed her medicine woman training to kick in before her thoughts mired down. Medicine women had to deal with many people at the same time. The ailments would range from minor to serious and had to be triaged so as to help the ones who needed it the most quickly. Keeping that in mind, she asked herself, *What is the most important thing to do right now*? As she looked over the collection of books that she had piled on the table, she had an answer. *Information. I wonder if there is any information in those that will help with what is going on now?* she thought. *So far, they seem to be history related.*

She looked down at the book that she had been reading. As she picked it up and studied it, she noted that the cover was black. Looking over the others, she saw that the others were different colors: purple, red, yellow, green, blue, orange, and white. She turned to find the Teigra sitting up, her tail curled around her feet, watching her intently. "You said something about colors."

The big cat nodded once. "The only thing that the previous Companion told me was that it was important to read the volumes in order." The black tip of her tail flicked back and forth as she thought further. "She said that you must determine the order."

Kilala nodded as she spread the books out on the table. As she handled all the volumes, she realized that they looked and felt new. She opened a few and fanned the pages. The spines were stiff as if they had been opened only once to write in them. The pages were pristine as if the words were written a few days ago. *Did any of the past Companions ever bother to read the books?* she wondered. *Or did they simply do what the previous one had taught?* She shook her head at that thought. She knew that not referring back to the original source would dilute or, worse yet, cause loss of valuable information and breed misinformation. She knew the result could be a diminishing or misuse of power. She glanced over at the white tigress as she asked, "Did she ever read the books?"

Teigra considered the question for a few moments then shook her head slowly. "No," she said carefully, "I had never seen her read them. I contacted Tiaret, who had spent more time with her, and she had never seen her read them." The big cat seemed to be searching her memory for something. After several minutes, she said, "In fact, there is nothing that has been passed down in our Lore about any of the Companions reading the books." She looked mystified as she glanced from Kilala to the books on the table.

Kilala was distracted from the discussion of the books by another unfamiliar term. "You mentioned the Lore. What is that?" she asked curiously.

"We have a verbal history of our tribe including that of our Companions from the time of the beginnings. It includes their strengths, their weaknesses, their wisdom, and their follies."

"Oh," she whispered as she thought, *Everything I do will be recorded for all time!* The idea of how she would be remembered frightened her.

Teigra picked up her concern. "Do not worry, Companion, do the best you know how. History judges all in the end."

Kilala gave her a tiny nod that she understood, then took a deep breath and let it out slowly. *That's the future. I need to stick with the problems and mysteries of today,* she thought as she looked down at the books again. "Maybe they were written in case a new Companion didn't have a mentor to teach them?" she observed, gesturing toward herself as an example.

When she looked back up, the brilliant blue eyes of the white tigress captured her gaze and bore into her. "Or is it because they were written for you?" Teigra asked her pointedly.

With a chill crawling up her spine and goosebumps popping up on her arms, she thought of the possibility that those books, many of which she knew were written so long ago, were specifically for her. She quickly shook off the creepy feeling and regarded that notion as being ridiculous. She knew she needed information and would consider it as that, not a message from the distant past.

As she stared at the volumes to see which one to read next, she suddenly had a whispered thought tug at her mind. Her eyes widened as she looked over at the white tigress.

"Do not worry, Mistress," Teigra purred. "That is the Sentinels contacting you with the daily reports."

Kilala smiled at her in relief; she had thought that the Death Hunter Spirit or some unknown enemy was trying to take over her thoughts. She relaxed and closed her eyes to concentrate on the messages. The Sentinels reported that all was quiet and there was no evidence of any of the other tribes entering into their territory. They also reported with sadness that they had not found any bear- or cat-kind cubs nor could they identify any of their kind that had entered into Dog Hunter territory. She thanked them, then opened her eyes. Teigra was watching her closely.

"Does that please you?" the big cat asked quietly.

Kilala nodded once, then frowned. She did like knowing that there were no other problems but was worried about the cubs that were missing. When she thought of the possibility of other problems emerging, she suddenly felt anxious. *What if something happened and it was up to me to do something, and I didn't know how?* she thought fearfully. *I still don't know my abilities as a Spirit!* She was surprised to hear her voice was steady when she answered Teigra who was still waiting. "For the most part I do. But I would like to hear that the cubs have been found. Why do you ask?"

The white tigress blinked as she looked away. "I do not disrespect your predecessor," she said as she ducked her head, then looked up at her. "Near the end, she had grown so old, her abilities had left her. She didn't want to be told about what was happening in the territory since she couldn't do anything about it."

Kilala hid her panic, furrowing her brow to appear confused about the information. She didn't want her attendant to know that she feared she would be the same way. "Couldn't she have commanded the Sentinels to do something in these events?"

"Oh, she would try," the white tigress tried to explain. "But she became easily confused and wasn't able to accurately direct the Sentinels."

Kilala nodded, feeling a bit relieved that the previous Companion's problem was not exactly like her own. She knew what Teigra was describing as she thought about the elders in the village. They would be encouraged by the younger to continue their work, but often the very aged would need help to do the things they had done well all their lives. "So the Spirits of the tribe age not only in body but also in mind just like anyone else."

Tigress nodded. "As I understand, the aging is much slower than the other human-kind of the tribe."

As she thought about her village, she wondered how her parents and grandmother were doing. She knew she should visit them as soon as she could to let them know how she was doing and to assure them that she hadn't forgotten them. As she thought about the misty barrier around her haven, she asked Teigra, "Can I leave haven?"

"Yes, Companion?" the big cat responded quickly.

"Is it only by projection? Or can I physically leave?"

"You can leave physically. You will need a Sentinel or a Shoku to escort you until you learn to navigate the Kuatrukai. This is so that you can safely arrive at your intended destination."

"The Kuatrukai?" she muttered to herself as she remembered the mists on her journey to the meeting place and to haven. "Is it different than the mists that come here at night?" she asked Teigra.

The big cat shook her head. "It is the same. But it is different than the mists you are used to that are in the forests around the villages."

Kilala nodded to herself as the white tigress confirmed her observations about the differences in the mists. "Is there something dangerous in the Kuatrukai?" she asked.

"No, it is neither good nor bad; they simply exist."

Kilala noted that Teigra made the same comment about the mists as Anong had. *Is that a pat reply they were taught to say?* she thought curiously. *Like I hear some humans say, 'It is what it is'?"* She focused back on what she wanted to learn. "Why the concern then?"

Teigra explained quickly. "The Kuatrukai that is between is very thick. It also swirls and can be misleading, causing a traveler to think they see something familiar when it is not."

"Oh, so I could get lost," she responded.

"Yes," Teigra confirmed.

"Where could I wind up?" Kilala asked. "In one of the other territories?"

"Yes," the white tigress answered. "And in places not known."

Kilala looked at her in confusion. "I thought all the land of Ritigabid was split up between the Hunter tribes."

"There are undesirable areas that none of the tribes wanted as part of their territories," Teigra explained.

"Ah," Kilala thought as she considered the implications. "I see. That is good to know when I desire to visit family," she said as she turned back to the task at hand.

When she looked down at the books she had laid side by side on the table top, she thought something about the colors looked familiar. She cocked her head as she tried to remember what they reminded her of. Suddenly, she gasped as she realized what it was.

Chapter Eighteen

"That's it," she cried out as she waved a hand over the books. In the corner of her eye, she saw Teigra glance from her to the books and back again. "These are colors found in rainbows! The order is how they appear in a rainbow," she explained to the great cat.

After she rearranged the pattern to match a rainbow, she held the black and white covered volumes. She looked up to see that Anong had joined them. She was watching silently as she sat on the table near the books, looking at each of the books, then up at her. Kilala turned her attention back to the two volumes in her hand. She stared at them for a long while, unsure of where to put the white volume. She set it aside then looked at the black volume. She wasn't sure which band of the rainbow to start, the upper or the lower. She looked at the white volume and again at the black. "I was instructed to read the black first," she muttered out loud. "Where would that fall into the pattern? And where does that put the white?" She sat at the table trying to contemplate her next move. "The black is the absence of light. So there is no color." She looked at the white. "And white has all the colors within." She looked up at the cats to explain, "That is what causes the rainbow when white light shines through water drops and causes the colors to be seen!" She smiled to herself as she placed the white volume at the end of the line, the black volume at the beginning and picked up the red one. "This is next."

She saw Teigra and Anong share a glance. Then the white tigress sniffed at the volumes as the old cat pawed gently at the ones nearest her. "How do you know?" Teigra asked curiously. Anong looked at her expectantly as she moved to curl up on one of the books.

Kilala smiled at them. "I will know for sure once I start reading. It should make sense if the information is in order."

"But why that one?" Anong asked.

"It seems to me," she answered while she pointed at the black volume, "that black is the start. That is the one I was directed to read first. It is the one that explains everything that happened to cause the tribes to form and the Spirits come into being. Then the order of the rainbow colors shows progression of some type of information. Maybe it is through time up to a certain point in history or the specifics of the development of the other Hunter tribes or words of wisdom to follow or something of that nature. The white could indicate the completion as everything comes together in whatever final outcome."

Teigra and Anong studied the books again, then looked up at her with concern. "There is an end?" Anong asked quietly.

For a moment, Kilala's excitement from the discovery was tempered. "It may not mean end of all things. Could be an end to what we know as another thing is beginning."

Teigra sat back on her haunches and licked a paw. Her ears flicked back and forth in agitation as the dark tip of her tail twitched irritably behind her. Anong quietly curled up more tightly while she rested her head on a paw to watch her.

"What are you thinking?" Kilala asked the white tigress since she seemed more agitated.

Teigra looked up at her in surprise. "I was thinking that a new beginning could be something good or bad."

Kilala nodded. "That is true." She sat down and opened the red volume. Before she started to read, she glanced over at the cats. "Right now, I'm just guessing about what I will find." She turned the pages back to the beginning. "I need to read more, then maybe I'll be able to tell..." her voice drifted off as the words on the page captured her attention. The script transported her mind back through time as she read more about the early history of Ritigabid.

The first thing Kilala noticed was the cold. When she looked up from the pages of the book, she saw that it was dark outside. No one was in the cave with her. She thought that odd. It seemed that there was always a big cat in there whether to guard her or keep her company; she wasn't sure which. She looked around for her ancient cat. When she couldn't find her, she began to panic. She called her name repeatedly while she walked around the cave and then outside. She looked out into the night and saw the Kuatrukai hanging around the trees and above her head. It was thick as porridge and the lights were large, brilliant flashes that nearly blinded her. She was confused, why was there such a change?

As her mind tried to focus and figure out what was going on, she heard a soft voice behind her calling her name. Whirling around in shocked surprise, she saw a young girl standing in the cave. She was not yet a woman but exuded confidence and authority that was beyond her years. Her hazel eyes shone brightly from an oval face that was framed by long blond hair that had a black stripe starting from the middle of her forehead. The girl lifted a slender hand and beckoned her back in.

Kilala followed her in and sat at the table as the young girl gracefully indicated one of two chairs. Two chairs? she thought. The detail seemed to capture her attention, causing her to look more closely around the cave and saw other differences. The cave floor was not covered, there was not a sleeping place, and there were no shelves. How can this be? she thought in confusion.

"Don't worry," the girl said, her voice soft but high-pitched with youth. "You will be back in the familiar soon." She picked up a stone pitcher. "Would you like some water?"

Kilala, still unable to speak, shook her head slightly.

"I know you have many questions." The girl poured water into a stone cup. Kilala recognized the cup as the one she had used earlier. As the youth sat down and took a few sips, she studied Kilala with eyes that were much older than she seemed. "There are many questions," she stated as she set the cup down on the table. "You are seeking the answers. Am I right?" She didn't seem to notice that Kilala hadn't been able to say a word.

"Keep reading the books," the girl said seriously, locking eyes with her. "It is all in there. Once you are done, you will know more than all the Companions before you." Then she smiled slyly. "Well, except for me."

Kilala finally found her voice. "Who are you?" she whispered.

"I wrote the books," the girl whispered back. She smiled secretively, and then she lifted a hand and waved.

Kilala woke up with a start. She had fallen asleep slumped over the book she was reading. She quickly opened each of the books and looked closer at the handwriting. Suddenly, she sat back in the chair with the weighty realization that they all had been written by the same hand. They were not written by a series of people as she had first thought. As her gaze focused on the sunshine outside the cave entrance, she thought about who she had met. "She was the first Companion," she whispered to herself in awe as a chill crawled up her spine and goosebumps popped up on her arms.

After she briskly rubbed her arms and shook off the awestruck feeling, she stacked the books in order as she planned out how much she needed to read each day to get through all the volumes as quickly as possible. She was relieved and encouraged that she had some direction to go and that the books would tell her everything she needed to know.

Chapter 19

Kilala brooded as she sat at the table looking out into her private garden. An empty stone plate and cup sat on the table in front of her as a silent testimony to her recent meal. As she sat with an elbow on the table and chin in hand, she knew her light mood from earlier had morphed into dark concern and wasn't completely sure why. So far, what she had read had not given her any ready answers for all her questions. That was frustrating, but she knew she hadn't finished reading all the books yet. But there was something more, something she couldn't put a finger on that was still bothering her. Something undefined that deeply disturbed her more and more as time passed. *Is it the predecessor's warning and the news from the Shoku?* she wondered, tapping the tabletop with one finger as she thought. *"Or is it because of the encounter with the First Companion? Or is it because of the encounter with the Spirit of the Death Hunters?*

She turned her thoughts back to the books left by the First Companion. She thought she had missed something in the first volume, the black-covered one, and had reread it. Even with that, she couldn't see anything else that would help in the information that detailed a sophisticated civilization that fell into chaos and, in the aftermath, the evolution of the Hunter Tribe system. After finishing that one and part of the red one, she became impatient for information and scanned through some of the other books. From what she picked up, they related to the formation of the other Hunter tribes, except the Death Hunters. They detailed territory disputes as well as various historical accounts. However, some of the writings puzzled her. They related to things that should have been beyond the lifespan of the First Companion. And some cryptic phrases seemed to be about events not yet happened. But those messages were so vague; she wasn't sure how helpful they would be for what she was dealing with now.

Maybe it's the lack of information about the Death Hunter tribe that is bothering me, she thought as she dropped her hand to reach for another volume. She could understand the need for the Hunter tribes and partitioning of Ritigabid and resources. Even with the reluctant information she had gotten from the Shoku, she still wasn't sure why the tribe of the Death Hunters was necessary. "Is taking care of the dead their only purpose? Did they really form because they were rejected from the other tribes? Even being outcasts, why would any human choose to be part of their group?" she muttered to herself.

Her encounter with the Spirit of the Death Hunters rose up in her memory, unbidden and disturbing. She felt again the fear exuded by the apparition, the sinister attitude in how he acted, and an implied threat that hung unformed and unknown. She tried to study the event dispassionately but had a hard time doing so because of the intense emotions of the whole encounter. After finally pushing it out of her mind, she concentrated on what she knew. So far, she hadn't found a clue to reveal the source of the unspoken threat except the mysterious disappearances reported by the other Spirits. "Could that be their work?" she wondered aloud

She thumbed through the volume as she rapidly scanned the pages. Reaching the end, she sighed and placed it back on the pile. She would read it in detail later. There had been nothing about the Death Hunters in it.

She sat back to stare outside the cave entrance again. As she thought further about what she was sensing deep within her, she had a sudden flash of revelation that something disastrous was brewing. It would not only affect her tribe, the Cat Hunters, but also all the other Hunter tribes. She didn't know where that thought came from but knew that it rang true. As she concentrated on it to try to glean more information, uncertainty and fear started to cast a shadow over her thoughts, trying to confuse and distract her. As the dark fog tried to close off her mind, she felt a warm muzzle nuzzle her face. The sensation dissipated as she opened her eyes to look straight into Tiega's anxious stare.

"Companion, your thoughts grew dark. Please forgive my intrusion, but I worried."

Kilala lifted a hand to gently stroke the black-and-white-striped face. "It is okay," she whispered huskily. "Thank you. I needed not to stay in that state."

The white tigress studied her closely. Soon the worried look cleared, and she returned to her space on the floor.

Kilala watched the big cat arranged her paws and tail as she lay back down on the floor. Before she was fully settled and started to close her eyes, Kilala wanted to ask her something. "May I ask you a question?"

The big cat looked up at her. "Of course. But I may not able to answer it."

She smiled at the white tigress, appreciating her eagerness to help. Her expression became more serious as she thought about how to phrase the question. "I know that this is a sensitive subject." She stopped to clear her throat. "Can you tell me anything else about the Death Hunters?"

She saw the bright blue eyes cloud a shade when she spoke the name. When Teigra started to lick a paw, Kilala knew it was a distraction tactic and waited. After several minutes, the front paws were thoroughly cleaned and the white tigress looked up at her and saw that her Companion was still waiting for an answer. After several heartbeats, she seemed to make a decision "We do not like to speak of them."

Kilala nodded that she understood. "I realize that it is uncomfortable."

The blue eyes snapped. "It is more than that. To say their name is to invite them in," she warned with a nervous growl.

Kilala pulled back in shock. "Oh," she exclaimed softly. She looked away to think. *They have that much power that they can simply respond to their name?* she thought warily. *What other powers could they wield?* When she caught a movement in her peripheral vision, she shied away slightly until she realized it was Teigra standing and padding to her side again. Feeling relieved it was only the white tigress, she thought, *I guess with everything going on, I'm a bit jumpy.*

"Companion," Teigra purred. "I am sorry." She sat on her haunches and looked at her. "I thought you had enough information from the previous discussion. Your encounter with their Spirit still deeply disturbs you?"

She nodded at the big cat silently. After a few minutes, she took a deep breath, then said, "It does. But there is something ominous that is stirring that will affect all the tribes. I sense it, but I don't know what it is. It may be because of the activity of the Death Hunters or someone else that we don't know of yet."

Teigra nodded once. "We feel it, too."

Kilala sat back in shocked surprise that someone else was sensing this darkness as well. "The Sentinels?" she asked urgently.

The white tigress nodded her head slightly. "Yes, the Sentinels and the Shoku," she clarified. "But it's not just us that sense the upcoming storm. It's felt by all animal-kind."

"You all can communicate together?" Kilala was amazed by the revelation.

"Not directly." The big cat started licking her shoulder. "The Spirits have a counsel, yes?" she asked as she glanced at her companion. When Kilala nodded, she continued, "Not only do the Sentinels have a council within their tribe, they also have a Council of Sentinels involving representatives from the five Hunter tribes."

"I see," Kilala was intrigued. "How long has this been going on?"

"It was formed centuries ago. But for a long time, it rarely met," Teigra responded as she moved her ears slightly. "They have been meeting more regularly ever since the disappearances started."

"Of the young ones?" Kilala asked as she leaned forward in her chair.

"Of the villages," Teigra answered.

Kilala sat back suddenly again. The white tigress had caught her off guard, causing thoughts and images to suddenly swirl around her. She couldn't harness it all. She tensed, and her throat tightened up.

Before she could try to say anything, Teigra spoke first, "Your birth village was not the first." The big cat placed a massive paw on her leg with her long claws carefully sheathed. Kilala met the earnest eyes of the great cat. "One village was destroyed before yours. The others were after your birth."

"Did the Dog Hunters destroy all the villages?" she asked, her voice harsh and higher pitched as she forced the words out.

"We are not sure it was Dog Hunters that destroyed yours," the white tigress said softly.

Kilala was confused. "But in the vision I had, there were dogs howling. Anong's memories show dogs tearing up my father, the villagers, and their cats."

Teigra's blue eyes earnestly sought hers. "Are you sure they were dogs from the Dog Hunters tribe?" the white tigress pushed. "Our Lore of that event is murky. Too many conflicting reports were made by the Sentinels who were there. They have since been replaced by younger ones as they had grown too old to serve."

"Oh, I see," Kilala muttered as she cast her mind back to the vision she had seen. As she picked through the memories, she was certain that it was dogs that had been howling. Then she took into consideration what Anong had shared with her. Taking the two visual accounts, she slowed down the action in her mind as she compared them to try to view the attackers in more detail. The effort in doing it caused her thoughts and memories to swirl like a whirlwind, making her head hurt and confusing her emotions. She clamped her eyelids shut and squeezed while she pressed clenched fists against her forehead to force the pain away. She had to remind herself to breathe deeply and slowly as she drew on all her willpower to push forward through the physical and mental pain. She wanted this information desperately; she needed it.

Just as she thought her head would burst, she felt great paws on both legs and a small weight in her lap. Suddenly, a sense of strength and communion flooded through her. The additional support enabled her to disperse the whirlwind and see the events in crystal clarity. What she saw made her gasp as she opened her eyes.

At first, she couldn't focus on anything except what had been revealed to her. As she calmed her breathing again, her eyes focused on three pairs of eyes focusing on her face; the blue eyes of the white tigress, the gold eyes of the lioness, and the brilliant green eyes of her ancient cat. As her body relaxed, she was able to smile at them. "I am okay," she stated in a hoarse whisper. "I saw clearly."

All three nodded mutely while Teigra and Tiaret sat back on their haunches and Anong nestled down into her lap. When she looked around the room, she saw it was filled with the Sentinels and the Shoku.

When Teigra saw Kilala's confusion, she started to explain, "Through our mental connection, we saw flashes of your vision but not enough to explain. When we could not grasp everything you saw, they sensed our confusion and your distress and came to add their support."

Kilala sighed heavily as she bowed her head and hid her face in her hands. To witness the carnage of that night and her parents dying again had been exhausting and difficult. She drew a deep breath, trying to cleanse herself from the effects of the ordeal, as she sat back to look around the room. She knew she needed to press forward. "I saw who destroyed my birth village." She drew another breath and let it out slowly. "It was not the Dog Hunters." She looked down to meet Anong's eyes. "Did you see what I saw? What was hidden from you when you were a kitten?" The ancient cat answered her with a nod. Kilala petted her as she looked up to meet the eyes of the great cats. "What was seen and heard were coyotes, jackals, and hyenas that were posing as Dog Hunters' animal-kind in their voice and mannerisms."

"Death Hunters," the lioness muttered darkly as she looked nervously around the cave.

Kilala nodded, a cold chill going through her thoughts and body as she and the other big cats also looked around. After a while, with no appearance from the Death Hunter Spirit, she confirmed, "Yes." After she gently moved Anong from her lap and set her on the floor, she found the strength to stand, feeling the need to move as she thought. Pacing through the assembly, she formed her thoughts into words. "With this revelation, I believe that they are responsible for not only destruction of the villages but also the kidnappings." Deep in her own thoughts and memories, she didn't notice the reaction of the big cats as they looked at each other, ears flattened and tails twitching irritably. Some growled to themselves as their fur bristled in anger and fear. "But why?" she muttered to herself and the others. "Why do all this destruction and killing? Their existence depends on the survival of the other tribes!"

"Parassssitessss ssssometimesss kill their hostsss," said a small voice from the cave entrance.

Chapter Twenty

All heads turned to the sound. When they saw the speaker, the instantaneous reaction of the Sentinels and Shoku stunned Kilala in what looked like an intense and elaborate dance. As the Sentinels moved to block the intruder and then crouched ready to spring on him, the Shoku moved around to stand as a protective barrier around their Companion.

"Pleassse, cat lady, ssspare me," the little green snake begged as he lowered his head to the ground in a bow.

Kilala raised a hand to silently command the Sentinels and the Shoku to stand down. They all obeyed as they sat, but none of them relaxed. Their postures were tense and ready for quick action, if needed.

She walked to the cave entrance as she spoke, "What are you doing here? How did you get past my barrier?"

"I don't know how I was able to enter. I was outside trying to figure out how to contact one of your Sentinels when suddenly there was a weak spot, and I took it." The little snake trembled slightly as he pulled himself into a tight coil. He raised his head enough to look up at her. "I have been banissshed." He looked around the room, briefly meeting all the eyes of the big cats in turn, then back to her. He started to tremble more as he saw the hostility that blazed in their eyes. "In truth, my mistress tried to kill me." He lay his head on the ground. "I have nowhere else to go."

After she made a mental note to check the barrier around her haven and territory, Kilala studied the little snake while she wondered if she could trust him. After a few minutes, she asked, "Why would she do such a thing?"

At first, the tight ball of green didn't answer. "I...I..." He drew a deep breath then let it out. "I opposssed her. I spoke out againssst what ssshe planned to do to you."

Kilala squatted down to pick up his head so she could look him in the eyes. "Why did you do that? Don't you support your mistress?"

"I have no choice, do I?" was the immediate answer from the little reptile. "I am sssnake-kind. Nothing will change that. Even a leopard cannot change hisss spotsss into stripesss!" He flicked his tail to point at the Sentinels. "But there are wrongsss and rightsss that are common to all kind whether cat, sssnake, eagle, dog, bear, or human. And ssshe wasss wrong!"

Kilala was caught by surprise with the thought that this snake seemed to have a moral standard. She also sensed that there was more to the betrayal of his kind. "Is there anything else?" she asked firmly. She met the snake's eyes unwaveringly.

The little snake met her stare then ducked his head. "I...I...," he visibly gulped. "I could not poissson you, my cat lady," he whispered.

When she realized how much danger she was in from the Snake Hunters Spirit, Kilala's mouth went dry, and she froze for a second. After a few moments, she licked her lips to moisten them. "She wanted to kill me?" she asked quietly as she thought, *Can she do that? Bemot seemed to suggest a Spirit couldn't be killed. But maybe she knows something that he doesn't?*

The snake's head ducked once in acknowledgement.

"When did she decide she wanted to kill me?"

"When ssshe could not posssesss you."

She knew what incident he was talking about when Chusi thought she was present for Kilala's first translation. Kilala remembered witnessing the Snake Spirit's shiny, semi-transparent body morphing from a young woman into a large snake. She shuddered slightly, then quickly suppressed the horror and fear she had felt at that time.

Focusing back on the present, she thought to herself, *I shouldn't be surprised that the Spirit of the Snakes would try something else.* She took a deep breath to relax, then looked down at the little snake. "Thank you for not poisoning me," she whispered softly. Then she had a sudden thought. "You are a non-venomous snake. How were you going to poison me?" she asked curiously.

"SSShe wasss going to place sssmall granulesss of poissson under my ssscalesss. Then all I would have to do wasss ssswim through your ssstream or dip a tail into your water cup for them to disssssolve."

Kilala was stunned by the ingenuity of the plan. She also realized that if the snake had poisoned the stream, anyone drinking out of it would have been killed. She felt the ripple of reaction through the big cats as they thought of the same thing. She held up a hand to signal them to be quiet and relax.

Thinking for several minutes to weigh the risk of the presence of the snake with his request for asylum, she thought of what Teigra had told her about the previous Companion keeping the little snake around as a way to keep an eye on the Snake Hunter tribe. She knew that he could be lying about why he was at her haven and could actually have been sent as a spy, but she couldn't be sure that he was not in danger. She studied the tightly coiled green reptile and saw that he was truly terrified. With all that in mind, she made her decision.

Turning to the others in the cavern, she announced her judgment. "He chose not to cause us harm against the orders of his Spirit," she said firmly as she met each pair of their eyes. "He can stay amongst us for now. He can find a place out in the gardens of my sanctuary. But he will be watched closely. If he does anything to threaten us, then he will be cast out." She glanced back at the snake. "I am sorry that I cannot fully trust you at this time. Perhaps, in time, I and all cat-kind will."

The snake's head dipped once. "Thank you, my cat lady. I will do whatever you asssk."

"Even if it is against your kind?" she asked softly.

"If it isss for the good of all, yesss," the snake replied. "If it isss for persssonal gain or vendetta, I will not."

Kilala studied the snake closely, surprised again at his scruples. "Yes," she said approvingly as she nodded at him. "That is most wise." She turned back to the others. "He may be of use to us in the coming days."

All of the Sentinels and Shoku nodded that they understood. Even though they relaxed at her command, Kilala could tell from their body language that many were not happy having the reptile amongst them again. But she had no doubt that they would honor her requests, especially the one about watching him closely.

"What is your name?" she asked him when she realized that nobody had mentioned it. "I don't want to keep thinking of you as the little green snake."

The reptile ducked his head in a bow again. "My name isss Yumie."

"Okay, Yumie," Kilala nodded at him and gestured to the area outside the cave. "Welcome back and make yourself at home." She didn't wait for his reply as she turned around.

With that business done, she slowly walked back to her chair and sat down. She had to figure out a way to find out what the Death Hunter tribe was up to. Since the trail of their destruction started before the day of her birth, she knew their plan was conceived long ago by someone thorough and patient. What *do they hope to accomplish?* she wondered again.

"My cat lady." The snake was still at the entrance. "May I ssspeak?"

Kilala looked up and nodded at him. *Would he share valuable information already?* she thought curiously.

"I heard you talking about thossse who walk amongssst the dead," he said as he looked about nervously.

"Yes?" She leaned forward in intense anticipation of what he wanted to share. She figured his nervousness was from the fact that snake-kind also didn't want to say the name of the secret tribe.

"I know of a hiding place for them on the border between Sssnake and Cat Hunter territory."

Kilala's eyebrows shot up with her surprise. "How did you find this place?"

"When I ran from my missstresssss," he said as a slight tremor passed along his slender body. "I had to hide and found a tunnel. I followed it deep into the ground and found a group of them."

"How did you avoid them?" Nemr spoke up abruptly. "You are still alive after encountering them. How can that be?" The other Sentinels nodded their heads in support of their comrade's question.

"I wasss very fortunate," the snake said softly as he faced the Sentinels. "There wasss a dissstraction on the other ssside of the cave ssso they did not sssee me. I wasss able to turn around and leave without them knowing." He watched them for a moment, then turned to face Kilala.

"I see." Kilala watched the snake with her chin in hand, elbow on the table. *I wonder if he's a double agent,* she thought. *For Snake Hunters and Death Hunters? Could they possibly be in league with each other?*

Yumie dared to slither inside the cave entrance a few feet, then stopped. "I wasssn't there too long," his voice rose in fear or excitement, Kilala couldn't tell which. "But I sssaw cubsss!"

Before Kilala could react, Teigra spoke up, "What kind of cubs?" Urgency hardened the tone of her voice as she stood up.

The snake looked over at her. "Many are there but they are of cat- and bear-kind. I did see white tiger cubsss," he reported with an anxious note in his voice. "And many othersss of the great catsss."

"You better not be lying," Nemr growled in warning at the little snake as he stood up. The Sentinels moved to stand with him.

As Kilala watched the reactions of the great cats, she noted their apprehensive excitement and wondered why their intense interest. As the two groups, the Sentinels and the Shoku, waited to see what their leaders were going to do, it dawned on her that the missing cubs could be close kin to them. She held her tongue as she waited for the little reptile's response.

Yumie shook violently with fear but stood his ground. "I ssswear that isss the truth. That isss why I dared to come back." He ducked his head respectively at the massive white tiger. "It is true that I have been threatened by my Ssspirit and needed sssomewhere to go. But I wanted to tell you what I sssaw and lead you to them!"

Without another word, Nemr started moving toward the cave entrance with the Sentinels following him. The Shoku hadn't moved but were watching Teigra for their cues.

Kilala had a bad feeling about the whole thing. It felt like a trap to her. She was stunned that they were moving without a plan of action and without consulting her. *Do they not trust me that much?* she inwardly cried in distress. Then the cold voice of reason spoke, *They are used to acting on their own with the previous Companion not able to direct them.* With that thought, she knew she had to take action. "Wait!" Kilala shouted at them.

The Sentinels stopped and turned to stare at her. The Shoku looked from Teigra to her. All of a sudden, Kilala felt an ice-cold tension in the air. Nemr stalked back toward her to stand next to his mate.

"You must not keep us from rescuing them," Nemr said so intensely that it sounded like a growl. "Do I need to remind you about your oath?"

Kilala was momentarily shocked into silence by the intense stare of his dark blue eyes. Then her medicine woman training kicked in. *This is like confronting the angry panic of a patient's family when their loved one is in serious shape and dying.* She took a deep breath and let it out slowly; she refused to allow herself to react in anger. "No, I do not forget my oath," she said quietly but firmly, directing her reply to all the great cats in the room. "In fact, I am acting on it."

She relaxed her posture, aware her body language needed to telegraph a message of authoritative calm as well as her words, so she leaned back in the chair to address them. She glanced around and noticed that Yumie had not left yet. She contacted Nemr and Teigra telepathically, hoping only they heard but not caring if the other great cats did. *I fear this is a trap. We need to make plans.* She saw they got the message when they relaxed and slowly blinked at her. She looked at the other great cats and saw they were waiting. Their anger had dissipated when they heard of her concerns. Then she spoke, "I need to contact Bear Hunters tribe. They will want to help."

She stared at Nemr and Teigra again. She had another issue she wanted to address. "Why did you not tell me about these cubs?" She looked over the group to meet each pair of eyes. "All the young of cat-kind are important, and I knew there was a search for them. But why did no one tell me the young ones that were in danger were cubs of the great cats?" All the big cats looked at each other, then at her.

"You are new to the position. You had enough on your mind to learn your power and how to protect your haven as well as Cat Hunter territory," Nemr said as Teigra padded over to nudge Kilala's leg. "We did not want to burden you further. We felt with everyone on watch for cubs, ours may be seen."

"They are truly your kin?" Kilala asked quietly, trying to keep the hurt out of her voice. She was deeply upset and still mystified as to why they had briefly given the report that cat-kind cubs were missing but didn't give her all the details. *Is this another clue that they do not trust me? I could have dealt with it – or could I?* she asked herself as doubt crept in.

"The missing ones are the cubs of the Sentinels and Shoku," Nemr confirmed sadly. Not wanting to meet her eyes, he and his mate bowed their heads and kept them down, their gaze on the floor at her feet. She saw that they knew she was hurt that they had not informed her and had not asked her for her help. She looked over the group of great cats again and saw they were doing the same.

"Yes, I am new to this, but I wish you had told me. The security of the Cat Hunters has been compromised by the taking of your cubs!" she said, she met their eyes as they looked up at her. "I know you have been doing the best you could, but it had to have taken a toll as you worried about them!" She suddenly started to feel their fear and panic that they had been masking up to that point. Her own emotions and fear heightened her feelings, causing her heart to ache painfully. Her voice dropped to a tortured whisper as she pressed both hands over her chest while she slumped over the table. "I would've tried something…" She squeezed her eyes shut, unable to stop the tears from streaming down her face. With her eyes closed, she couldn't see the group of great cats staring at her with great interest and suppressed excitement while silent messages rapidly passed between them.

Earlier, Anong had moved to Kilala's sleeping place to watch the discussion. When she saw what was happening, she moved as quickly as she could through the crowd of big cats to jump up on the table. She started to purr as loudly as she could while she rubbed Kilala's wet cheeks, drying them with her fur. Turning to face the Sentinels and the Shoku, she growled, "Tone it down, will you? You need to continue to shield her from your distress. She is too sensitive."

As the intensity dialed down, Kilala was able to catch her breath and sit up. After wiping her face with a cool, damp cloth the puma had brought her, she opened her eyes to see the great cats staring at her. "Oh, I am so sorry, Nemr and Teigra!" She met the eyes of every great cat in the cavern.

"And for those of you whose cubs are missing! This situation greatly saddens me."

They all remained silent as the Sentinels and their mates looked at each other, then at her. Kilala felt confused as they purred and bowed as one. She sensed something had deeply changed but couldn't put her finger on what it was. As each pair left the cave, they rubbed against her legs until all that were left were the white tigers, Anong, and the small green snake.

"What just happened?" she asked anxiously. "Are they going to get the cubs?"

Nemr bowed to her. "Soon, Companion. We have taken your wise advice to heart. We have contacted the Bear Hunters Sentinels so we can meet and coordinate on a plan. We thought it would be best for you to contact the Spirit of the Bear Hunters."

"Other than contacting their Spirit, what else can I do?" she asked. She didn't feel right sitting safely in her haven while they went to go against the Death Hunters.

"Companion." Teigra padded up to her. "You have done more than you can imagine. You are more than you know."

Kilala was perplexed as she tried to figure out what the white tigress was talking about and what had happened.

"My mate speaks riddles right now," Nemr purred. "It will become clear soon enough. For now, we need you there not in body. You will need to be there to deal with the Spirit of the Death Hunters."

Inwardly, Kilala shuddered with fear and revulsion at the thought of encountering that horrific Spirit for a second time. She had never wanted to see it again. Outwardly, she steeled her gaze and voice. She sensed she had their trust and she would not let them down. "I will be there. I will go to where Yumie leads you." The white tigers bowed to her in response.

"Once the little Snake Hunter shows us where the cubs are, I will contact you as to where we will be meeting the Bear Hunter Sentinels," Nemr said before he rubbed her legs and then left the cave.

"I will be meeting with the Shoku to instruct them. I will be back later," Teigra said, then looked at Anong. "Guard her well. I will be back." Anong nodded that she understood. Then the white tigress rubbed her face on Kilala's legs respectfully before she left the cave.

Yumie bowed to her while he looked at her strangely. She was about to ask what was wrong when he suddenly turned to slither out of the cave to join the waiting Sentinels.

Kilala sat back, still confused. She looked down at her ancient cat in her lap and started petting her.

"You are a true Companion," Anong whispered as she purred.

She stopped petting her in surprise. "What do you mean?"

Anong bumped her hand, signaling her to keep petting her. "All the others before you were Companions, but they did not have the deep union to cat-kind. All, except the first one," she added as she stretched up on arthritic hind legs to rub her face on Kilala's. "You are truly melded with cat-kind."

"Oh," was all Kilala could say. Overall, she didn't know what that meant, but she was inwardly satisfied with that revelation. She smiled at her ancient cat, then gently picked her up and walked over to her sleeping loft. "I am lying down for this."

"Good plan," her cat agreed. Anong waited patiently until Kilala lay down on the pallet and covered herself with blankets. When she was settled, the old cat curled up with her back nestled against Kilala's side and her head resting on her front paws. Slitting her eyelids open a bit, she kept watch while her mistress was doing her job.

Chapter 21

Without a thought of how projecting had become second nature in such a short time, Kilala simply sighed, and her translated self immediately hovered over her body. She didn't look back as she headed for her destination, thankful that one of the books had specified where Bear Spirit's haven was located. She was now used to, and barely noticed, the floating freedom and the silvered curls that floated in and out of her view. In a very short time, she stopped to float near the Spirit of the Bear's sanctuary barrier and tapped on it. She had no idea whether that was the correct protocol or not, but she figured that with the news she had, he wouldn't mind.

"What," a gruff voice answered.

"It's me, Kilala," she responded. "The Spirit of the Cat Hunters," she added quickly in case he forgot her name. "I have news of the bear cubs."

All of a sudden, the apparition of the Bear Hunters Spirit flew out of his haven to float in front of her. His glowing countenance seemed brighter with anticipation. "What? Are they found? Are they alive?"

She held up a hand to stop him so she could speak. "They are found. Last seen, they are still alive. But they need to be rescued."

"Rescued?!" the Spirit of the Bear Hunters growled. His aura suddenly changed to burn with red and orange hues. "They are still in danger?!"

She nodded silently, then said quietly, "Along with some of our cubs."

The Bear Spirit drew back in surprise. The angry overcast to his apparition dissipated quickly. "Cat-kind as well?" he whispered hoarsely. Then his face grew dark with anger against a common foe. "Who dares threaten our young?" he growled.

Kilala had trouble controlling her anger as she saw and felt his rage growing into a white heat. "Death Hunters tribe has them."

"What!!" he shouted. "What?" he said more softly as the impact of the news hit him. "What could they possibly want with our young?" He looked extremely confused.

"I do not know," she said as shook her head. "But we must join together to get them."

"Yes, yes." The shaggy head nodded. "I have just contacted my Sentinels. They report that yours have informed them and they are already in transit to meet with them. Where are our cubs?"

"Follow me," she said as flew away toward where she was told the Sentinels were meeting.

They found them in a meadow near the cave where their cubs were being held. A thick stand of large trees hid them from the cave entrance.

As the two Spirits hovered side by side, Kilala scanned the large group. She saw that on one side were bears of different sizes and colors standing together while on the other side were gathered her Sentinels.

Both Spirits silently listened as their Sentinels debated on different plans of action. They spoke to each other in the common tongue of all animal-kind; one Kilala was surprised to find that she understood. She drew closer to Bemot to ask, "How do I understand them?" she whispered, not wanting to disturb the others.

Bear Hunter Spirit smiled at her. "It comes with the territory," he whispered back gruffly. "Rank has its privileges, or so they say."

After a quick nod, she smiled back at him, then drifted to hover over her Sentinels. As she passed over the group, she picked up more of the subtle threads of the conversation concerning their plans and disagreements. The bears wanted to do a frontal assault with a rush into the cave, strong arm any resistance, and find their cubs. The big cats wanted to be a bit more subtle and lure as many of the captors out as they could before they mounted a raid. The only thing they could agree on was that there was only one entrance large enough for them. Representatives from both groups of Sentinels had already scouted around the area and couldn't locate any other ways into the cavern except the narrow tunnel the little snake had found.

A sudden silence surrounded them as they stalled on points of procedure without agreement and stood staring at each other.

As the silence lengthened and the tension increased, Kilala remembered her initial thoughts when she heard about the cubs. "Has anyone considered this could be a trap?" she asked as the bears and great cats lifted their heads to look up at her.

Bemot spoke up first. "Why do you think that? I thought your source was reliable."

Kilala searched the group and around the area. She didn't see the little snake anywhere. *He must have left once he led the Sentinels here,* she thought, mildly disturbed by his absence. "My source is a snake. Although he is reported to be a friend of the Cat Hunters, I do not have total trust in him."

Bemot shook his glowing shaggy head and tugged on his massive beard. "Do you think the cubs are even there?"

She nodded thoughtfully. "I do. A trap needs bait."

"What do you think we ought to do?" the Spirit of the Bear Hunters asked urgently. Below them, the eyes of the bears and big cats were following the conversation between the two Spirits as they looked from one to the other.

Kilala thought a while as she hovered. A plan began to form as she thought about what she knew and what she suspected. She met the Spirit of the Bear Hunter's eyes. "I propose that we, you and I, check out what is in there and how many are involved. With more information, we can formulate a better plan that will hopefully cut down on causalities and increase our chances of a successful mission."

She could see that Bemot thought hard about what she had said before he answered. "Problem is, we can be seen. It will tip them off that their hiding place has been found," he pointed out.

Kilala nodded at him, acknowledging this fact as a question popped into her mind. "You told me the Spirits can look like anything they wanted to."

Kilala saw confusion flicker in his eyes with the sudden change in subjects. But then he nodded slowly as he answered, "That is true."

"What about wishing to look like nothing?" she asked as she quirked a glowing, silver eyebrow at him.

At first, his face pinched up into a scowl as he quickly spat out, "Lunacy! That is crazy!" Then a thoughtful expression smoothed his features. He tugged at his beard as he contemplated what she had said. "But," he started to mutter, "no one that I ever heard of has tried that." He looked down at the Sentinels, who had been watching their leaders with great interest. "Have any of you ever heard of that in your Lore?"

Bear-kind and cat-kind looked at each other thoughtfully, then looked back up at their Spirits and shook their heads.

Kilala looked at Bemot and his Sentinels curiously. "Bear Hunters tribe has the Lore as well?"

A huge grizzly answered, "All of the Sentinels of the Hunter tribes have this tradition."

Bemot spoke up, "Animal-kind felt that they needed to keep their own history. Through the centuries, they had noticed the human tendency of not keeping to facts when it came to historical accounts."

Kilala nodded as she thought about the writings in her haven that had an account of the history of the Hunter tribes. She started to wonder how true to fact they were, especially since they were written by one person. *Did she have the facts of everything going on and be able to look into the future?* she thought as she remembered some of what she had seen in the books. She made a mental note to consult with her Sentinels and their mates to see if their Lore matched what was in the books. She put those thoughts away as she focused on the problem at hand. "Okay, now, to do what we are here for." She met the dark eyes of the Spirit of the Bear Hunters. "Would you like to try, or shall I?"

The glowing visage frowned a bit in worry and shrugged. "It is said 'ladies first.'"

Kilala smiled and nodded. "It was my idea, so I will certainly try first." She thought a while then whispered to Bemot. "I don't know the first thing about how to change my appearance." She glanced at him in embarrassment.

He grinned widely at her, then whispered back, "Concentrate on what you want to look like."

She nodded, then started getting nervous about her idea, which earlier seemed brilliant. She thought about it further and considered what could happen if she thought about nothing. *What if I think of nothing and I become nothing?* she worried. *Maybe I want something like simply being unseen?* When that idea seemed to make more sense, she concentrated on being unseen. She thought on being unseen as hard as she could, the effort causing her face to scrunch up tight and prune like.

"You don't have to think that hard," she heard Bemot as he grunted a short, gruff laugh. Then she heard him stop suddenly and gasp in surprise.

She opened her eyes to find that the world around her seemed as wispy as a Spirit appeared in the state of translation. All the Sentinels and the Bear Hunter Spirit were looking around as they tried to find her. She glided around them to see if they could see movement or sense her in any way. She was thinking about having fun with it, but then she saw how worried her Sentinels looked. *Plus,* she chided herself, *we have frightened cubs to save.*

She was about to concentrate on reappearing, or being seen, when she heard Bemot whisper, "Kilala, did thinking about nothing make you go away all together?" His expression radiated intense concern as his glowing form searched the air, looking for her.

This time she didn't concentrate too hard. She simply thought about being seen. She knew instantly that she had popped back into view when all of them gasped in reaction and the surroundings looked as they should. She turned to smile at her Sentinels, glad to see they had relaxed.

"I didn't think about being nothing," she told Bemot after she had turned to face him. "Simply being unseen. Apparently, that did the trick."

He nodded his shaggy head and then closed his eyes. Suddenly, he disappeared from view. After a few minutes, he popped back into view. "Did anyone hear me shouting when you couldn't see me?" Everyone shook their heads. He glanced at Kilala. "Very useful," he muttered, then paused and looked thoughtful. "Why haven't we ever thought of doing that before?"

She shrugged her shoulders slightly as she smiled at him. "Necessity is the mother of innovation? Anyway, we know it now!" Her mind quickly turned to the task at hand. "Time to check on the cubs." Bemot nodded in agreement. When they popped out of sight to their Sentinels, they were relieved to find out that they could see and hear each other.

"This will work out quite well," Bemot commented as they flew through the trees to approach the cavern.

Kilala smiled at him in agreement. Then she suddenly thought that this ability should be kept a secret. "Let's not tell any one else about this quite yet," she whispered to him urgently. When he glanced at her, she emphasized her request with an intensely serious look.

Bemot nodded slowly. "I agree. Not until everything that is going on comes into the light."

<u>Chapter Twenty-two</u>

Being in the translated state, they had no problems sliding through the earth and rock that made up the walls of the cavern. Once they entered the stalactite- and -stalagmite-ridden space, they found a large pack of hyenas, jackals, Tasmanian devils, and coyotes that were broken up into smaller groups as they hid in the many nooks and crannies of the large cave. As the two Spirits hovered near the ceiling, they also saw a variety of vultures, ravens, and crows that were perched up high on small, naturally formed ledges that were scattered across the cavern walls. There was no doubt that an ambush had been set up to attack anyone that entered the cave.

"Good thing we did reconnaissance," Bemot growled as they moved deeper into the cavern looking for the cubs. "There would be too many casualties."

Kilala nodded silently to him, then started to look into every dark recess of the cave. When they went in deep enough to find the back wall, they found a narrow passage that connected with another cavern. After they entered the larger one illuminated with the soft light of luminescent vegetation, they hovered together as they looked around. In the strange, bluish green glow, they were able see dark shapes huddled by the far wall.

Slowly, Kilala and Bemot moved closer to the shadows until they could see that it was a large group of bear- and cat-kind cubs huddled together. As they continued to cautiously approach the group, Kilala saw a low partition stretching from one area of the cavern wall to another area, fencing in the cubs. She wondered why there were no guards present since the barrier didn't seem to be high enough to keep the cubs from escaping. When she could see the cubs' faces and postures, she recognized stark fear as they pushed against each other and up against the irregular cave wall as they looked around with wide, fearful eyes. They were doing all they could to avoid getting close to the barrier.

As Kilala stared at the boundary, she felt deep unease. In the eerie light, she thought she saw sections that were moving. At first, she thought it was her imagination until they got close enough to see what it was.

At the same time she realized what was wrong with the wall, Bemot growled fiercely, "It is a wall of snakes!"

Kilala was immediately repulsed, then blazed with anger and fear as she studied the boundary more closely and saw large and small venomous snakes intertwined and woven together. To maintain the wall-like structure, they had to continually move as they writhed and coiled as a unit.

"That is sick, horrifically sick," Bemot rumbled. Kilala could tell he was as angered and scared as she was. "As soon as we attack, they will strike our cubs!" he howled in agony. With a heavy heart, Kilala had to agree with his assessment.

"Do you think Snake Hunters are part of this?" Kilala asked him quietly. Although she was as upset as he was, she was fighting for calm so that she could think of a solution. She needed for him to help. "Or do you think these are renegades?"

Before he answered, Spirit of the Bear Hunters drew up and huffed loudly. "Snakes will say they are renegades, whether they are or not."

Kilala nodded, trying to keep her fear and anger from influencing her thoughts. She knew those strong emotions would cloud her judgment and endanger everyone concerned. As she started to analyze the situation, she could feel the eyes of the Spirit of the Bears on her, as he watched her closely. "Do you have any ideas?" she asked him quietly.

The gruff personality growled impatiently as he looked away. Then he sighed deeply and turned back to her. "I was all for a frontal attack," he admitted as he looked toward the scared cubs. "That would not only have caused the loss of many of our Sentinels, but the cubs would have surely died." He looked back at her. "You have the cooler head. What do you think we should do?"

She could tell that not only his admission of being wrong but also seeking her advice was hard on him. She was too upset to give him a full-on appreciative smile, so she did the best she could with a slight upturning of the corners of her lips. "I would appreciate any ideas," she said quietly.

The shaggy, glowing face tensely smiled at her. "If I have any good ones, I'll let you know," he promised.

"Good." She turned back to look at the cubs, the wall of snakes, and around the cavern. She thought about the passageway and the other cave filled with hyenas, dingoes, and vultures. "I have two questions," she said quietly.

"What's that?" Bemot asked as he watched her intently.

"How hungry is everyone in these caverns? And what would serve as a distraction that they couldn't resist?" She met his eyes as she waited for his answer. She wanted him to think of the solution, the one she had already worked out.

He thought for a while before he answered. "If everyone has been in here since the bear cubs have been missing, I would say they're pretty hungry." He cut his eyes to meet hers. "But what leader would have guards that are not relieved at certain intervals to keep them fresh?"

"One that promised that they would have a feast if they held out," she quietly answered.

Spirit of the Bear Hunters' eyes grew wide at the sudden revelation of what her statement implied. Hot, red wrath flamed up within his apparition as he shouted in rage, "That is monstrous! This is a trap so that they can feast on our Sentinels and our cubs!!"

"And weaken our tribes and our position in Ritigabid," she added quietly.

The blazing eyes of the Bear Spirit bored into hers. "For someone to take over," he growled dangerously. She nodded mutely; glad his anger was not directed at her. "But who?" he asked sharply.

Kilala shook her head slowly. "I have my suspicions, but no proof right now." She gestured back to the cubs. "Right now, we need to rescue them and keep our Sentinels safe."

She could see that Bemot barely contained his rage and had a need for immediate action. "What do we do?" he asked her.

"We need to bait our own trap," she said, then told him her plans. After she was finished, he nodded to her, then left quickly to inform their Sentinels as to what needed to be done. They had both agreed that she would stay to watch over the cubs.

She moved to hover directly over them. As she looked down at the bear and cat cubs that she estimated were between two and six of the greater moon, she was overwhelmed with a deep desire to hold all of them. She wanted to comfort them and let them know rescue was on the way. When she looked at the ever-moving snake fence, she worried whether her plan would work without loss of any of their tribe members' lives. As she dropped down to be closer to the huddled dark shapes, she had an unexpected impulse to beseech the unnamed one, "Please let this work so we can bring our little ones home without any loss of our Sentinels." To her surprise, her worry suddenly lifted, and she had the distinct feeling that she had been heard.

When she couldn't resist her maternal urge to join their tight, fearful group, she nestled amongst them and wrapped her arms around as many as she could. She had expected that her arms would be ineffective and fall right through them. When that didn't happen, she found that she could hold them as long as she didn't squeeze too hard. Once she settled, she was amazed when their tense and shaking bodies start to relax and lean into her. *They know I'm here!* she thought in excited relief.

After the cubs had settled around her, she glared at the snake fence, watching it to see if the reptiles noticed the change in the cubs. After several minutes, she saw no indication that they were aware of it as they continued to slither in, out, and through their intricately designed barrier. Relieved, she continued to hug and pet each cub as best she could while she was in the translated state.

"You all are going to be okay," she told them quietly even though she didn't think they could hear her. "The Sentinels will be coming to rescue you soon." She was surprised to see their ears swivel around as they heard her. *Huh?* she thought as she wondered why they seemed to feel and hear her.

As she continued to cuddle them, the answer came to her. *I'm in contact with them!* She nodded to herself in satisfaction. *That is what is making the difference! Well, I'll have to keep that in mind.*

As she waited for her plan to be put into action, she talked gently to the little ones. She let them know who she was and told them the stories that she had been told when she was little. She thought about singing them a lullaby but then changed her mind. She couldn't risk them falling asleep right before their rescue.

About the time she thought her plan should be going into action, she stopped moving and talking when she saw an apparition glide into the cavern. Following it were a few of the larger hyenas. She suppressed her fear and wished she could physically shield the cubs as she glared at the Spirit of the Death Hunters.

"Any word on the Sentinels' movements?" the skull-headed, black-tattered Spirit asked his Sentinels.

"No, Master," responded the largest of the hyenas.

"Didn't that little snake get back to spread the word?" The Spirit snapped at him as he asked.

"Yes, Master!" the hyena answered with his head hung down, but his eyes were swiveled upward to watch his master warily.

The Spirit acted like it spat away a bad taste. "Count on snakes not to be reliable," he grumbled darkly.

In response to his words, the snake fence hissed angrily. The slithering stopped as the wall slumped into individual snakes writhing on the floor looking up at him while they struck frenziedly at the air toward him.

"Oh, shut up and get back to work!" the Spirit shouted at them. "You know who masters you!" He hovered closer to glare at them with blazing eyes out of a skeletal face. They stopped their movement suddenly, frozen in fear. "And you don't want to anger her!"

Kilala could hear the snakes grumble fearfully under their breaths as they proceeded to start weaving their bodies back into the form of a fence. She had her proof that the Snake Hunters were part of this plot. *There's only one 'she' that could possibly master the snakes.* She looked up sharply as she saw the Spirit of the Death Hunters set his intense glare on the cubs.

"Why are they not shaking in fear?" he shouted angrily. The snake fence briefly stopped as all the lidless eyes stared at the cubs. Then they hissed in unison as they didn't care what the cubs were doing. They were tired, hungry, and blamed the cubs for their discomfort.

The Death Hunter Spirit started to glide in closer to the huddled cubs, causing them to shake in fear as they watched him. "Well, that's more like it," he sneered at them. Then his head cocked in confusion. "But there's something not quite right," he muttered suspiciously.

Kilala could see he was about to move in closer to investigate when they heard a loud noise echo throughout the cavern. It was coming from the adjoining cave. The death head whipped around to look toward the sound. "Idiots!" he screamed at his Sentinels who stood in frozen confusion. "Go see what is going on!" When they didn't move fast enough, the Spirit sped away and quickly passed through the thick rock wall.

Kilala had to smile as she watched a large mob of varmints running into the cave. Part of her plan was for her Sentinels to hunt for and round up as many as they could of rats, voles, and small mammals, those that snakes preyed on. The Bear Sentinels' task was to hunt for the sick and maimed prey, those who were about to die anyway, and any dead animals they could find and place those outside the cave. They needed to be close enough for the carrion eaters to smell but far enough away for them not to see the Sentinels ready to charge in. Once the first cavern had been cleared, then the big cats were to drive the vermin through the first cave into the cave where she was with the cubs.

As she expected to happen, the snake fence quickly fell apart as they went hunting after the prey that ran over the rocky cave floor. As soon as all of the snakes were distracted, she made herself seen to the cubs. "Okay, little ones." She smiled at each of them and petted them. "Once you see the Sentinels come in, you do as they say and go with them." All of cubs looked at her with rounded eyes and nodded that they understood.

They didn't have to wait long. The Bear and Cat Hunter Sentinels came running out of the connecting tunnel at full speed. She knew it wouldn't be all of them since they had to leave a few to guard the entrance of the other cavern for their escape. But the group was large enough that the floor of the cave rumbled as their huge paws pounded toward them. If any vermin or snake got in their way, they grabbed it in their teeth and flung it aside. Nothing was going to stop them from getting to their young.

When they slid to a stop in front of the huddle of cubs, several turned outward to keep a wary eye on the snakes while the others picked up any cub they could reach with gentle mouths. They put the older cubs on the backs of those standing guard and their own backs, while the younger ones they held in their mouths. They had no care whether the cub was of their own kind or not. They were determined to save them all.

With all the cubs secured, Kilala sprang up to hover above them. "Okay, lets go!" she shouted as she sped toward the exit with them following. She flew through the connecting tunnel and into the other cavern. As she neared the exit, she saw the Sentinels that stood guard along with the Spirit of the Bear Hunters. She nodded at him as she flew past with the Sentinels carrying the young thundering behind in her wake. When she looked back to see if everyone was out of the cave, she saw Bemot signal the guards to follow the group as a rear guard.

As she led the group through the forest to the clearing where they had gathered to make their plans, she watched for the Spirit of the Death Hunters and any Death or Snake Hunter tribesmen. She was glad when their escape wasn't impeded, but after she reached the meeting spot, she hovered anxiously looking back the way she came. She didn't know where the Spirit of the Death Hunters was. She was fairly sure his animal-kind were feasting happily and wouldn't be in pursuit.

She smiled in relief when she saw all the Sentinels emerging out of the forest with their rescued cubs. The guards were close behind and joined the milling group. Once everyone was accounted for, all the Sentinels formed a ring and the ones carrying cubs in their mouths placed their charges in the middle. Those carrying the cubs on their back lay down so they could scamper off. Bear-and Cat-kind cubs happily tumbled over each other as they ran to their fathers.

Kilala was trying not to cry with joy when the Spirit of the Bear Hunters glided over to hover near her. She looked over at him, nodded, and smiled. "Good job," she congratulated him.

"Great plan!" he grinned widely at her. His face sobered as he said in heartfelt sincerity, "Thank you, Kilala. We would've failed miserably without you." He bowed his head to her.

"Thank you, Bemot." She smiled at him when he lifted his head again. "But everyone worked together to pull it off. It is a victory for us all! I am very glad it worked out."

She looked down at the group that was breaking up and going separate ways after fathers and cubs were reunited. She pulled her lower lip in between her teeth as she thought about what she had learned. She glanced at the Spirit of the Bear Hunters and knew she could trust him enough to share it with him. "Bemot." She glanced around, expecting the Death Hunter Spirit to appear. "I learned something while I was waiting. But we can't have anyone eavesdrop on us."

He nodded that he understood. Suddenly, he disappeared a split-second before she did.

Chapter 23

In the vague world of the unseen Spirits, she told him what she had learned. As she explained the link between the Death Hunters and the Snake Hunters, she stopped and pointed as she saw the Spirit of the Death Hunters drift into the now empty clearing. He was clearly looking for someone. When he didn't see anyone, he drifted back the way he came. Kilala could see that he was full of rage. His plan had failed, and it made him look the fool.

"So that is the Spirit of the Death Hunters tribe," Bemot remarked. He had watched the apparition with tense concern.

"Yes," Kilala answered, confirming with a nod.

"I hope he doesn't look like that in reality," the Bear Spirit said as he shook his head.

"I agree."

"He is dangerous," Bemot concluded when the Spirit left. "He is even more deadly now that his plan has been thwarted."

"Again, I agree."

"How can we protect ourselves against this threat?" Bemot asked as he turned toward Kilala. She saw that his dark eyes looked worried and fearful.

She thought for a while, then said what first came to her mind. "To be protected, we need to clear the threat."

Bemot smiled wickedly. "A frontal assault?" he growled menacingly. "Sounds like my kind of plan."

Kilala could see he was primed for more action. She nodded, then added reasonably, "Eventually. We do need more information."

"Reconnaissance," he stated with a nod.

"And…" Kilala hesitated before she asked, "Do you believe in a power greater than all?"

The Bear Hunter Spirit stared at her in confusion at the sudden change in conversation. Then his expression cleared as he thoughtfully watched her. After a few moments, he said, "You can't have been a Spirit as long as I have and not know that there is a power greater than we are." He looked around, then met her gaze again. "However, I do know of some Spirits that are too stubborn or dense to recognize that reality." He cocked his shaggy head as he asked, "Why bring that up?"

Kilala smiled then said, "Because I feel we need to ask that power above all for guidance and wisdom."

"Do you think he or she will give us that?" he asked, looking thoughtful. "I'm not sure if anyone's tried to interact with the Greater Power before."

"Why is that?" Kilala asked sincerely. She was curious why this hadn't been done. She thought again about how all her life she hadn't been told of the Greater Power, or Eternal One, or whatever the name. She wondered again why that was.

Bemot thought hard before he answered, "I can only speak for myself," he started slowly. "I've always been under the impression that although everything was created by the Greater Power, he or she moved on." He scratched his beard as he tried to be clearer in his explanation. Then he shrugged his broad shoulders helplessly.

"Were you ever told about the Greater Power when you were growing up?"

He thought a bit, then looked at her as realization lit his eyes. "No, there was never a mention." He looked down as he seemed to dredge up more memories. "I do remember my mentor mentioning the Greater Power and how it didn't like to be bothered. So I never did."

"It?"

"That's how he referred to the Greater Power," he said with another shrug of broad shoulders.

"Interesting," Kilala whispered, looking at the ground below them as she thought. "I wonder why that is? I'm not calling him an 'it.'"

"Why not her?" he asked as his dark eyes studied her.

"The pronoun he or him has been used to reference all people, no matter the sex. We don't even know if the Higher Power, Greater Power, whatever, has a gender. So I chose to use the pronoun 'him.'" She thought further, then added, "I think that is how my Sentinel's mate referred to the Higher Power. Animal-kind teaches their young, and they seem to interact with him on a regular basis."

"Really?!" Bemot exclaimed. Kilala looked up and saw his eyes wide with surprise. "I never knew that!" He scratched and pulled on his beard as he considered this information. "I wonder why my Sentinels never mentioned it." He turned to her. "Are you sure it is all animal-kind?"

Kilala nodded in confirmation, her silvery, glowing hair undulating with the movement.

"I'll have to ask them about this," he muttered more to himself. Then he looked up sharply at her. "Why did you think of this? This praying to the Greater Power?"

"Well…" She met his eyes without flinching. "While I was waiting for you to instigate the plan, I said a prayer to him." She held up a hand when she saw him opening his mouth to say something. "I truly felt that he heard and did help."

Bemot looked away as he thought about what she said. "It is true that the plan, although well crafted, relied on several things to work perfectly right to pull it off." He met her eyes again. "Perhaps we did have help from the Greater Power. Do you think he will listen again?"

"We can only try." This time, Kilala was the one to shrug her shoulders.

Bemot looked toward his territory. "I need to make sure all my Bear-kind got home safely." He bowed to her, then hesitated. "Why don't you pray to the Greater Power? He seems to listen to you."

Kilala smiled at him and returned his bow. "I will." The Spirit of the Bears smiled at her, then sped toward his haven.

Kilala looked around at the indistinct world of being unseen and laughed. "I hope he remembers to become seen again!" she said out loud. Then she sped toward her haven and remembered to be seen as she drew closer.

Chapter Twenty-four

After trying every trick she knew, Chusi hovered in angry frustration outside the barrier blocking her from entering Kilala's haven. "How could she have put up such a powerful barricade that defies all my tricks?" she muttered angrily, scowling deeply.

She decided to wait for the Spirit of the Cat Hunters and attack her outside her haven. She wasn't sure what she could do to her in her translated form, but she was going to try. She felt the need to exact some sort of revenge and get rid of her hated rival. As she hovered behind a stand of trees, she refused to admit to the fact that she feared this new Spirit. *She is so unexpected in her abilities so early in her role, especially without the benefit of a mentor.* Frustrated, she shook her head. *How can this be?* she pondered further. *The predecessor was so old because she had to hang on for so long after I deceived her previous replacement into not taking on the position of the Spirit of the Cat Hunters! This new one should be weak and naïve! She should be easy to manipulate!*

As her wait lengthened, she started to dwell on her suspicions that Kilala was the only one instrumental in stopping her grand plan in its tracks and the fact that she had not gotten the satisfaction of vengeance from her hurriedly conceived plan of assassination. The original plan she had considered perfect, one that she had been carefully putting into place for generations, hinged on destroying the Bear and Cat Hunter's Sentinels by using their cubs as bait for her trap. When this was done, she would have been able to easily move into their territories. From there, she would take full control of the Eagle and Dog Hunters and achieve what she desired, to be the sole leader of Ritigabid. When her trap didn't work, she tried to invade the Cat Spirit's haven to kill the mates of the Sentinels while Kilala was incapacitated. She knew this would instill distrust and rebellion amongst the Sentinels and destabilize the protective structure of the Cat Hunter tribe. This situation would make it easy for her to move in to take over, and then she could work on a plan to eliminate the Sentinels of the Bear Hunters.

Now that her replacement plan hadn't worked, she was completely stymied, an experience she was not used to. Her reaction to this predicament was hot and volatile as she smoldered with anger and frustration. When she sensed the Death Hunters Spirit speed up behind her, she turned quickly, ready to strike out with her full fury. She was unaware that she had allowed her human image to slip and was showing her true self.

The Spirit of the Death Hunters stopped quickly where he was and hovered at what he hoped was a safe distance. He stared at the apparition of the Spirit in front of him and realized he was seeing the true form of the Snake Hunter Spirit. Her usually beautiful translated form was now a man-sized, deep black reptile without any humanity evident. The sickly green, lidless eyes with slit pupils blazed with evil that even he feared.

He bowed hastily so he could hide his surprised reaction. "My queen," he said quickly, hoping he sounded respectful enough. The snake image had deeply unsettled him as all the little things about her and the dark secrets he knew about her started to fall into place and make sense. He hastily pushed those thoughts aside as he dared not reveal that he knew the truth about her and knew not to look up at her until she gave permission.

"Yesssss," Chusi hissed at him.

"Your plan did not work out as you desired," he said as he steeled himself for a powerful backlash. When it didn't happen, he glanced up at her.

She looked pensive now. "I am aware," she muttered. "Ssshe is more of an adversssary than I thought ssshe would be." The tail end of her thick body flicked furiously back and forth as she thought deeply. "I will have to reassess her and think of a new approach."

"Does she still view you as a friend?"

"Ssshe doesss not. Ssshe ordered me out of her haven. Ssshe never did trussst me." He saw Chusi look around, then focus back on Kilala's haven. When she startled with shocked surprise, he jumped back in reaction. When she looked toward him, he saw that her slit pupils were fully dilated in fear. "How did ssssshe do that?" she hissed at him in amazement.

The Death Hunter Spirit looked about him. When he turned to look in the same direction she had, he saw Kilala as she slipped through her protective barrier into her haven. "Do what? She's just going into her haven."

"No," she said as she shook her reptilian head. "Ssshe jussst appeared out of nowhere."

The Death Hunter Spirit stared at the snake apparition. He didn't quite believe her. Any Spirits in the same area were able to see each other, no matter what. It had always been that way. He was glad that all she could see was his body language since his facial expressions and emotions were covered by the skull death mask that she ordered him to wear. She stared long and hard at him when he hadn't said anything, and he bowed his head again. "As you wish, my queen."

"You don't believe me!" she yelled at him as she swung her tail end around to try to hit him. When he had sped away to hover at a safe distance, she glared at him, then spat, "You didn't see it so you are unable to believe." She turned away from him to stare at Kilala's haven. "I need to go back to my haven and rest." She glared at the Death Hunter Spirit before she left. "We will meet again soon. We need to devise another plan; otherwise, we will fail to take over Ritigabid."

The Death Hunter Spirit bowed his head again. "Yes, my queen. I understand." He watched her speed off, then slumped in relief. Shaking his skull head slightly, he thought of how the centuries of dealing with her taught him that when she referred to 'we' it truly meant herself. *And now*, he wondered, *how did I become so deceived to commit my tribe to her and her desire for domination?* He sighed deeply and shook his head in dismay when no immediate answer came to mind.

Out of curiosity, he probed around Kilala's haven boundaries and found all of the typical hidden avenues blocked. Nodding his head, he realized that what had contributed to the Snake Spirit's foul mood besides the fact her trap hadn't worked was that she couldn't get in. "And it's a new Spirit that has no mentor or any training in the craft," he muttered in amazement. He hovered in place while he thought, and he was glad that he hadn't given the Spirit of the Snake Hunters all the access he had to the havens of the Spirits. Since he was the Spirit of the Death Hunters, he had been specially gifted to enter into any domain, no matter the protective boundaries that had been set up. He knew he could get past Kilala's powerful defense but decided not to.

He thought of how Chusi had demanded that he terrorize Kilala after the Council of the Hunter Spirits had met. Since he didn't know who he was going to encounter, he reluctantly had done as he was ordered. When he had confronted the Spirit of the Cat Hunters, he had been startled by her beauty and the innate power she had radiated. "Yes, my queen," he whispered to no one, "she will be a very difficult adversary." When he thought of the Snake Hunter Spirit's claim that Kilala had popped suddenly into view, he shook his head as he stared at Kilala's haven. *Is that true?* he wondered to himself. Shaking his skull head in bewilderment, he left for his haven. He had to rest and contemplate what he had seen and learned today before he had to meet with Chusi again.

Chapter 25

After Kilala had reintegrated into her physical body, she lay on her pallet and stared at the top of the sleeping slot that had been carved out of the cavern wall. Thoughts and ideas whirled around in her mind until the activities of the day caught up with her. She became so tired that she drifted off to sleep.

In the state of dreams, where everything was usually vague, she saw a figure in sharp relief walking toward her. As the person approached, Kilala could see that it was the young girl again, the first Cat Hunter Companion.

"It has begun," the girl stated as her eyes met Kilala's and seemed to bore into her thoughts.

Kilala nodded mutely. She didn't know what to say.

"Such as it was in the beginning." The youth stopped to stand in front of her. "Have you read all the books?"

Kilala nodded, still unable to say anything.

The girl cocked her head to study her closely. "Did you read the books?" she repeated. This time, she emphasized the word 'read.'

Kilala thought about how she scanned the pages of the books, speed reading to get as much information as fast as possible just to get an overall feel for what was going on. She found her voice to say, "I read through them quickly. I thought I had a good grasp of the situation."

The young girl shook her head slightly and sighed. "A quick read gives superficial information. A careful read imparts hidden knowledge and deeper understanding." She turned to walk off into the dreamscape.

"But which book do I need to study right now?" Kilala called after her.

The youth stopped and turned slightly to answer her. "As I said, such as it was in the beginning. Beware of the coming chaos." She turned again to walk off, then stopped to look over her shoulder. "You need to seek the Greater Power. The words are there."

Kilala was going to ask her other questions, but the girl disappeared. She looked around the dreamscape and recognized the forest around her laden with the Kuatrukai, thick and heavy as it flashed with bursts of energy.

When she woke up, she lay quietly for a while thinking about her dream. As she started to move to get out of bed, she found Anong had curled up on her belly while she slept. Slowly, she moved her ancient cat off of her and rolled up to a sitting position. Slipping out of the sleeping place, she carefully padded over the carpet squares and around the sleeping tigress and lioness over to the table. After sitting down in the wooden chair, she reached over to the shelves and pulled the black-covered book out of its spot and placed it on the table.

She didn't open it right away. She sat and stared at the front cover as she thought about what the young girl had said. She felt a need, a desire to fully understand what was in the book. But she wasn't ready to confront it all yet. She looked around the room then outside the cave entrance. The sky was darkening, and she could see the Kuatrukai had started to gather and thicken in the dusk. As she considered all of Ritigabid and the heavens, she felt totally inadequate. She was simply a speck in all of Creation.

With her elbows on the table, placed on either side of the book, she buried her face in her hands. She could sense that the balance between the tribes had been disturbed and it was shifting into chaos. *Somehow I'm supposed to know what to do?* she silently fretted, feeling overwhelmed by the heavy responsibility placed on her.

After several minutes, she sighed deeply, knowing she couldn't bear the burden or the responsibility of all the tribes. On the edges of her awareness, she sensed a stirring. In the emptiness of her inadequacy, she mentally reached out to that disturbance and touched it with her mind. Suddenly, she felt a consciousness greater and more powerful than herself. It instilled in her uplifting strength and a greater calm. It didn't take her long to realize that she had connected with the Greater Power. At first, he was a presence with no words, no demands, just deep comfort and an introductory revelation of himself.

Comparing this interaction to her experience with the old man in the forests with the dark powers, she sensed neither deceit nor evil. This helped her to relax her guard and allowed herself to know that she was not alone in this task. With that assurance, she opened the book in front of her and began to read.

As the night deepened, she continued to read carefully and store away the bits and pieces that seemed important. She soon realized that, although there was information, there were questions that were brought up in her mind, questions that needed answers to try to fill in the gaps so she could see the bigger picture. She knew she needed to start with knowing who were her allies and who were not. As she looked over at the sleeping females, she knew she also needed the Lore of the Sentinels.

After she closed the book, she stretched as she considered what she was going to do the rest of the night. She needed a break from reading but wasn't tired enough to go back to bed, and she was unwilling to wake up the females. She stood up from her chair and walked out into her garden where the Kuatrukai had thickened around her orchards, vines, and stands of grain. She walked up to stand by the edge of the mists, then stopped to watch the bursts of energy within the light grey to white swirls.

Sensing that the greater presence was still with her, she silently asked a question about what the energy bursts were. Suddenly, she had the desire to reach for one to find out. She hesitated momentarily, a little afraid of confronting the unknown, then she thought, *I won't know anything unless I try*. With that in mind, she slowly and carefully walked through a thin, transparent barrier to enter into the thick, murky depths.

As she moved through the swirling grays and whites, she felt the moisture of the suspended water drops dampen her hair, skin, and tunic. After stopping, she reached for a bright flash of energy that was nearby, but it moved away as it avoided her touch. She dropped her hand and wondered why she had been rejected. She tried again to reach for another, but it, too, moved away. She dropped her arm again and felt like giving up. She was about to turn and leave when she saw a bright yellow flash that was located farther out on the upper edge of the Kuatrukai move toward her. When it reached her, it hovered in front of her. Slowly, she lifted her hand to reach for it with a finger. It did not move away from her; in fact, she saw that it moved to meet her. When she made contact with it, she saw the energy disappear into the flesh of her finger, illuminating it with an inner glow in which the tendon and bone were shadows before it dissipated into her being. With its joining, she felt a burst of power and heightened insight.

With that enhancement of her powers as a Spirit, she gasped with amazement and joy. "They are gifts!" she exclaimed aloud, directing it toward the mysterious entity. "They are special gifts and powers!"

Just at the limit of the range of audible sound, she heard a voice, deep and resonant. "They are. They have been there from the dawn of time, but so many have not been used and are fading away."

She knew it was the Greater Power who had answered her. She hugged herself in delight. "Can anyone claim these gifts?"

"Many can claim a gift, one or more, if it is appropriate for them at that time."

Kilala thought of the flashes that moved away from her. She nodded as she realized that those were not for her or not for her at that time. "Who do I tell of these gifts?" she asked the Greater Power.

"Part of your gift is discernment. With that, you will know who needs to hear the meaning of the energy that is bound in the Kuatrukai," the voice answered.

She looked around, wanting to see some form or face to identify with the voice. But there was nothing to see even though she felt his presence and heard him clearly. "I understand," she said as she bowed her head.

She had no idea how long she stood in the moisture-laden, power-enhanced grayish white when she felt a muzzle nudge her hand. She opened her eyes and saw Teigra looking up at her, deep concern in her light blue eyes.

"Companion," she said to Kilala, "Come in. You are wet and shivering."

Kilala looked down at the long, dark green tunic she was wearing and saw that the white tigress was right. She was completely drenched and was cold, very cold. Shivering, she made her way back into the cavern to sit in the wooden chair by the table. The lioness offered a thick, fluffy blanket that had been warmed by the small fire in the fireplace. Kilala nodded gratefully at Tiaret as she wrapped it around her body. As she soaked in the warmth, she smiled at both of them. "Thank you," she whispered as her thoughts moved away from her discomfort to dwell on all the revelations she had had that night.

"Do you have further need of us?" Teigra asked softly.

Kilala looked from one to the other as she weighed whether she should ask them about their Lore. Since they seemed wide awake, she decided to try. "I have learned several things tonight," she started. Both big cats nodded their heads for her to continue. "I need more information, and it may be in the Lore of the Sentinels."

As the white tigress turned to look at the lioness, Kilala watched the subtle twitching and shifting of whiskers, ears, and eyes, the secret language of cat-kind. After a few minutes, they turned toward her.

"The Lore of the Sentinels is specific to each tribe," Teigra started. "There is not one source that relates all the tribes' Lore."

Kilala nodded that she understood and waited for her to continue. "The mothers of each tribe are required to pass their Lore to their cubs when they are old enough to understand," Tiaret explained. "But what is included in our Lore is decided upon by the Sentinels themselves."

"When something happens that is considered important enough to be remembered, all the observations of cat-kind are examined. Once the Sentinels establish the facts, it becomes part of our Lore," Teigra added.

Kilala nodded again. She had her answer to the accuracy of the Lore. "I am sure the body of this Lore is very extensive since it has been gathered over the centuries."

The females shared a glance, then the lioness spoke. "It is concise. We do not embellish the truth with details."

The white tigress spoke next, "For example, as far as what the Lore records about our Companions, humans in general can be placed within certain personality characteristics and behavior groups. They have certain coded names attributed to each that designate their overall performance in the office of Spirit of the Cat Hunters."

Kilala felt wide-eyed open astonishment at their explanation. She had known cat-kind was intelligent but finding out the level of sophistication of their Lore surprised her. "That is amazing," she whispered. After thinking a while, she asked, "I need information from the very beginning of the Lore, around the time there was a need for humanity to split into the Hunter tribes."

The Teigra and Tiaret looked at each other in shock and confusion. Then they turned toward her. "Why is this needed?" Teigra asked cautiously.

Kilala looked around the cavern then outside. She could see the dark sky turning slightly grey, the hints that dawn was approaching. She leaned toward the big cats to explain. "I have seen the first Companion two times," she started. Both cats looked surprised but held their tongues. "The last time, she said that what is happening had happened before. I need to know what happened before. That information could be very important for us to know so that we can be more prepared for what is happening now."

Both females sat back on their haunches. As the end of their tails flicked back and forth, one picked up a massive paw and cleaned it; the other licked her paw and washed her face. Kilala waited patiently. She could see that her request bothered them greatly and they were considering how to deal with it. Teigra set her paw down and met her eyes. "Did not the first Companion write of those times?" she said as she cut her eyes to the books on the shelves.

"Yes, she did. But I have more questions. I am hoping that the information passed down from the Sentinels who had witnessed the very beginning will help fill in the gaps."

Tiaret sighed as she lay down. Teigra glanced at her, then lay down as well. After she settled, she spoke, "It was a time of great sorrow."

"There have been many times of great sorrow," the lioness grumbled.

Kilala held out a hand to quiet the two. After she pulled it back under the blanket she huddled in, she said, "I know of the very beginning. All the land and heavens were created perfect. Then it was marred by the coming of evil into human-kind. Many disasters came upon all life, but human- and animal-kind rebounded as they adapted to the imperfections in creation. But then human-kind advanced to the point that they could harness the power of the imperfect creation to use for their purposes. But when they did this, they further imbalanced and twisted creation, and it morphed into chaos. This destroyed the civilizations and the creations of human-kind. Because of that, the Hunter tribes came to be, and the land was divided into territories, establishing Ritigabid." Kilala paused and saw that the big cats nodded that they agreed with the concise account. She started again, "Now, something happened during the formation of the tribes. Something or someone tried to interfere with its balance and purposes. What does the Lore say about that?"

The females looked at each other. They seemed to be thinking deeply, but Kilala could tell there was something wrong. They seemed baffled.

Teigra spoke up. "I am sorry, Mistress. We both have thought about the beginning of our Lore, and it does not include any specifics of that time. It talks of how the Hunter tribe system was first started and then after it was complete and stable."

"Where can I go to find out?" Kilala asked as her hopes were dashed. She was deeply disappointed.

The females shook their heads sadly. "We do not know."

"Would some of the other tribes' Sentinels have that in their Lore?" she asked. She was desperate to know what could be in animal-kind's distant memories.

"It is unlikely," another voice spoke from the cavern entrance. There stood her village's Sentinel, the white tiger. He bowed his head to her as he approached where she was sitting. "I am sorry, Companion. I did not mean to interrupt," Nemr said as he sat on his haunches next to his mate. When he didn't say anything else for a while, Kilala could see that the three big cats were silently communicating with each other in their body language. She felt sure, and was glad, that the females were bringing him up to speed about what they had discussed so far.

When they seemed to have stopped communicating and were thinking, she decided to ask, "Why do you say that?"

The big male turned toward her as his eyes sought hers. "The Cat Hunters were the first tribe formed. From that template, the others came to be." He studied her closely. "But you are already aware of that. Why do you want to know about the before time?"

"I believe what is happening now has some link to back then." She kept it simple, not wanting to divulge everything she suspected.

He nodded at her that he understood. He looked at the females and communicated something to them. Reluctantly, they both stood, bowed to her, and left the cavern.

"They go to hunt for their cubs," he explained to her. "It is a good time to do that." He nodded to the lightening sky outside the cave. "And what I am about to share with you, they do not need to hear. This is the part of the Lore the Sentinels have kept to themselves."

Kilala wondered why that was. She knew Nemr could read in her expressions that she was confused and had questions.

"It is not something we want to burden our families with," he explained briefly. "But since no part of history should be forgotten, we teach the young males that are selected to be Sentinels as they are being trained." He lay down, stretching out his long frame on the carpeted floor. "It is regarded as a prologue to our Lore."

"What can you tell me about that time?" Kilala asked quietly. She tensed slightly in anticipation, hoping that he would know what she needed.

Nemr looked away as he considered her question. "Our kind, the great cats, were either in cages or in the wild. Some were made to perform for humans. Some were altered to be pets," he said slowly, his expression grave and sad. He sighed heavily, then continued. "When humans started to destroy each other, they forgot about animal-kind. When their creations failed, the survivors had to learn to live off the land. Many were not capable. Some of cat-kind, mainly the house cats who had been well treated by humans, took pity on them. They contacted the rest of cat-kind to see if there was some way for cat- and human-kind to work together so they all could survive and thrive. When the Cat Hunter tribe was formed, there were other humans who did not want to join with cat-kind, so they found their preferred predator and made their own tribes." He stopped for a few moments to gather his thoughts.

Tears sprang in her eyes as Kilala nodded at him to continue. The abuse of cat-kind was new to her, but the tribe's formation matched the writings. She waited quietly for him to continue, glad that the time of their abuse was long, long ago.

"During this time," he started again, his voice strained so that he almost growled the words. "There was a group that tried to deceive the others and take over all of Ritigabid. They were being driven and helped by the evil one."

"Who was that?" Kilala asked, even though she thought she knew the answer.

"Snake-kind," the tiger said harshly. This confirmed her thoughts. "They have been and always will be devious."

"Does all of snake-kind follow the evil one?" she asked. She still wondered about the little green snake and whose side he was on.

"Not all," he said with finality. "Just as we have within our ranks some tribe members, human and animal, who do not heed the Greater Power and prefer the evil one, so the Snake Hunters have those who would prefer to follow the Greater Power."

"Can you tell which ones are which?"

The white tiger sighed deeply. "That is the problem. Snake-kind lie so well it's hard to tell if they ever speak the truth!"

Kilala sat back to look out of the cavern and saw the day brightening sunny and clear. "I believe Snake Hunters are trying to take over again," she said quietly but firmly.

Nemr cocked his head as he watched her, his ears forward. "So you do think she was behind the kidnapped cubs?"

"I know she was," she admitted. "And I need to figure out what she might do next and what we need to do to stop her." She pulled the blanket more tightly around herself as she thought. Looking up, she met the white tiger's deep blue eyes. "How did snake-kind try to take over? What tactics did they use?"

After a few moments, the tiger said, "I will consult with the others. That was not compiled into a cohesive account by the first ones."

"Are you going to consult with the other Cat Hunter Sentinels?" she asked curiously.

He shook his head slowly. "No. For this I will need to consult with all the Sentinels of the Hunter tribes." He stood up to leave. "I will try to find out as quickly as possible." As he walked toward the cavern entrance, he looked back over his shoulder. "I will not be consulting with Snake-kind; they would lie anyway."

"Understood," she said as she smiled at him. *Now all I have to do is wait*, she thought as she stood up and draped the blanket on the chair. She moved around the cavern to make her breakfast and get ready for the day.

Chapter Twenty-six

Greatly relieved that their cubs were safely back home, Bemot, the Bear Spirit, sped his way over Bear Hunter territory to his haven. Thinking of how big a part the new Spirit of the Cat Hunters played in the rescue and the powers she had displayed had distracted him so completely that he was back in his haven before he realized he hadn't become seen again. His Sentinels jumped in surprise when he popped back into view, and then they immediately gathered around to thank him and celebrate their victory. Hovering slightly above their heads, he smiled widely and threw back his head as he belly laughed with joy at their victory.

As his cave started to empty with jovial bear-kind moving back to their homes, he knew he should rest. With a sigh, he viewed his physical body lying on a raised wood-framed bed. He was swaddled in a cocoon of bear skin pelts, those granted to him from the Sentinels he had lost over the years. His thick grey hair fell like a scruff, framing his deeply lined face that sprouted a thick white beard and mustache. He knew his body was getting frailer with age. Because of this, he preferred to stay in the translated state much of the time instead of being bound to the weakness of mortality. He sighed again, knowing he needed to reintegrate so he could eat and take care of bodily functions.

When he opened his physical eyes, he gazed up at the stalactite-decorated ceiling of his cave while a thought hit him. He wondered what the Spirit of the Snake Hunters really looked like. As he rolled out of his bed, feeling his joints pop and crackle, he thought of how young and beautiful Kilala was. All the Spirits knew how she really looked because of their impromptu meeting once she had taken her position as the Spirit of the Cat Hunters. Other than the semi-transparent and silver glow that was common to all of them in the translated state, he was glad she didn't change her form even though she knew she could.

He walked carefully to his lone chair, a large, elaborately carved, dark wooden, high-backed and -armed seat that easily supported his bulk when he was younger but now engulfed him with its size. He gingerly sat down, adjusting the goose down-filled cushion under his backside. Once settled, he tried to remember when the Council of Spirits had greeted any new Snake Hunter Spirit to the group. As he thought further back, his forehead wrinkled even more with concern as he couldn't remember when they had done that. He called Kuruk, the leader of his Sentinels, to him. Looking up into the grizzly's eyes, he asked, "My friend, does the Lore tell of the last time a new Spirit of the Snakes was inducted into the Council of the Spirits?"

The huge grizzled brown bear sat on his massive haunches as he considered the question. Bemot was dismayed as he sensed Kuruk reach out to the other Sentinels to check with them. After a while, the bear's massive, shaggy head shook slowly from side to side. "The Lore indicates that it has been several Spirit lifetimes since a new one was welcomed into the Council from the Snake Hunters tribe."

Bemot started scratching and pulling at his beard. "That is very strange," he muttered. "Very unnatural for the way of things." He was very worried about what that could mean.

As the old man hunched over, thinking, he hadn't noticed that the grizzly waited to see if he needed anything else. He was completely taken aback with the fact that a new Spirit of the Snake Hunters had not emerged in such a very long time. This revelation added to his previous worries that things were not right, not balanced, in Ritigabid. He wondered if he should contact the Dog Hunter Spirit and the Eagle Hunter Spirit when he stopped himself. He didn't know who he could trust except for Kilala. He glanced up to see that his Sentinel still attended him. "I am sorry," he murmured to the big bear. "Would you mind hunting for me? I seem to be very weak right now."

"I wouldn't doubt it," a sharp voice spoke from behind the grizzly bear. Kuruk moved to hush the speaker. Instead of quieting, another bear, a female grizzly, came around him to face the Spirit.

"You neglected your body far too long," she chastised him. Bemot nodded to his Sentinel's mate mutely. He was about to open his mouth when she lifted a paw to have him be quiet. "I know it was for noble reasons." She bowed her head. "We respect that. Now it is time to take care of you!"

The Spirit of the Bear Hunters nodded to her. "Thank you." Within a few minutes he had berries and nuts in front of him along with a stone cup of fresh spring water. He knew that the berries and nuts were something for him to start eating while they hunted some game. While he ate, his thoughts drifted back to their darker paths to consider that things were not right and that, somehow, they needed to be set straight.

Chapter 27

Destroying the furnishings that she kept around as if the Snake Spirit were still human, Chusi furiously lashed her tail about while she slithered angrily around her haven. Her tongue flicked in and out rapidly, spattering venomous spittle everywhere while she muttered to herself. Although she was still fuming about how her carefully organized plan didn't work, she was more aggravated and fearful about what she had seen.

"How did she do that?" she muttered to no one in particular as the image of Kilala appearing from nowhere replayed in her mind. "Did she transport through the ether? Or was she invisible?" She knew that her enemy's having this ability was dangerous. It could unravel the rest of her plans that she had been putting into place for centuries. She was jerked out of her thoughts by a creepy, hollow voice.

"Didn't go according to plan," the voice said matter-of-factly.

Chusi jerked her head around to face the Spirit of the Death Hunters hovering high above her.

"No! It didn't!" she spat back. "Why are you even mentioning it again?! Want to rub my face in it?!" She had a strong urge to strike at the apparition but knew it would be fruitless. Instead, she turned her bulky, serpentine body so she didn't have to look at the skull face staring out from the black tattered cowl. Even though she had demanded that he adopt that creepy appearance to terrorize others, she was uncomfortable with seeing him like that in her haven. As she moved, the end of her tail swished through the apparition, causing it to shudder with the force of the impact. "Why are you here?" she hissed irritably. "We've already had this discussion!"

The specter glided around her so she had to face him. "To see if you had another plan, of course," he answered in his strange, hollow voice. "I am here at your orders."

She glared at him. Even though she couldn't see his expression, she felt that he was laughing at her, jeering at her because of her inadequacy with the failure of her recent plans. In her agitation and frustration, she threw out the first question that came to her mind to try to unsettle him. "Why is the Spirit of the Cat Hunters able to appear out of thin air?" She stared at him, challenging him to answer it.

The Spirit of the Death Hunters did not expect that and seemed visually taken aback. "What do you mean?" he asked, his voice sounding more normal. "Are you still thinking you saw that happen?"

She glared up at him with her tongue flicking in and out. "I know what I saw! I saw her as she approached her haven. She appeared out of thin air."

The skull head cocked to one side as he studied her. "Are you sure you didn't miss her approach?" he asked, the voice resuming the hollow quality. "After all, your eyes may be losing some sight because of the many years you have lived." He started to drift around her as he seemed to study her aging form.

Chusi shuttered, feeling that those hollow spaces where the eyes should be seemed to be sizing her up for a post death meal. "Stop that!" She shouted at him. "You know I can live forever!"

The apparition nodded knowingly. "Yes, I know. I finally figured out how you do it. With every human life you sap out from those who are sent here to be the Spirit of the Snake Hunters, you add to your own." He shook his head slowly. "This is not the way it should be," he said, thinking it over. "Dominion was given to humans. Only they should be able to attain to be Spirit of their tribes. You have upset the order of things by being a Spirit and not of human-kind."

"Sssssoo?!" She raised her body to elevate her head to the same height as the Death Spirit hovered. "What doessss that matter?" She stared at him with her lidless eyes, her slit pupils narrowed to slashes through her dull green irises.

The Death Hunter Spirit wasn't fazed by her reaction. He calmly hovered as he regarded her through skull socket eyes. "It has been a secret you have kept well hidden. Centuries ago, you never told me the truth about yourself when we made our agreement." He cocked his skull head to regard her, then continued. "I believe that at this time, it could matter very much to the Counsel of the Spirits," he stage whispered, the hollow sound to his voice deeper and more dramatic. "And just think how the human-kind of your tribe would react to the thought of your eating their daughters."

The fear of her longstanding deception being revealed caused her reaction to be instant and fierce. "You. Wouldn't. Dare!" she shouted out each word, accompanied by a torrential shower of venomous droplets. "What of our agreement? What about the prosperity of your tribe?" Her upper body started to wave back and forth in agitation. "I am the only one that cares about your tribe!"

Spirit of the Death Hunters glided away, putting a little space between him and the upset serpent. He slowly shook his head as he contemplated the situation. "You are mistaken," he said quietly, the added vocal effects dropped. "We don't need you. You needed us to be successful with your plan." He dodged aside as the thick tail swung at him. "You couldn't get any of the other Spirits to support you for your quest for ultimate power."

He started to slowly circle her, causing her to swivel her upper body to keep facing him. She had to keep her eyes on him. Even after all the years of dealing with the Death Hunter Spirit, she wasn't sure of the full extent of his powers. She felt more nervous as he moved slowly toward her. She had nothing else she could say and waited to see what he would say and do next.

Finally, he spoke, his voice deep and echoing, "You hunted me down. Remember?" He stopped as he stared into her eyes, his face inches from her flickering tongue. So close she could taste his essence; it tasted of death.

She squelched her fear as she lowered her body to coil it on top of the lower half. The Death Hunter Spirit stayed hovering where he was as he watched her settle down. "You are not my only ally," she hissed spitefully. "I have many believersss interspersssed amongssst the other tribesss. And I do have one of the Spiritsss under my control."

The apparition jumped slightly in surprise. Then he gently floated down to her level. As he faced her, his head cocked slightly to the side. She knew he was curious about this revelation.

"Sssoooo," she hissed quietly, pleased with his reaction. "You are not my only ally." She moved to turn her back to him. She had to telegraph to him that he was not as important to her as he thought. "You don't know everything about me or my plan."

The Death Hunter Spirit didn't bother to reposition himself in front of her. "Apparently not," he said. When he didn't say anything more, Chusi looked behind her. He was gone.

She lay coiled up for a while as she thought about the encounter with the Death Hunter Spirit. "Why is he challenging me after all this time?" she muttered fearfully to herself. "What has changed? Why has he come into my haven? He's never done that before. He's seen my true form now. What will he do? What does he know? Is it because of the Cat Spirit?" All this added to her agitation as she smoldered in her thoughts.

Some of her Sentinels, a cobra, a boomslang, and a coral snake, dared to venture in when they saw that she had quieted down. They had needed to talk to her but had huddled fearfully outside the entry to her chambers, knowing it was better that they let their queen work out her angst.

Before she noticed that they were approaching her, she hissed loudly and violently, springing up like a tightly wound spring. She resumed her version of pacing around the battered room as she slithered in tight circles. Her Sentinels quickly reversed their direction and slithered out of her reach. They posted themselves outside again as they waited for another chance to speak with her.

Chapter Twenty-eight

After she had eaten breakfast, Kilala spent most of the day patrolling Cat Hunter territory. With this task done and not seeing anything amiss, she went back to her haven. After reintegrating with her physical form, she left her sleeping area and sat at the table. As she ate some fruit, her thoughts returned to what she had seen and experienced the day before. She knew the Snake Hunter Spirit was helping the Death Hunter Spirit to some end game that she wasn't sure of. *More death? More corpses?* She looked at the peach she was eating, dripping its sweetness from where she had taken a bite. She set it down for a moment as she tried to reframe her thoughts so she could finish eating it without thinking of beings that ate corpses. She drank some spring water out of her stone mug and stared out of the cave entrance to see if the late afternoon sunshine of a beautiful day would help cleanse her thoughts.

Placing the cup back on the table, she sat back into the chair as she allowed her thoughts to run free. She hoped she could mine more information out of what she had already heard and seen. Suddenly, the memory of the young girl came to mind. "As it was in the beginning," Kilala whispered as she repeated what the first Companion had told her.

Kilala sat up straight. She thought of what Nemr had shared with her from their secret Lore, that in the beginning of the Hunter tribe system formation, the Spirit of the Snake Hunters had tried to take over all of Ritigabid. "Could it be that the Death Hunters are helping the Snake Hunters?" As she thought about it, she saw that it would fit better than the other way around. The ominous feeling that something very wrong was brewing in the Land grew even stronger. Putting her elbows on the table, she rested her chin in her hands as she continued to contemplate what she knew and what she didn't. She needed to know where everyone stood. "Does she have anyone else helping her?" she wondered aloud as she thought about the other Spirits on the Council. Whom could she trust? She felt that Bemot could be trusted after what they had just gone through. He had displayed a genuine concern for all the cubs and was very much in favor of immediate and drastic action to rescue them. Suddenly, she heard a small, sibilant voice at her feet.

"Mistressss cat lady?" She looked down to see the little green snake coiled up next to the huge paws of her Sentinel.

Her surprise at seeing Yumie again after his sudden and unexplained disappearance caused her anger to flare at whoever had allowed him in. Jumping up out of her chair, she glared furiously at Nemr. She couldn't understand why the white tiger had let him in. She knew the Sentinels had their suspicions of him and were aware of her concerns when the little reptile had led the Sentinels into an ambush. She had started to regret her earlier acceptance of the snake, and now he was in her haven again.

The white tiger simply bowed his head and blinked. "I am sorry, Companion. He was insistent about seeing you, and you hadn't given firm orders about him."

She knew he was right; she hadn't given them any instructions on what to do if they saw the reptile again. She nodded at him as her anger quickly cooled. Slowly, she sat back down in the chair. "You are correct. We do need to determine what to do with him considering the latest events." She glanced around the cavern and was surprised to see that all the Sentinels had assembled. Even as large as they were, they had entered the cave and gathered as a group in absolute silence.

"Good." She nodded to each one as she met his eyes. "I am glad you all are here." She turned in her chair to face them directly. "First of all, how are the cubs?"

The fathers of the rescued cubs spoke in turn. They all reported that their little ones were unharmed and happily at home with their mothers. "I am glad," she said with a smile when they were finished. Then she looked down at the snake. Inwardly, she sighed in frustration that she had to make another decision about him. As she thought, she studied him closely and saw that his slender body was coiled tightly in fear and was shaking. He kept his head low and wouldn't look up at her.

"Why are you back here?" she asked him directly.

He still didn't look up as he answered meekly, "I have nowhere to go."

She nodded, tapping her lips with a forefinger as she thought. "Yes. You did mention that before." She thought a bit then asked, "How did you come across the cubs?"

"As I mentioned, I happened upon them on my way here," he said in a quiet, nervous voice.

"Snake!" When she yelled abruptly, she saw the little reptile nearly jump out of his skin. "Tell me the whole truth!" This time, he trembled violently, then started to slither around in a tight circle. Kilala wondered if it was a nervous reaction or if he was trying to find a way to escape. "Why do you hesitate?!"

He stopped moving and laid his head on the floor. "I have been trained since hatching from the egg to be loyal to the tribe. I cannot speak the whole truth without being disloyal to them."

She bent down to look more closely at him and felt stark fear rising from his small body. She decided to be more direct and ask yes or no questions. *Maybe he would feel less disloyal if I could guess some things,* she thought. "Were you sent as a spy to lead us into an ambush?" she asked, lowering her voice but keeping it firm.

"No!" The little snake's answer was immediate and emphatic.

She sat back as she watched him. He had lifted his head and met her eyes without wavering. To her, he seemed to have answered truthfully. She decided to see how he would react and respond to more questions. "Was the finding of the cubs intentional?"

He lifted his head slightly higher and cocked it as if questioning what she meant. "Were you looking for the cubs?" she clarified.

He dropped his head a bit and nodded. He didn't say anything.

"Did you hear something before you were thrown out to give you reason to look in that particular cave?"

"Yess, mistressss cat lady," he said quietly. "But when I was there, I didn't see any one else but a small group of hyenas that guarded the cubs."

Kilala nodded as she thought. She was starting to get a clearer picture of what had happened. Yumie spoke again, "I am sorry I couldn't rescue them when I was there. I'm non-venomous you see, and so very small. They would've torn me to shreds."

"You did the right thing telling us where they were." She leaned over again, elbows resting against knees. "Is there any way that someone saw you either eavesdropping on the conversation before you were thrown out or there at the cavern where the cubs were?"

"I didn't think so, mistressss cat lady," he whispered as he spoke. "But I can't guarantee it. I don't have eyes on the end of my tail."

Finally, she had to ask the question that bothered her most of all. "Where did you go after you lead the Sentinels to the cave?"

The little snake shivered fearfully but picked up his head again to meet her eyes. "As I said before, I am a little snake with no poison. I was scared and could see that I was no use to the rescue effort," he answered quietly as he looked down, obviously ashamed of his cowardly act.

Again, she felt that he was speaking the truth. Kilala nodded that she understood then sat back in her chair to think further about the situation.

Nemr asked her telepathically, *What are you thinking?*

She looked around the room as she mentally linked with all the Sentinels, finding it easy to do when they were all present. *This is what I think happened*. Then she explained the scenario of the little snake hearing about the cubs either on purpose or accidentally. *Either way, the ambush was set after he had left to come to tell us. I think he is innocent of the deception, but he was used by those who wanted to harm us.*

She saw each of the Sentinels nod his head in agreement. "So what do we do with him?" she asked them out loud so Yumie could hear the rest of the conversation.

The panther spoke up, "He has been rejected by his tribe. He should go to the Death Hunters as an outcast."

"But," the lynx spoke up, "he has helped our tribe and should be welcomed as an ally."

Nemr injected his thoughts, "He has helped save our cubs. We should extend our hospitality to him for however long he needs it."

Tau added his opinion. "I think he needs to pledge his fealty to the Cat Hunter tribe and its Spirit." Then they all heard him mutter, "I still don't trust him completely. He's still a snake. He can't change his scales into fur."

"Don't forget the lack of legs!" the leopard sniggered. Some of the others snorted as they tried to keep from laughing.

Suddenly, silence fell over the cavern as everyone's attention was captured by a white tiger cub who wove amongst them carrying a field mouse. Right behind him was his mother, Teigra. She followed her offspring as she eyed the males, daring them to say or do anything to get in her cub's way.

Kilala watched Nemr as he turned toward his mate. His expression showed surprise and curiosity. His mate simply nodded at him and then toward their cub as if to say, 'Wait and watch.'

The cub walked up to Kilala but stopped by the snake. He carefully put down the mouse. When the rodent didn't make a move to run away, Kilala looked closer and saw that it had been stunned. Then the cub started to speak. "Here is a thank you present," he said, his childlike voice high-pitched and unashamed. He looked at the little snake and nodded at him. "We saw you when you came into the cave." The cub then looked around at his elders and his Spirit. "He hid from the hyenas. When they were arguing about something, he was able to signal us that he would tell you where we were." He nudged the mouse closer to the snake. "Go ahead and eat," he urged, "I know you are hungry." He looked back up and continued. "As he was sneaking out of the cave, the Snake Spirit came into the cave and saw him. He couldn't see her. That's when she surrounded us with a fence of snakes." A visible shiver went up his spine with the memory.

Kilala glanced at Yumie and saw that he had circled the prey with his slender body but hadn't eaten it yet. She looked up as Teigra approached.

"He helped save our cubs," she murmured to Kilala. "He should be given sanctuary."

Kilala met her eyes as she nodded. "I will consider it." The white tigress nodded once, then gathered her cub and left the cave.

The Spirit of the Cat Hunters looked around at the others and stood up. "I will consider all that was said here. I will let you know my decision soon." With that said, all the Sentinels nodded, bowed to her, and left the cave. Once they were gone, she looked down at Yumie again. He still hadn't eaten. "Aren't you hungry?"

The dark, lidless eyes looked up at her. "I am famisssshed, cat lady!" he said quickly. "It's just that mammalsss do not like to watch usss eat. It takesss awhile to consssume our mealsss and the method isss very foreign to them."

"Ah, I see," she said as she nodded to him. "Would you like me to leave?"

"Oh no! Mistresssss cat lady, never!" he reacted, horrified at the thought. "If you could provide a bit of cover? That would sssuffice."

"Cover?"

"Throw a blanket over me," the little snake suggested.

"Oh, okay." She went to the big, cushioned chair that had been repositioned in the center of the room and grabbed a blanket. She casually tossed it over Yumie and his meal as she walked toward the cave entrance. She needed to feel the sunshine and the breeze while she thought.

Chapter 29

Kilala took the opportunity to walk around her garden area. She checked on the fruit trees and stands of grain. As she walked along the rows of vegetables, she gathered some ripe squash, matured beans pods, and pulled some carrots that were ready to be eaten. While she was at it, she pulled the few weeds that had grown. She liked working outside amongst growing things. It reminded her of home.

Thinking of home, she wondered how her parents were doing. Even though she knew they were not her natural parents, she still loved them and appreciated their patient and loving upbringing. Then she thought of her grandmother. She smiled at the memory of Mamm's kind and gentle face. The old medicine woman had also been a big part of her childhood, even through Kilala hadn't known she was her grandmother all that time. Seeing their faces in her mind's eye, the feeling of impending crisis deepened further. As she thought of the other villagers and all those in the Cat Hunter tribe, she felt the weight of responsibility for them and knew she must solve what was going on and help protect those under her care. With that in mind, she took her gathered vegetables into the cave and placed them on the table. Later, she would wash them in the clear flowing stream outside the cave before she cooked and ate them.

Standing by the table as she stared down at the lump under the blanket, she didn't see any movement and hoped the little snake had eaten. As she continued to watch, she wondered what she should do with him. *Is he a threat?* she wondered. *Or can he be an asset?* She knew this decision and every decision she made would impact her ability to perform her job as Spirit to her people. Determined not to jump to hasty decisions or freeze in indecision, she pondered the different scenarios. She couldn't send him back. If he had told her the truth, he would be killed by his own kind. She couldn't send him to any of the other Hunter tribes; he would automatically be killed or shunned.

He did help us with the cubs, she thought, feeling very grateful toward the reptile. *Can I send him to Death Hunters as a spy?* As she considered this idea, her fingers started to tap lightly on the table top. After a few moments, she shook her head slightly. *No. They're working with the Snake Hunters. He would be spotted immediately.*

While she contemplated the information she had at her disposal as logically as possible, she refocused on the lump under the blanket. When she saw movement, her attention was drawn to it, and she waited to see what was going to happen next. Soon a little, green head poked out from under the edge. His tongue flicked in and out as he looked up at her.

"Wondering what to do with me?" Yumie asked quietly.

Kilala smiled at him as she reached over to move the straight-backed wooden chair so she could sit down facing him. "Are you feeling better?" she asked as she sat down and then bent over with elbows on knees to talk to him.

"Yesss," he responded as he nodded his head slightly. "It'ssss very much appreciated."

"Good!" She nodded at him. "I am glad. Apparently, you made an impression on the cubs."

The little snake slithered out to where Kilala could see the bulge in the middle of his body. She tried to think of it as his meal and not the mouse. Her thoughts flickered over to ponder why the thought bothered her. *Cats eat mice,* she chastised herself. Then the realization of why it did bother her hit her. *True,* she thought further, *when cats eat a mouse, you don't see it while it's being digested!* She hid a slight shudder by tapping the tabletop again with her fingertips as she returned to her contemplations of what to do with the little snake. She was so deep in her thoughts that she jumped slightly when he spoke.

"I wissh I could gain the trussst of your Sssentinelsss."

When she looked at him, she thought his reptilian face actually appeared earnest. "It is hard to combat centuries of distrust," she answered gently. The little green head nodded in agreement as she returned back to wondering what to do with him. Suddenly, she thought she should ask him. "What do you think I should do with you?"

Yumie drew back his head and upper body in shock. "Me?" He cocked his head; his lidless eyes stared at her as his tongue flicked in and out more rapidly. "Why do you ask me?"

She studied him as he carefully coiled his body with the bulge under his front half. "Your kind has a different way of thinking," she started as she tried to explain her logic in asking him. "You have a different perspective. I wanted to see if you could offer me more options than what I can think of."

"Oh," he said as he dropped his head. Kilala waited patiently, giving him time to consider how to answer her. He raised his head slightly and met her gaze when he was ready. "If you consider my strengthsss, I am sssmall; I can move into sssmall ssspacesss relatively quietly. And I don't have to eat but once a week. My weaknesssss isss that I cannot regulate my temperature. If I get too cold, I get lethargic and if I get too hot, I can be paralyzzzed."

Kilala nodded as she thought about these facts. "Do you think you can function as a spy?"

"That isss an idea I wasss thinking on," Yumie answered with a slight nod. "But where?"

"Yes, where," she mumbled absent-mindedly as her fingers started tapping again. After a few minutes, her thoughts were whirling with ideas, but none of them seemed to be the right answer. Suddenly, she felt so frustrated by the lack of ready answers to everything she had been confronted with since she became Spirit that she slammed her hand down on the tabletop. She was distracted from the sharp pain in her palm when she saw the little snake jump at the sudden noise. "Sorry," she apologized. "I need more information." Using her mental link with Nemr, she summoned him into her haven.

After several minutes, he padded through the cave entrance. "Yes, Companion?" he asked as he walked over to her side.

"Thank you for coming," she said, reaching over to rub his ears as he sat down next to her. He responded by rubbing his face on her arm. "I need to ask you your opinion and see if you have any ideas." She nodded at Yumie. "I'm thinking, and he agrees, that he can help us by being a spy. But I'm not sure where to use him."

The white tiger's gaze intensified as he locked eyes with her. "So you've decided to trust him?" he asked pointedly, requesting clarification.

That direct question made Kilala realize that she needed to make a decision without any more contemplation. She looked from him to the little snake then back again. "Yes." She nodded to him as well as affirming it to herself. "I am willing to trust him. I cannot ignore the fact that not only did he help save our cubs but also that he didn't go through with the plan to poison us."

The large black-and-white-striped head nodded in agreement. "I am inclined to agree." When he turned to stare at the snake, Kilala could feel his massive body tense up. "I am giving you a chance because I am indebted to you because of your help in saving my cubs. Don't make me regret my decision to trust you," Nemr sternly warned Yumie in a low growl.

The little snake lowered his head in a bow as he turned away from the white tiger's hard stare. "I will earnessstly endeavor to work to keep your trussst," he answered respectfully.

Nemr relaxed as he looked at Kilala then back at Yumie. Kilala could tell he was thinking about what she asked of him. After a while, the white tiger turned his head to address her. "Whom can we trust and whom can we not?"

"Well," Kilala started, "We can't trust the Snake Hunters or the Death Hunters. But he is known to them because of their association."

The white tiger nodded again. "Can you trust the Bear Hunters?"

"I think so," Kilala answered, then shared her previous thoughts of the Spirit of the Bear Hunters with him.

"What about Dog Hunters and Eagle Hunters?" Nemr asked her as he focused on her completely.

Kilala thought about it and shook her head slightly. "I really don't know. I haven't had much interaction with them."

"Excusssse me," Yumie spoke up to get their attention. "I have heard that there is another Spirit that is under the Snake Queen's control." He stopped as Nemr and Kilala shared shocked looks with each other, then turned to stare at him. The reptile added, "And she has people amongst all the tribes that will obey her."

That was the last thing Kilala wanted to hear. She closed her eyes and took a deep breath to calm herself. After she opened her eyes, she looked at the snake and asked, "Do you know which one of the Spirits?"

"Do you know which individuals in each tribe are under her command?" Nemr asked immediately after her.

"No." Yumie looked from one to the other, meeting their eyes without flinching.

Kilala looked away as she thought of the medicine women from the villages closest to the Snake Hunters territory. The former Spirit of the Cat Hunters had not trusted them. "I think I know a few of them," she muttered as she suddenly slumped down in her chair and put her face in her hands. "Oh, what are we going to do?!" she cried as her attempts at trying to remain calm were shattered by a sudden surge of desperate worry. "How are we going to figure this out and react appropriately?" She felt the white tiger rub against her shoulder as he purred.

"We will get more information to work with," he said confidently. He looked at the snake and asked, "How much do you know of the Snake Spirit's plans?"

"Ssshe prefers to be called Sssnake Queen by sssnake-kind," he muttered, looking embarrassed. "I am young, ssso I have not been in her ssservice long," he started to answer the white tiger, "but I have had a sssenssse that there hasss been a plan for the queen to dominate for a long time." He looked from one to the other before he continued. "Neither one of you have ssseen her in perssson, correct?"

Kilala and Nemr nodded. "I have just seen her translated form," Kilala said. "She said that it was pretty much what she looked like."

Yumie shook his head. "You cannot trussst a sssnake, my cat lady," he said sadly. "I know I'm of sssnake-kind, but it iss a truth." He took a deep breath and let it out in a sibilant sigh. "What I'm about to tell you iss the deepesst sssecret of sssnake-kind. I will be a traitor to ssshare it. Even our human tribesssmen do not know thisss." He stopped as he prepared himself to commit treason.

Kilala glanced at her Sentinel. She could see that he was as intensely curious as she was at what was obviously a very serious secret that the little snake would reveal. They didn't say a word or move while they waited.

"The Ssspirit of the Sssnake Huntersss, our queen," Yumie blurted out abruptly. As he continued speaking, his voice quavered slightly, "isss not human-kind. SSShe is a sssnake!"

Kilala felt her Sentinel react as he bristled and growled. She gasped in horror as her hands flew to her mouth and her eyes widened in fear. She couldn't say a word as her mind blanked out in shock with the realization that things were much worse than she thought. She barely heard what her Sentinel said next.

"That is against the foundational code of the Hunter tribes!" Nemr snarled at Yumie.

After the immediate, intense sense of shock had dulled to a point that Kilala could think again, she became aware of her surroundings. Although Nemr was still close to her, he was standing stock still, his black-and-white-striped fur bristling, as he stared at the snake. Yumie had wisely moved several feet away from them before he stopped and tightly coiled up again. He had stayed silent as he watched their reactions to the news.

"Nemr, sit down and relax," she whispered to her Sentinel. "He didn't create the situation; he just revealed it to us." The white tiger turned to look at her over his broad shoulder. After a few moments, he nodded at her and sat down.

So, she thought to herself as she considered the revelation of the little reptile, *I did see her true form. It wasn't my imagination.* With that, cold logic clicked in as she considered all the facts she had learned and what she should do with the information. All she could think of was to contact the Council of the Spirits but she couldn't because there was a Spirit who was under the Snake Queen's control. Then she thought of the Spirit of the Bears. She nodded to herself as she thought of reaching out to him. Her thoughts switched back to her original problem as she looked at the snake again. *He's given us vital information so far,* she thought, *but what more can he do? A spy, yes, but where?* When she looked away, the little snake's words about not trusting snake-kind came back to her. *Can I trust him? Did he speak the truth?* she asked herself as she wondered how she could verify what he had said.

As she continued to contemplate the situation with the information she had been told, she couldn't stay still. She knew that there were several variables that had to be considered. As she stood up and started to pace around the cave, her fabric slippers hardly made a sound on the thick carpet squares of multiple colors. When she passed by the cave entrance, she looked out. She was surprised to see that the sky was nearly black and the mists had started to thicken. Seeing the Kuatrukai triggered a thought that she was missing something. She abruptly stopped her pacing as she realized that she should be contacting someone else. As she watched the flashes of energy within the mists, she sent a quick prayer to the Greater Power for guidance. Suddenly, a random thought blossomed in her mind.

Chapter Thirty

She stepped out of the cave and moved to within arm's reach of the Kuatrukai. Turning her head, she called over her shoulder to Nemr and Yumie. "Come out here. Both of you." She turned back to watch the swirling opaque gray-white thicken more as the tail end of dusk moved into deep night. When she felt the presence of the white tiger and the little snake near her, she asked without looking at them, "Do either of you know what the flashing lights are in the Kuatrukai?" She heard them both say they didn't. Smiling to herself, she stepped through the thin barrier that marked the boundary and into the moisture laden fog. She gestured to the lights floating around her as she turned to face them. "They are gifts given to us by the Greater Power," she told them. "If one of them is for you, it will seek you out." She stopped as she watched one of the flashes of energy draw near to her but didn't approach her when she reached out for it. "If it is not for you or you are not ready for it yet, it will stay out of reach." She stepped back out through the boundary. "I want each of you to step into the Kuatrukai."

"But, surely, it is just for human-kind," Nemr commented as he watched the flashes suspiciously.

"I don't know," Kilala had to admit. "But we won't find out until someone tries."

Yumie seemed even more nervous about the mists and energy flashes. "I have never ssseen the like," he admitted. "What if it'sss not for sssnake-kind? Will it kill?"

"I don't know," Kilala repeated. She watched Nemr and Yumie size up the situation warily. Finally, the little green snake slithered forward toward the mist.

After Yumie entered the Kuatrukai, he stopped and coiled his body under him. As he lifted his head upward, Kilala held her breath and clenched her fists. Her sudden feelings of concern for the snake and what would happen to him surprised her. But she didn't dwell on it as she saw one of the energy sparks move toward him.

She watched in nervous fascination as the bright light seemed to be seeking. It slowly moved around the snake as if it was looking him over. *Searching for something?* she wondered. Then it slowly moved toward him and lightly touched him on the end of his snout.

Immediately, the shock caused the reptile to uncoil. His body looked like a slender green rod as it fell flat on the ground. Kilala gasped in horror as she ran into the mist to scoop him up. "Oh no!" she cried, tears suddenly flooding down her cheeks. "What have I done?"

A sudden, sharp, high-pitched burst of sound drew her attention to the spark that had touched the snake. She looked up at it and saw that it wanted her attention. As she stared into the blinking brightness, she could almost make out a voice. It was a whisper, barely audible, almost telepathic in nature. It asked her permission to impart a gift to the stranger.

When she heard the query, Kilala's eyes widened in shock as she looked down at the still, reptilian body then up at the spark. "He's still alive?" she asked in a whisper. The energy burst hovered silently. Hoping it would answer her innermost concerns about the snake, she added, "Can you tell if there is deceit in him? Can he be trusted to help? To be trusted with a gift?"

The spark suddenly moved. It was so fast that she didn't realize what happened until after it was done. The energy pulse had swept through the snake's head and into hers. With that action, Kilala saw what the snake had seen and felt when he had served his queen. She gulped heavily as his memories detailed events that surprised and horrified her. She had to put those revelations aside for the time being until she knew what to do with it and with whom to share it. Focusing her thoughts back on whether he could be trusted or not, she recognized that the information that was shared showed her that he had told her the truth. She shook her head to clear her mind and looked around.

The energy pulse was waiting for her. After it had deposited the memories in her mind, it had left and hovered between her and the snake.

"What gift are you?" she asked the spark.

Again, a barely heard whisper emanated from the blinking light, "Communication."

Of course, she thought as she considered what had just happened. "How can you help him as a spy?"

The energy burst seemed to laugh at her as it jiggled slightly in place. "Communication is everything. He can see others' thoughts. And he can use the gifts to better convince others of things that are true."

Kilala had to smile. "Yes, that would be a benefit."

"Do you give your permission?"

"I do," she whispered as she nodded. Before she could think or react, the energy flash dove for the snake. Instantly, it entered his body on impact. As Kilala held him and watched, Yumie faintly glowed as he absorbed the energy.

After a few moments, she felt his body stretch as his muscles started to move. She set him down on the ground and stepped away to let him recover. When she saw him start to look around, she moved out of the Kuatrukai. Soon he slithered out looking confused.

When they stopped next to Nemr, Kilala waited to see if Yumie had any questions. The snake didn't say anything as he rested his head on top of his coiled body. Since he looked tired and weak, she decided to let him rest as she turned her Sentinel. "Your turn."

Blue eyes filled with concern turned toward her. "Will I have to go through that?" he asked her as he cut his eyes toward the little snake. "Is it necessary?"

Kilala looked away to stare into the Kuatrukai. As she watched, she saw three of the flashing energy bursts move closer to them. "I think you are expected," she said as she looked at him and nodded toward the mists.

Nemr swung his massive head to look at the bursts of light. Suddenly, his body relaxed a bit while his ears pricked forward. "Are they talking to you?" she asked quietly as she watched him. He nodded slightly, then started to move slowly toward the Kuatrukai.

As soon as he entered the mists, the three bursts of power glided around him. They seemed joyous as they started to dance. The white tiger stood quietly as he watched them. As one came near, he raised a paw; the light flew into it, causing the paw to glow for a moment as it was absorbed. Then another entered his head, causing his head to briefly shine. The third entered his chest. After a few moments, Kilala saw a bright radiant aura around his heart, and then it subsided.

After the energy bursts had imparted their power, Nemr seemed to be in a trance for several minutes. He stood as stiff and still as a statue, staring at nothing in particular. Suddenly, he snapped out of it and moved as fluid as water as he glided out through the barrier to stand by her.

"Are you all right?" she asked him quietly. She wanted to place a hand on his shoulder but was uncertain if she would be disturbing something that was happening with the big cat.

When he looked up at her, his blue eyes glowed faintly with a hint of power. "Yes, Companion, I am more than well." He shook his head and sat down on his haunches as he looked at the thick mists with the drifting points of energy. "I never knew those lights in the Kuatrukai were for us," he said thoughtfully.

"Considering the situation that is unfolding, maybe it is time for us to know so we can use them," she offered as she followed his gaze to watch the bright multi-colored lights drift randomly as the grayish white fog swirled around them.

"Perhaps," he agreed, then looked up at her. The movement caught her attention, so she looked over to meet his eyes; they had returned to their normal color. "Or we could have been using them all along and were prevented from the knowledge until now," he said gravely.

Kilala's heart sank as his words had a ring of truth. "That may be true," she said, nodding. She thought for a while, then replied, "But the past can't be changed. All we can do is move forward from here."

The white tiger nodded, then looked at the snake. "He looks very tired." He looked back at the Kuatrukai then at her. "I found the experience invigorating."

Kilala studied Yumie for a few moments as she thought about her personal experience with the gift she had received. "The gifts may have not been meant for his kind," she said quietly. "They asked for my permission to impart it."

"You truly trusted him enough to give your permission," the Sentinel stated rather then asked as he met her gaze with serious eyes.

She nodded. "That gift he just received showed me what he had seen and felt when he served the queen. He can be trusted."

Nemr nodded thoughtfully. After a few moments, he looked up at her, his expression serious and intent. "So you saw through his memories her true form?"

Kilala shuddered slightly as she thought of Yumie's memories that had been shared with her. "Yes," she said decisively. "Yumie spoke the truth. She is not human."

Nemr turned sharp eyes on her, his face more serious and stern. "What are you going to do about it?"

She thought about it a while as she looked at her garden shrouded in the Kuatrukai, then glanced at the coiled snake sleeping soundly at her feet. She looked back at her Sentinel and met his eyes. "I will need to uncover her deception in front of the Council of Spirits," she said. "Otherwise, they will not believe me."

"What about the Spirit that is under her control?" Nemr asked.

She shook her head slightly as she turned away from the Kuatrukai to enter the cave. "I don't know," she said quietly. As an afterthought, she turned back to scoop up the small reptile to take into the warmth of the cave and out of the cool night air. "I hope that revealing her true nature will shock whoever it is out of her control."

Nemr walked beside her as she went to sit down by the table. Reaching down, she picked up the blanket that had covered the snake during his meal time and piled it up near the bookcase. She gently laid the coiled reptile onto it for warmth. Moving him hadn't jarred him from his deep sleep.

She sat down in the wooden chair to think. Nemr lay down beside her in companionable silence, each of them thinking about the situation from his or her own frame of reference. Later into the night, Teigra came into the cave. Kilala watched her as she approached her mate cautiously.

"Is there something wrong?" Kilala asked her quietly. Nemr sat up as she approached.

"He seems different," the white tigress muttered as she sniffed him over. "It is him, but somehow not." She met Kilala's gaze, her eyes perplexed. "What happened?"

Kilala smiled at her, trying to reassure her. "He has received gifts from the All Power."

Teigra crinkled up her black-and-white-striped brow as she telegraphed her confusion. "What gifts?"

Kilala pointed to the Kuatrukai outside. "Those flashing lights are gifts." She met Teigra's eyes. "Remember when you found me in the mists? That's when it had been revealed to me what they were. I was too distracted by other things at the time to think of what to do about them or who to tell."

The white tigress swung her head around to look out the cavern entrance. Kilala watched her as she studied the Kuatrukai closer. "Really?" Teigra whispered in awe. "They were there all this time?"

"Yes," Kilala confirmed. "But only the ones you are ready for. It seems that once you pass through the barrier that confines it, if there are gifts waiting for you, they will contact you."

"I see," the white tigress whispered more to herself than anyone else. Kilala saw how tense but yet attentive the big cat was as she continued to stare at the flashes of energy suspended in the thick grayish white fog.

"Do you want to see if there is a gift waiting for you?" Kilala asked her quietly as Nemr stood up and walked to stand by his mate. She saw Teigra look over at him, her expression apprehensive.

After a few minutes of discussing something in their secret communication, Teigra heaved a big sigh and turned away. She gave a slight shake of her head to her mate. When Kilala saw that they were discussing something else that seemed to be of a different nature, she silently watched and waited.

After several minutes, Nemr turned to her. "She was updating me about news she has heard. Word has gotten around about the rescue of the cubs and who had them. A widespread panic has started to spread amongst cat-kind. They worry that their cubs and kittens will be kidnapped."

Teigra spoke up next, "How do you protect against such an adversary?" Kilala knew that she was referring to the Death Hunters and didn't want to say their name out loud. She looked from one to the other as she realized it didn't sound as if anyone had any suspicions about the Snake Hunters' part in the kidnapping. She decided that she would rather keep it in that way.

As she thought about the news Teigra had passed on, Kilala's face fell. She knew fear was the worst enemy of all. Fear and panic made individuals do things that could propel them into danger instead of away. Thinking about what could be done to try to dispel the fear before it caused harm, she took a deep breath and let it out slowly. She had to make sure she was thinking with a calm and logical mind.

As she sat in silence with Nemr and Teigra watching, her mind whirled with different thoughts and options. Suddenly out of the chaos, a single thought emerged. With it, a certain calmness and sense of rightness descended on her. She turned in her chair to look at both of them. "There must be a way through this," she started. "But it is one that needs to be revealed to us." She lifted her hands to spread them out before her. "We cannot see the whole picture of what is going on." The pair of black-and-white-striped big cats nodded in agreement. "We must contact the All Power." She looked away from them to scan the bookshelves. She was looking to see if she had missed any other books. "Is there anything written down about this Supreme Being?"

The white tigress shook her head. "As I said before, our kind do not use or care for such things as writing."

"Anything in your Lore that could help?" Kilala asked hopefully.

"Didn't you ask help from the All Power for wisdom and help in rescuing the cubs?" Nemr asked. He seemed confused by her sudden request for more information about the mystical entity.

"I did," Kilala said as she nodded slightly. "But I had a good idea of what we needed then. With this situation, I am not sure what to even ask for." She rested her hands on the table as she sat back again. "There are too many things I don't have the facts about."

"Companion," Teigra said gently. She gestured with a paw toward the cavern entrance. The night was lightening into dawn. "It is nearly sunrise. Have you slept at all?"

Kilala saw that the white tigress was right; the night was done. Not only had she not slept, but also she had had no sense that it had passed so quickly. "I am tired," she said absent-mindedly.

"I suggest you sleep." Teigra padded over to her Companion's sleeping loft and pulled the covers back. "Rest will help you organize your thoughts. And you never know," she said as she walked to the cave entrance, "The All Power may speak with you through your dreams."

Kilala nodded at her, then slowly stood up. When she moved, she suddenly felt bone-weary tired. She sorely needed her bed. She didn't bother to change into her night clothes as she slipped in between the blankets and lay down. Quicker than a thought, she was sound asleep.

<u>*Chapter 31*</u>

Her worries chased her into the world of dreams. It started off disjointed and nightmarish, simply a jumble of images, clips of conversation, and thoughts. Then it coalesced into a stark and memorable experience.

She ran through a misty forest looking for something. She didn't know what it was, but she knew she had to find it. Suddenly, she was chased by the Death Hunter Spirit and had to fly across Ritigabid to escape it. When she looked down, she could see the Death Hunter tribe. Many of them were sad or angry. Suddenly, a huge snake erupted from under the ground, shattered the Land, and chased her into the territory of the Snake Hunter tribe with its unhinged mouth gaping wide, venom dripping from blood-red fangs. As she flew away from the snake, she looked down and saw that many of the Snake Hunter tribe members were also angry or sad.

Suddenly, the great snake was gone. As she flew through the sky of the dream-world, she saw the other Spirits. The Eagle Hunter Spirit, high on a mountain peak, his eyes trained on the sky, not seeing what was below him. The Dog Hunter Spirit as he surveyed his pack and tribe, not caring about any others. Then she saw the Bear Hunter Spirit as he cared for his tribe, but his eyes looked about him. There was a question in his gaze, a wondering. It was as if he were trying to find an answer.

Then she flew higher than the sky. She wanted to escape all that was going on. She felt it was her responsibility to fix whatever was happening, but she couldn't. She didn't have the knowledge or the power.

Suddenly, a being brighter than the sun appeared before her. She stopped her aimless flight and hovered. She couldn't make out his face or any details of his appearance; the golden-hued white light was too intense. She had to turn her face and cover her eyes with a hand.

She sensed that he wanted to ask her questions. But there was no voice and no telepathic connection. She didn't know how to answer since she couldn't hear the questions. She could feel him reaching out to her, but she didn't know what he wanted. As she felt the frustration born of not being able to communicate or to understand and not knowing what to do, she could do nothing else but burst into tears. As she started to cry, she felt the entity stop his questing for answers.

With tears still in her eyes, she kept them shielded as she looked at the blazing being. She could see movement as his luminous arm swept out, not to strike her, but to hold out his closed hand. As his hand opened, three bright flashes of color were released. She watched them and waited. They hovered between her and the entity as their strobe-like flashes blinked red, yellow, and blue. Moments or minutes or hours went by; dreams do not gauge time. The being watched her, and she watched the brilliant lights. Finally, she reached out her hand and opened it. Instantly, the three vivid spots of energy flew to her and nestled in her hand. She looked up at the mystic entity for explanation. There was none. Then as suddenly as he appeared, he disappeared. Then the dreamland was gone, and she slept deeply and dreamlessly until the next morning light.

Chapter Thirty-two

When she awoke, the memory of the dream didn't fade like her other dreams. She could remember her flight across Ritigabid and the bright being. She looked at her hand that in her dream had held the three bright lights. There was nothing to see. "Maybe it was symbolic," she muttered to herself as she sat down to eat the oatmeal she had prepared. Looking out into the dawning day, she thought about the images of the Death Hunter and Snake Hunter tribes. Many looked sad and angry. *Why is that?* she wondered. *Are they unhappy because their leaders hadn't conquered* Ritigabid*? Or are they unhappy because they are trying to?*

By the end of her meal, Kilala had come to the same conclusion as she had after reading more of the books, that she needed more information. It was if the books and the dream hinted at deeper things but didn't fill in enough for her to see the whole picture. With that in mind, she considered her next steps. She needed to know who the Snake Queen was controlling on the Counsel of Spirits. She also needed to warn the other members of the Council that the Snake Hunter Spirit was not a human. She wondered who she could trust to help her get more information. Her Sentinels were loyal, she felt sure of that. She felt that cat-kind throughout their territory would help. But their allegiances were known. Who would tell one of her kind the secrets that she needed to know?

She felt the need to move and pushed back from the table. Then she stood up and started to pace around the cave as she thought, trying to fit the mental pieces of the puzzle together. As she passed the blanket on the floor by the bookshelves, she didn't notice a small, green, scaly head pop up to look over the bunched-up material.

Kilala thought of her grandmother and her parents. She shook her head. She didn't want to endanger them in any way. She felt that none of the villagers could help her. Her thoughts skipped to the meeting of the medicine women when she was installed in the office of the Spirit of the Cat Hunters. Her thoughts zeroed in on the two medicine women that were from the villages that bordered Snake Hunters territory. The previous Companion had asked them point blank if they had been spending time with Snake Hunters. Kilala nodded to herself. They had reacted suspiciously and had never given a satisfactory answer to the question. She knew that they were untrustworthy.

As she continued to think about them, she stopped by the table and sank down slowly to sit in the wooden chair. Her fingers started to drum lightly on the flat surface of the table. *Somehow, I should be able to find out something from those two,* she thought to herself. *I would not be breaking into someone else's territory that way.* She started to nod as she thought about how she could try to extract information from them. Her thoughts were interrupted as she heard her old cat meow.

Kilala looked up from her sightless contemplation of the floor and saw that Anong had jumped up on the table and was sitting upright on her haunches, tail swishing, as her green eyes stared at her. She reached over to pet her but Anong ducked her head to avoid her touch. "What's wrong?" she asked her ancient cat.

The brilliant green eyes changed as her pupils grew large, causing her eyes to look black. "The Chaos is approaching," she meowed in a hollow-sounding voice.

Kilala felt a chill run through her. Chaos, that was what the first Companion had called that time before the establishment of the tribes and had warned her that it was approaching. She studied the old cat and wondered where she had gotten that message. "Who told you that Chaos was coming?"

"The All Power," her old cat meowed in answer.

Kilala stared at her, noticing how stiff she seemed to be. Her eyes still looked black and seemed to look through her. She started to wonder If something was wrong with her, and then it dawned on her that the old cat was waiting for something.

"Anong," she started cautiously. "What should I do? Will the All Power help?"

"Only if asked. Only if wisdom is truly sought," the cat said in response.

"What should I do?" she asked.

"Seek the truth. Seek your enemies."

"How do I that?" Kilala asked quickly.

"Trust the All Power."

Kilala sat back to put a hand over her eyes in frustration. She felt like she was going around in circles and not getting anywhere. "Can't I have a list of instructions to follow? So I don't make a mistake?"

When she didn't hear an answer, she dropped her hand to look at her cat. Anong was more relaxed, her eyes back to normal, and was licking a paw, then wiping her face. Kilala sighed deeply; she could see that her question wouldn't be answered.

Anong looked up from her grooming. "What's wrong?" she asked sharply.

Kilala sighed again, planting an elbow on the table to cup her chin as she looked at her cat. "Apparently, you were in touch with the Great Power. I was hoping to get more information when the link was broken."

Anong stood up to walk to her and rubbed her face against Kilala's face. "Apparently, you didn't need any more information," she purred soothingly.

Kilala reached up with her other hand to rub the old cat's ears gently. "It would be nice to have a list of things to do so I can be sure I'm doing the right thing," she muttered.

Anong pulled away from her hand and sat down on the table again to stare at her. "You have all the equipment you need. You were born with the gifts to figure out how to handle this. All you need now is to trust in the All Power to guide you each step of the way."

"It's never easy, is it?" Kilala asked.

"That would be boring," Anong said as she stood up, walked to the edge of the table, and then jumped down with a soft groan. "I'm going hunting," she said over her shoulder.

Kilala watched the small cat as she left the cave. When she was out of sight, she sat back in her chair. Leaning her head back against the head rest, she stared up at the rocky cave ceiling overhead. Her mind swirled between silently praying to the All Power and trying to figure out what to do next. After several minutes, her thoughts were disrupted.

"My cat lady," a voice hissed on the ground behind her. She turned in her chair to look down at the coiled green snake. His flicking tongue pointed right at her as he regarded her with lidless, dark eyes.

"Oh," she said softly, "You're awake. How do you feel?"

The snake uncoiled slowly and moved out of the blanket he had slept on. He re-coiled near her feet. "I am confusssed but unharmed."

"Do you feel different?" Kilala asked; she was curious to know how the gift had changed him, if any. She was also wanted to know if he knew what happened.

The small, green head nodded slightly. He looked away as if he were thinking. Without looking back, he started to speak again. "I feel…expanded," he said, then stopped. "It'sss like there'sss more of me than before."

"Do you know what gift you received?"

He shook his head again. "Not entirely. But I do know I can sssee the turmoil in your mind."

Kilala was slightly disturbed by the thought of the snake prowling through her thoughts. She ducked her head, then replied, "Well, don't look too closely. You never know what you may find."

"Undersssstood," he said agreeably. "I can alssso sssee the thoughtsss of cat-kind and bear-kind."

Kilala looked at him again, then nodded thoughtfully. "That can be useful. How about eagle- and dog-kind?"

The little snake sat still for awhile, all but his flicking tongue. Then he shook his head. "I don't know," he said quietly. "I guesssss I need to be near them to sssee."

Kilala furrowed her brow in confusion. "How do you know that you can link with bear-kind then?"

"While you were sssleeping, a Sssentinel from the Ssspirit of the Bear Huntersss came to visit. He wasss essscorted in by your Sssentinel. When they sssaw that you ssslept, they decided to leave and come back later." The little snake turned to look toward the cave entrance. "That wasss when I found I could read their thoughtsss." He turned to look back at her. "I dissscovered I could read yoursss when your dreamsss woke me up."

Kilala had followed his gaze to the cave entrance but snapped back to stare at the little snake. "You saw my dreams?"

He nodded. "Yessss, in much detail."

At first, she froze. She felt that her personal thoughts and very mind had been violated. Then a sudden thought occurred to her. *He saw everything I did; he is a perfect witness and may be able to help interpret.* She focused back on him. "Well?" She didn't bother to fill in the details since she figured he was reading her thoughts.

The snake looked confused. "Well, what?" he asked suspiciously.

"Aren't you reading my thoughts?" she asked quickly.

"No, my cat lady," he said as he shook his head. "I ressspected your wissshesss and found how not to read your thoughtsss."

"Oh," she said quietly. "That's good to know." She smiled at him warmly appreciating that he respected her wishes. "I was thinking since you had seen the dream, you could help interpret it." She watched him closely, hoping he would agree to help her with the perplexing images. But his answer was interrupted by the entrance of the white tiger and a grizzly bear.

"Hello, Companion," Nemr greeted her as he approached. "I hope this is a good time to hear from our friend from bear-kind. This is Kuruk, the leader of Bear Hunter Sentinels.

Kilala straightened up in the chair and smiled. "Of course," she said. "Hello, Kuruk, how is your Spirit doing?"

"He is doing well but would like an audience with you." The bear's gruff voice filled the cavern.

"Is everything okay? Are there any more cubs missing?" she asked as anxiety tightened her throat.

"No, Mistress," Kuruk shook his head. "I am sorry to worry you. All bear-kind is safe, for now." He settled down on his haunches beside Nemr who had sat down near Kilala. Yumie had slithered under the table, out of the way of their huge paws.

Kilala expelled a sigh of relief, but then caught the 'for now' ending of the bear's statement. "What is happening?"

"There is much discord throughout **Ritigabid**," Kuruk started then stopped. He glanced at Nemr who nodded for him to continue. "The Sentinels feel it. We have sensed it for quite a while but could not find the source."

"The situation has worsened," Nemr picked up when Kuruk stopped. "We are beginning to realize that the source is centered in Snake Hunter territory."

"The Council of Sentinels has not been in touch with the Sentinels of the Snake Hunters for decades," the bear added. "And recently the Sentinels of the Eagle Hunters have not been in contact."

"Eagle Hunters?" Kilala gasped as she thought, *Is that whose Spirit is under the control of the Snake Queen?* She felt her heart grow heavy at the thought of the eagles, the majestic birds that she always enjoyed seeing flying in the sky so free and powerful, being under control of snake-kind. *Could it be?* she almost whispered aloud.

"Companion?" Nemr called to her, snapping her attention back to them. "Can the Spirit of the Bear Hunters have entry into your haven? Or would you like to meet him elsewhere?"

Kilala thought awhile. "Tell him I will meet him where we talked earlier."

Kuruk nodded his head in acknowledgement. "Yes, mistress. It is done." He stood up and nodded to Nemr. "I will take my leave. Thank you for showing me the berry patch. It was a good snack!"

Nemr stood and nodded at him. "My pleasure. Let me escort you back to the border." Both Sentinels bowed to Kilala. After she nodded to them, they turned to leave the cavern.

As soon as they were out of sight, Kilala stood to move to her sleeping place to prepare for translation. When she heard a soft hissing sound, she stopped and looked under the table. When she met the dark, lidless snake eyes she asked, "What did you say?"

"The dream isss not for me but for you."

Kilala thought for a moment trying to figure out what he was talking about. When she realized it was a delayed answer to her request from him about the dream, she nodded that she understood. She knew he was right and that she needed to quit trying to get others to shoulder her responsibilities. She stood up as she squared her shoulders, accepting the weight of more accountability. She started to move away when she heard the snake speak again.

"Both of them are noble and there are no deceitful thoughtsss."

"Who? The Sentinels?" she asked as she glanced at the cave entrance. She turned to see the little green snake nod.

Kilala smiled at him. "Just as I thought. But it is good to have verification." She made her way to her sleeping place and lay down on her back with the blankets over her. Before she closed her eyes, she looked across the cave to the little green snake who had moved back to the blanket by the bookshelf. "Thank you for respecting the privacy of my thoughts," she called out to him.

"Asss you wisssh, my cat lady," he answered back.

She nodded at him, settled her head so her neck was straight so she wouldn't have a crick in her neck when she came back, then relaxed and translated smoothly into her ethereal form.

Chapter 33

As Kilala floated above the old stump in the meadow, waiting for Bemot, she watched as the butterflies and bees flitted by her as they went about their business. No one noticed her, as she had intended. She debated about going into the seen mode while she waited, but they were very near Snake Hunter territory. She figured Bemot would understand and would do the same once he reached their meeting place and didn't see her.

Soon she saw the translated form of the Spirit of the Bear Hunters glide into the meadow. She watched as he looked around for a bit then looked confused. She was about to reveal herself when she saw him realize where she was. Soon he was in the unseen mode and drifted to her side while he scanned the meadow and the forest around them.

"Hello, Kilala," Bemot greeted her with a gruff but kind voice. "Thank you for meeting me."

"Hello, Bemot," Kilala responded, smiling. She couldn't help but trust this person. "It is my pleasure. Your Sentinel said little but hinted much. What can you tell me?"

The Spirit's shaggy head wagged slowly back and forth, his silvery beard and long dreads waving gently as they followed the movement. "Since our encounter with the rescue of the cubs, I have been thinking and remembering a few things. I am very concerned that we have a snake in our council."

She nodded, not surprised at his suspicions. "I know you are not using that as a colloquialism," she said quietly. "It has been recently revealed to me that the Spirit of the Snake Hunters is not a human."

Bemot looked at her closely with dark eyes under upraised bushy eyebrows. "Is your source reliable?"

She nodded her head slightly. "It is the little green snake that she had sent to spy on me. The one that helped us save the cubs."

"Yes, yes," he muttered as he ran a hand over his mustache, stroking it back into place. "My cubs have been singing praises of the reptile. They want to send him gifts!" He shook his head slowly at the thought. "An amazing thing, a reptile with a heart!"

Kilala smiled at him then said, "Yes, he is very surprising individual. But he does seem to be truly horrified by what is going on in his tribe."

"He can confirm the Snake Hunters have a snake for a Spirit?"

"Yes," she emphasized by nodding her head. "Snake-kind calls her the Snake Queen. The human-kind of the tribe thinks they are picking their new Spirit every few years." Her voice fell as she prepared herself to share what she had learned from Yumie's memories. The thought of what she was going to say made her incredibly sad and angry. "But the young girls are being devoured by this snake. Somehow the Snake Queen is able to steal life from them to feed her own existence."

Bemot beat his breast and groaned loudly. "NO! I could not think or imagine such horror!" As his ethereal being hung dejectedly in the air, he whispered. "It has only been the last few days that I have remembered that we had not officially welcomed a new Spirit from the Snake Hunters into the Council for a very long time." He lifted his head to meet her eyes. "I asked the Bear Hunter Sentinels if they had such an occurrence in their Lore." He shook his head as he looked away. "They had not." Suddenly, he pounded a fist into an open hand in anger. "Why did I not see?! Why did I not think of this before?!"

Kilala hovered midair, thinking of what he had said. "But Bemot, you are not the only member of the Council of Spirits. The others should have noticed and started to investigate."

The Bear Hunter Spirit hung his head again. "We have been too focused on our tribes and plots of Ritigabid that make up our territories. I am as guilty as the rest."

Kilala pursed her lips as she thought further. "Who is the oldest of the Spirits right now, not including Snake Hunter Spirit?"

Bemot looked up at her with questioning eyes. But instead of asking why she changed the subject, he answered, "The Spirit of the Eagle Hunters, Amaud."

"Okay," she nodded. "Who is the youngest, besides me?"

"Spirit of the Dog Hunters, Tahmores."

Kilala nodded once, then started to tap her chin in thought. She was so deep into her contemplations that she didn't realize that she had started to glide in tight circles around the stump and Bemot until he spoke. "Can you please quit doing that? You're making me dizzy," he growled in annoyance.

"Oh, sorry," she said as she stopped to hover beside him. "So the order according to age is Eagle Hunter, Bear Hunter, Dog Hunter, and me, Cat Hunter. With Snake Hunter being the oldest but not human."

Bemot thought a moment, then nodded. "That is correct."

"Who out of those Spirits do you think the Snake Queen could've gotten under her power?" she asked him directly, looking deep into his eyes, wishing that Yumie could see Bemot to assess him like he did the others.

The Spirit of the Bear Hunters acted surprised, then shocked. "Well, it's not me!!" His face fell suddenly into anxious lines as he realized why she had asked such a question. "There is a Spirit that is under her control?" he whispered hoarsely as he asked. "How can that be?"

Kilala nodded at him silently. After a few moments, she said, "I don't know how it happened, but yes, I have undeniable knowledge that the Snake Queen has one of the other Spirits in her control." Then she smiled and put out a hand to calm him. "I really didn't think it was you. I saw your character when we worked together to get our cubs back."

She could see that he tried to control his growing fear and anger as he gave her a tight smile. "And I know it's not you." He leaned closer to her to whisper with a twinkle in his eyes, "For the same reason that you trust in me."

She smiled back. "Thanks for the vote of confidence!" She met his eyes, then asked seriously, "But how do you know for sure?"

He looked away for a moment to think. The shift in conversation had allowed him to calm down to consider things rationally. Then he met her eyes again. "You are different than us. You are unique amongst the Spirits both present and past." He thought more, then shrugged his broad shoulders. "Don't ask me to explain it further. I just know."

Kilala sensed the silvery glow emanating from her translated form shift to a pinkish hue. *Oh no!* she thought in surprise, *Being embarrassed is obvious in this form, too!* She saw Bemot smile slightly and was relieved when he didn't make a comment.

Suddenly, she heard a noise, like something heavy and rough being pushed through dry sticks and leaves. She looked toward the sound and realized that it was coming from the edge of the meadow closest to Snake Hunter territory. As she watched, she saw two large snakes, a king cobra and an anaconda, break through the forest underbrush and move onto the short grass. *How did they break through my boundary?* she thought in shock. When she glanced at Bemot, she saw that he had heard them and was watching them intently. As the two reptiles made their way across the meadow, they talked loudly enough for the two Spirits to hear them.

"The Sssnake Queen wantsss usss to do what?" the cobra asked the other snake. He sounded as if he couldn't believe what he was hearing.

"Ssshe wantssss usss to kidnap the little sssnake sssspy," the anaconda answered, his sibilant voice deep and harsh.

"But ssshe threw him out!"

"Yeah, but now sssshe thinksss he could be valuable. He may have ssseen sssome of the Cat Huntersss Ssspirit'sss sssecretsss."

"Have you ever ssseen her ssscared of anyone?"

"Not until the new Cat Hunter Ssspirit came along. Ssshe sssseemsss terrified of her!"

They slithered across the rest of the clearing without a word as they looked around to see if they were being watched by cat-kind. As they entered the cover of the forest again, the anaconda asked the cobra, "Do you think ssshe will sssucceed in taking over all Ritigabid and enssslaving all the tribesss under her?"

"Only if sssshe can do away with the Sssspirit of the Cat Huntersss," the other one said as they slithered out of sight into the thick forest undergrowth.

Kilala's mouth dropped open in amazement. There was the enemies' entire plan, along with their next move, dropped at her feet with a witness nearby. She looked over at the Spirit of the Bear Hunters and had no doubt he had heard them. His pent-up anger was obvious as his silver glow had turned into a burning red, his face scowled fiercely, and his fists clenched tightly by his sides.

He turned blazing eyes to meet hers. "Well, there it is." His gruff voice strained with the effort of controlling his anger. "I told you, you are special. The Spirit of the Snake Hunters fears you. And there's our evidence of what her plans are."

"I see," she said quietly as she studied him. She knew he wasn't angry at her but at the Snake Queen and her plan. "I don't know why she is afraid of me. But I hope we can use it to our advantage."

She glanced over to where the two snakes had disappeared into the forest. "Yes," she said thoughtfully. "We now have confirmation of her plan. But we need to find the Spirit who is under her control!" Her thoughts whirled with all that she needed to do. She needed to protect herself, the little snake, protect Ritigabid from this invasion and find the Spirit under the Snake Queen's control. Her thoughts settled onto one question out of the many. "How can we find out which one?"

"Uh," the Spirit of the Bear Hunters cleared his throat as he looked down at the ground. Kilala was surprised to see the bright red anger of his ethereal glow turn into an embarrassed pink. "I might as well tell you, I found out something by mistake."

"Oh?" Kilala responded quietly as she waited for him to look up at her. But he didn't; he continued to speak while he looked at the ground below them.

"Before I sent my Sentinel to request an audience, I thought I would show up outside your haven and contact you. I traveled in unseen mode so that no one could see that I was visiting you. Well, my thoughts were so distracted by all that I wanted to talk to you about that I wasn't paying attention to where I was. All of a sudden, I found that I was in your haven! Somehow the unseen mode enables you to bypass the security fence set up by the Spirit that dwells there!" He glanced up to see how she reacted.

Kilala was shocked. Not only the fact that he had been in her haven while she slept, but that it was even possible. "Wow, that's even more of a dangerous ability than we thought," she finally said as she considered how it could also be an advantage for them. Finally, a plan emerged in her mind. But she knew she would have to do some experimenting to see if it would work. She felt a little hope as she thought she could see a light at the end of a long, confusing, and distressing tunnel. "Yes," she said as she smiled at a confused Bemot. "I think I know what we can do."

Unseen to the world, they hovered over the old tree stump as she described to him the bare bones of her plan. While the sun began to set and darkness started to settle over the forest, Bemot thought about the plan and nodded. "It could work," he said quietly. "Let me know what you find out from the experiment."

"I will," she said with a smile. She was profoundly relieved that she had a direction to travel. She didn't know where it would wind up but at least it was somewhere to start. They bid each other farewell and went back to their havens. Both of them agreed not to become seen until they were safely within their security fences.

Chapter Thirty-four

Heading back to her haven, Kilala kept an eye out for the two big snakes as she telepathically warned her Sentinels of their intrusion and their intent, hoping that only the big cats had received it and she would not panic all cat-kind. She was relieved when she was able to contact Yumie through the lioness to warn him. Tiaret replied that he was very frightened because he knew that those two snakes were the queen's assassins as well as her Sentinels.

Once she arrived at her haven, she switched out of the unseen mode and reintegrated into her body. Sitting up, she shoved the blankets off and got out of bed. As she searched for the little snake in the cavern and out in her garden, she called out to him, "Where are you? Are you okay?"

After several minutes, she stood quietly as she continued to scan around for him and heard a sibilant whisper. She moved with light steps as she followed the sound to one of the berry bushes. Woven into the green branches of the bush was the little snake. "Good camouflage," she commented then said, "I need you out here. I need to try something to see if you can safely help us."

She heard a muffled reply as Yumie unwrapped himself from the bush and dropped to the ground. He constantly moved his head to look around as he slithered over to her.

"Let's go into the cave." She gestured for him to enter first. She looked behind her and around the garden just in case the big snakes were able to get past her personal security fences.

Satisfied that all was well, she entered the cave and found that Yumie had slithered his way up onto the tabletop. "Good." She nodded at him. After she sat on the chair, she said, "Now, with your new gift, you can be valuable to us if we can take you with us safely."

The little snake nodded at her. "I would be happy to be of ssservice. But how? Apparently the queen hasss sssent her personal guardsss after me," he pointed out as his little body shivered with fear.

She smiled at him as she added, "I have discovered that I can make myself unseen in the translated state."

The little snake abruptly stopped his shivering to stare at her in surprised disbelief. Kilala held up a hand for him to not speak as she continued. "This is what I want to try. While I'm in the unseen state, I will touch you and see if that will make you unseen as well."

Yumie continued to stare at her. She wasn't sure but he seemed frozen in shock. She was about to give him a nudge when she saw him move his head slightly. After that he was able to speak. "Can you hold anything while you are in the form of a Ssspirit?" he asked quietly.

With a quick movement, she shrugged her shoulders. "I don't know. I haven't been the Spirit of the Cat Hunter's very long." She smiled at him and added, "No one has said I can't. And I'm willing to experiment."

Yumie nodded slightly. "Okay, if you want to try, I'm willing. I jussst don't think it will work."

"Well," she said as she sat back in the chair, "let's see what happens." With a quick thought, she translated and hovered over the little snake.

She was reaching down to touch him, when he asked, "How do we know if I become unssseen?"

Kilala pulled back her hand and contacted Teigra. The white tigress replied quickly and told her that she was already on her way to haven to check on her. She appeared at the cave entrance within minutes.

The blue eyes of the white tigress studied the scene in front of her. After she padded quietly over to the table, she sniffed at the little snake, then looked up at Kilala. "Companion, you may need to fill me in on what's going on. I have not been in attendance recently since I've been with my cubs until they were settled after their ordeal."

Kilala nodded at her. "I understand why you haven't been around lately, and I will bring you up to date. But right now, can you see if the little snake becomes unseen?"

Teigra sat down on her haunches while she kept her eyes on her. "And how are you planning to do that?"

"By becoming unseen myself while I'm touching him."

Teigra shook her head slowly back and forth. "I've been away too long. I think you've lost your senses."

Kilala looked at her quickly. She was surprised by her response. *I guess her mate didn't tell her about the ability to becoming unseen*, she thought, then smiled at her. "You will see." Then she thought about it further. "But you must not tell anyone. You've got to help us keep this ability I discovered secret right now."

The tigress' eyes widened in surprise. "So you've done this before?"

Kilala gave her a mysterious smile, then got back on task. "Okay, Yumie, I'm going to touch you. After that I will switch to unseen mode." She looked back at Teigra. "And you will tell us if it worked or not."

The white tigress nodded her head slowly, then kept her eyes on them while she waited.

Kilala reached out her hand again. Just before she touched the snake, she asked, "Ready?"

"Ssssure," Yumie said nervously, doubt filliing his voice.

When Kilala touched him, she experienced an odd sensation as her fingertips slightly slipped into his body. He didn't feel completely solid but like a very thick gelatin.

Yumie shivered with the touch. "That feelsss weird," he complained.

"Does it hurt?" she asked with curious concern.

"No. Jussst a tingly, pressssure sssensssation."

"Okay. I'm going into the unseen mode," she warned him. She didn't wait for his reaction as she wanted to get this experiment over as soon as possible. As she triggered the unseen mode, she made sure that she didn't move a bit.

She instantly felt the now familiar sensation of being unseen. She looked around at the vague cavern and furnishings around her to confirm, then looked down at Yumie. She thought he looked more solid than the table but wanted to make sure he was totally unseen. When she glanced over at Teigra, she saw that the white tigress' light blue eyes were wide with huge pupils. She had put her paws up on the table and was sniffing around where she had last seen them as she looked for them. "I guess it works!" Kilala exclaimed happily.

Yumie looked up at her. He had heard her without problems. "It did," he said as awe filled his voice. He looked back Teigra. "Ssshe can't sssee or sssmell me!"

"Now." Kilala wanted to try something else. She had to know the extent of this ability. "I'm going to move away from you and see if you remain unseen." The little snake nodded at her.

Moving her hand away from him slowly, she drew back as she watched Teigra. As soon as her fingertips were no longer touching Yumie, the white tigress startled in surprise. "There you are!" she exclaimed to the snake. She then looked up and around for her Companion. Kilala left the unseen mode and appeared before both of them. She was a bit disappointed that Yumie could only remain unseen if she stayed in contact with him. She sighed deeply but then smiled as she thought that her experiment was successful in other ways.

"Okay," she said confidently, "now we know what we can and cannot do." After she reintegrated into her body, she flexed her arms and moved her legs. Once she banished the slight stiffness, she put her elbows on top of the table top so she could rest her chin on her hands. "Now, time to formulate a definite plan."

Chapter 35

She met Bemot again over the ancient stump in the clearing to fill him in on what she had found out. When she ran out of information, he simply nodded but didn't comment as he looked around to think. She did the same, using the companionable silence as they hovered unseen. After she chased her thoughts until she could find no end and no absolute answers, she turned to look at him. She could see he was doing the same by the expressions that flitted across his broad face. "What do you think?" she asked him quietly. "You know my basic plan. What do you think we should do?"

The Bear Hunter Spirit's brown eyes focused on hers. His broad shoulders shrugged slightly. "Your plan is good. It is sound. But whether we split up or stay together is the big question." He looked at the forest around them and then met her eyes again. "How much faith do you have in the little snake's ability?"

Kilala responded immediately, "I feel he is reliable and important enough to have him present as we evaluate the other Spirits." She moved to hover closer to him to say, "I feel that he will prevent us from being deceived. He received a gift from the All Power that will help us. Perhaps this gift was bestowed on him because he is snake-kind. As we know, fire fights fire. Maybe it takes a snake to uncover snake deception?" she asked as she spread out her glowing silver hands in front of her, beseeching him to understand.

Bemot pursed his lips and didn't say anything for awhile. Then he slowly nodded his shaggy head, his thick, brown, glowing dreads floating back and forth in reaction to the movement. "That makes sense." He squared his shoulders as he made his decision. "Yes, we need to go together so the snake can be with us."

Kilala nodded once at him. "Agreed!"

They were about to go their separate ways again until they could implement their plan when the Spirit of the Bear Hunters called to her. "Kilala," he said, concern etching his face, "What of those snake assassins? Have you seen them again?"

Kilala shook her head. "No. I have warned the little snake. He knows who they are and what they are capable of. I have cat-kind looking for them as well."

Bemot nodded. "Good. Would hate to lose him right now." Then he muttered as he looked at the ground to shake his head in mock dismay. "Never thought I'd be trusting a snake, much less working with one for the greater good!"

Kilala smiled and waved to him as she moved off. "I agree!" she shouted back over her shoulder.

Chapter Thirty-six

When Kilala arrived at her haven, she commanded the unseen mode off and looked around. The entire area was empty. She figured Teigra was back with her cubs until she was summoned and Anong was likely hunting. But she wondered where the reptile was. "Yumie," she called as she walked around her gardens, peering into bushes and then into trees as she entered her orchard. "Yumie!" After several minutes of calling and searching, she became more and more concerned about where he could be. With reluctance, she had to give up. She walked back into the cavern after looking around once more, and then sat at the table to think.

"Why is he not here?" she muttered to herself, fighting off worry as she tried to stay logical. "He knows it's not safe for him outside of my haven." Since she had no information to work with, she was undecided what to do. "Should I wait? Or should I go looking for him? If I do that, where would I look?" She wasn't even sure where to tell her Sentinels to look. "Why did he leave?!" she grumbled angrily into the empty cave.

"Maybe he didn't leave on his own." The hoarsely whispered voice, spoken from behind her, startled her. She stood up and whipped around in the fluid, lightning-fast reflexes of a frightened cat. She found herself staring at the apparition of the Spirit of the Death Hunters as he hovered a few feet away from her. Much too close for her comfort.

As she stared at him in shock, it dawned on her that he made no attempts to hide from her. He wasn't playing any games, and he made no threatening moves toward her. He was acting completely differently from their last encounter. She eventually found her voice. "What are you doing here?" she asked gruffly as she tried to hide her fear. "How did you get in here?"

The skull-like head very slightly shook back and forth at her. "Death cannot be blocked out of anywhere," he stated simply. Although he spoke in a hoarse whisper, it didn't have the eerie, hollow tones like before.

"You have access to all of Ritigabid, no matter what?" she asked in disbelief.

As she watched, the apparition in front of her morphed from a figure shrouded in tattered black shadows wrapped around a skull head into a very old man. His was gaunt from his face to the frame of his body. He stooped a bit as if he should have a cane supporting him. "I show you who I am," he said quietly in the same hoarse whisper. "I trust that you can see I am offering a hand of cooperation."

She hadn't realized that her jaw had dropped in open-mouthed surprise until she had to snap it shut. Overwhelmed by the dual whammy of the revelation of the Death Spirit's true self and what he had said, she was stunned into speechlessness. Without taking her eyes off him, she reached around behind her to find the chair so she could sit down. She couldn't trust her weak, shaky legs. "I see," she managed to say through a tightened throat. She wasn't sure if it was fright or shock that plagued her. Determined to adjust to this new event, she cleared her throat and willfully threw off whatever had her in its grip. "Why are you here?" she asked, working hard to strike a conversational tone.

"I have come for your help." He slowly descended so he could hover near the floor. "May I join you at your table? I mean you no harm."

"Um," she stopped and glanced around the room. "I have only this one chair that will fit under the table." When she realized what she said, she felt stupid. His translated form didn't need a chair.

The old man smiled gently at her; he knew it was unnecessary to point out the fact he didn't need one. He floated around to the other side of the table to hover in a sitting position. "This seems much more civilized."

Kilala swiveled in her chair so she could face him. With him that close, she could see that his eyes were brown and gentle. They seemed to hold such sadness but mercy. "I…I…don't understand any of this," she stammered. "You tried to terrorize me after the Council meeting. Why are you here now and wanting to be friendly? Well, not friendly as such," she added hastily as she fumbled for words. "Shall we say, not as creepy?"

The Spirit simply looked away from her to regard the nearby bookshelf with its collection of journals. "We are not mentioned in those, are we?" He seemed either not to have heard her question or simply ignored her.

"You mean the Death Hunter tribe?" she glanced at the books, then at him. "No, you are not."

He sighed, shaking his head slightly. "Lack of information leads to tales, half-truths, and outright lies." He met her gaze as he continued. "The only things I have done shamefully are to be deceived by the Snake Queen and having to do her bidding." He looked down at the table as he added, "She was the one who wanted to terrorize you."

Kilala stared at him. She was shocked to hear him admit to his alliance with the Snake Queen. "So, why did you do it?" She left her question opened-ended to see what he would talk about.

He cocked his head to one side while he started to explain. "If you mean doing her bidding, she came to me with a plan. She felt that Ritigabid would be better united under one leader, one Spirit. She made an argument that it would benefit everyone by pooling the strengths of all the tribes, therefore negating the weaknesses." He glanced at her to see her reaction. Kilala nodded for him to continue. "She knew that the Death Hunters had to have, by right, the ability to access all the Land, including the Havens." He met her eyes again. His eyes were so full of regret and remorse, Kilala had to look away. "Her idea seemed to have merit."

Kilala studied her hands resting on the table in front of her as she thought. She nodded once then looked up to meet his eyes again. "Yes, it does seem to be a good plan." She sat back in her chair and asked, "So you allied your tribe with hers."

The old man nodded sadly. His gaze dropped to the table. "Unfortunately. Over the centuries, she has used the alliance to demand more and more from my tribe and started to take over leadership."

"How did she take over leadership?" Kilala asked quickly as she sat forward. "The tribes are supposed to follow their Spirit and no other."

"True," the Death Spirit nodded in agreement. "That is how the Hunter tribe system is set up. But the Snake Queen is very persuasive. After she gained access to my tribe through our alliance, she started to turn them against me." He looked up briefly, then looked away. "There are a few that remain loyal to me. But at times, even they are deceived because she has willed her Spirit form to appear like me."

"How did she get them to turn away from you? What could she have promised them to betray you?" Kilala asked while she thought of her own tribe. She knew of at least a few of her tribe that were likely under the Snake Queen's influence, the two untrustworthy medicine women. She questioned what the Snake Queen could have offered them to turn against their Spirit and their fellow tribesmen to follow her. Then she wondered if there were any more and how many there could be.

The old man appeared surprised by her question. "Why, corpses, of course," he said blithely.

Kilala felt herself pale while queasiness clenched her stomach into a hard knot. The Death Spirit noticed her reaction.

"No, no, my dear," he said in a consoling tone. He shifted to lean over the table a bit as he stared into her eyes. She automatically drew back from him. "Death is inevitable. All things die. We help tidy up the land. Unburied, rotting bodies disease Ritigabid."

As she stared back at him, the images of human-kind eating corpses had popped back into her mind. She felt nauseous and knew her complexion had turned green. "But the humans of the tribe…they…they…" She swallowed back the bile that was trying to come up.

The old man stared at her in surprise, then horror. "What do you think my humans do?" he demanded abruptly.

She gulped several times, then forced out the words. "Eat corpses?" she hoarsely whispered uncertainly.

The old man's jaw dropped open as his eyes widened in shock and disbelief. "What?!" he shouted abruptly. "What did you say?!"

Kilala was startled by his reaction. He had heard her and was honestly surprised at the question. She straightened up suddenly and leaned forward a bit. "Your humans don't eat corpses?" she asked curiously.

"By the Higher Power, no!!" he barked sharply between clenched teeth. "Is that what people think of us?"

Kilala couldn't meet his furious stare and had to look down at the table top as she answered, "That is what is said." She looked up at him and met his hard eyes straight on. "As you said, without information, disinformation is created." She saw his eyes soften slightly after he was reminded of his own words. She felt a sudden compassion toward the old man. "What do your humans eat? I know the animal-kind eat the corpses." She was careful to keep her tone curious and non-judgmental.

"The human-kind of my tribe eats only plant life and they bury the rare, unclaimed dead of human-kind. Animal-kind only eats the corpses of animal-kind," he answered as his hard, offended stance melted away. He slumped over as his brown eyes looked even sadder than before. "Our job has always been in the shadows," he muttered lowly. "Grief is such a personal thing to so many living beings that we don't intrude on that grief. But an unclaimed body of any kind is for us to take care of." He lapsed into a sudden silence as he stared into space.

For a few moments, she allowed him to drift in his own internal thoughts. Then she interrupted him to find out why he was in her haven. "So you are saying that the animal-kind of your tribe was persuaded by her because of promise of more corpses?" she asked loud enough to get his attention.

He instantly snapped out of his reverie and focused on her. "Yes. That is what I believe."

"To your knowledge, does she have influence over the animal-kind in other tribes?" she asked cautiously, hoping he would share the information.

He nodded to her. "Yes, she does. And some of the human-kind in them as well."

The deep dread that she had been feeling grew even more burdensome as what she had been told by Yumie was confirmed. "What is promised to them?"

"For animal-kind, prey. For human-kind, power."

She could understand the draw and temptation of the promise of power to human-kind. "Prey?" she asked wanting clarification.

"She has rounded up most of the prey in Ritigabid," the Spirit told her.

With this revelation, Kilala sat back in her chair, hard. "The other Spirits in the Council were reporting less prey in their territories."

"Yes," the bald head shook sadly. "She had snake-kind round up many of them. Then she had those she controlled in my tribe to help. She knew that since snake-kind ate so infrequently and my animal-kind rarely kills anything to eat, the prey they hoarded would be safe. Then she would use them as incentive for other animal-kind to rebel against their tribes, their Sentinels, and their Spirits as their hunger grew."

Kilala looked away as she put together all the pieces of information she had learned. The Snake Queen's plan was beginning to take shape. When she met the Death Spirit's sad, brown eyes again, she asked, "When did you realize that it was herself that she wanted to put into power?"

"I had suspicions soon after our alliance was agreed. But it wasn't until recently that I started to understand the full depth of her depravity and what she wanted to do with the Land and everyone in it." He shook his head again as his gaze dropped to the table top. When his looked up and locked eyes with hers, his eyes had changed. They had sharpened and burned intensely. "I was hopeless until I saw that she is afraid of you."

It wasn't just his words, but how he said them that had her frozen for a moment. She was amazed that the Spirit of the Death Hunters felt hopeless. Then she grasped what else he had said. Even though she had heard the same from the snake spies, the idea of the Snake Queen being afraid of her still mystified her. "Why is she afraid of me?" she finally asked.

"You are an unknown. You are not like any of the other Spirits that she has studied and dealt with for the past several centuries." The gaze softened as his thin lips curved upward in slight smile. "You display powers that she cannot understand. Because she cannot understand you, she has no idea how she can control you."

She considered his words and then nodded decisively as she responded, "I am glad to hear that!" She didn't let her thoughts dwell on what the Snake Queen thought about her; she had more important things to find out. She leaned slightly forward to ask, "Do you know which one of the other Spirits she has control over?"

The old man shook his head slightly. "I know there is one. But she has managed to keep it a secret."

Suddenly, she thought of Yumie. "You said that the little snake may not have left of his own accord." The old man nodded. "Where is he?

"Snake Queen sent her minions and captured him."

"How?!" she asked angrily. "They cannot get into my haven! And he knew better than to leave!"

The Spirit of the Death Hunters looked at the table as his apparition sagged dejectedly. After a few moments, he spoke. "Some of my tribe helped." He looked up at her, his eyes sad. "Remember, we can access any part of Ritigabid."

"So you had said," Kilala whispered as she looked away. She had to think. Her mind whirled with what she had been told. *No one is safe while she controls the Death Hunters,* she thought. *This situation must be dealt with quickly!*

When she looked over at the Spirit of the Death Hunters again, he was watching her intensely. "Are you willing to form an alliance with me and break the one with her?"

He straightened up, his face serious, as his eyes started to burn again with an inner fire. "That is why I am here. I wanted to see if you would accept whatever help I could offer so that the balance of the Land of Ritigabid could be restored."

"What help can you offer?" she asked as she wondered how much of his tribe was under the influence of the Snake Queen.

The old man shook his head slowly. "As much as I can," he said quietly. "I am hoping those of my tribe who are under her influence will open their eyes and see what she truly is."

"What do you think she truly is?" Kilala asked curiously.

"A monster," the Spirit of the Death Hunters stated firmly.

Kilala nodded. "With what I know, I tend to agree." She stood up from her chair while the visiting apparition rose to match her stance as he hovered in front of her. "How can I get the little snake back? He can be useful."

The old man looked a bit amused. "Trust a snake?"

"This one is a special snake," she countered but wouldn't tell him more. The Spirit seemed to be satisfied with the answer.

"They took him back to her haven," he said sadly. "Do you need me to get him?"

Kilala thought a moment, then said, "Thank you for the offer. But I know of another way."

The Spirit of the Death Hunters cocked his head curiously and stared at her. She could tell that he was intensely interested in how she was going to do it. When she offered no explanation, he shrugged and said, "Well, let me know if you need my help."

"I will," she said as she smiled at him. "How do I contact you to coordinate plans?"

"Just say our name," he said solemnly, then flew out of her haven.

She stood staring after him, focusing on the spot where he had gone through her wall. "So, it is true," she muttered darkly. "Saying their name does summon them." After she shook off the creepy feeling that bit of knowledge caused, she paced around as she finalized a plan to get Yumie back.

Chapter 37

Yumie was terrified. He had wrapped himself into the smallest ball he could as he faced his queen's wrath. He wished he could be braver and stand up to her. But her shouting at him, with venomous spit hitting the ground close around him, caused his instincts to take over. So now he looked like a ball of twine instead of a brave spy.

"Why can't you tell me how ssshe does it!" The huge, black snake yelled at him again, her sharp fanged-mouth wide open and very close to him.

He rolled a little more away from her, trying to gain some space. The king cobra standing behind him batted him with his head so that he rolled closer to the Snake Queen. This caused him to squeak a bit when he answered, "My queen." He gulped loudly, then continued, "I truly don't know!! Can't you asssk me another question? One that I might know the anssswer, ssso I can pleassse my queen?"

"No!" she shouted and spat back. "That. Isss. What. I. Want. To. Know!" Suddenly, she struck at him with bared, dripping fangs. With lightning-fast reflexes so he wouldn't be bitten, the cobra batted the little snake ball out of her reach.

"Why did you do that?" she screeched furiously at her Sentinel.

"My queen," he said respectfully as he dropped his head into a deep bow. "He may have other information that isss valuable."

The little snake could feel her blazing, lidless eyes focus on him as he continued to roll across the rough surface of the cave floor. He heard her snort in derision at the thought that he could know anything to help her.

"Well," she said snidely as she turned her back on them, "question him yourssself. Let me know if you didn't wassste your time!" As they watched, she pushed past bits of shattered furniture, slithering deeper into the cavern to a large depression carved out of the rock floor. Once there, she positioned her body so it rested in the concave area, making sure that when she laid her head on her coils, she wasn't facing them.

The cobra stifled a sigh as he slithered to where Yumie had loosened from a ball and sat coiled up. "Come with me," he said, disgust dripping from his words. He signaled for him to slither alongside as they both left the queen's cavern. When they entered the main tunnel, the cobra herded the little snake to take a sharp left to enter another cavern. Once they got to the center of the large space, the cobra turned to the little snake. "You ssstink like cat," he grumbled darkly.

The little, green reptile tightly coiled his body underneath himself, prepared to spring away at any sign of danger. As he barely lifted his head to watch the cobra, he decided to stay quiet until he could see what the larger snake would do.

As the cobra started to slowly slither around him in a tight circle, he looked amused as the smaller reptile swiveled his head so he could follow him. "Ssso, you don't know how the Cat Hunter Sssspirit disappearsss."

Yumie gave him a brief, quick nod.

"Okay." The cobra circled once more, then stopped to face the little snake. "What elssse can you tell me?"

Yumie cocked his head at the larger one. "What isss it that you want to know?"

As he thought, the cobra's tongue flicked in and out rapidly. "Anything you learned while you were with the Cat Huntersss," he stated as he tried to sound tough and official.

"They didn't tell me anything," Yumie said as he met the other snake's eyes steadily. He was starting to find his courage. "You do know that sssnake-kind is not trusssted amongssst the other Hunter tribesss, don't you?"

The cobra laughed at that. "We don't even trussst each other!" The thought seemed to amuse the larger snake even more as he continued his hissing laughter.

Yumie watched him quietly. He wasn't laughing. He was thinking hard about how he could possibly get information from one of the snakes closest to the queen. "That isss true," he cocked his head again to look thoughtful. Then he added, as if he had just had the thought, "I bet the Sssnake Queen trussstsss you! After all, you mussst trussst her. You are one of her mossst trusssted servants!" he exclaimed as he emphasized the word 'trust' every time he said it.

The cobra abruptly stopped laughing to stare at him with cold, hard eyes. He seemed to think about what the little snake had said. Soon he nodded his head agreeably. "Yesss, I am one of her most trusssted servantsss." He looked away. He seemed to be thinking of something that bothered him. "But ssshe doesssn't ssshare much with me."

"Oh!" Yumie exclaimed as he acted as surprised as he could. "I'm sssorry. I must be missstaken." He tried to arrange his expression to look sorry for the other snake. "I guesssss she confidesss in the anaconda." He looked away, seeming to study the floor of the cave. "I was just curiousss if some of the thingsss I heard by eavesssdropping on the Cat Huntersss were true."

The cobra was totally taken in. "What'sss that?! Maybe I do know sssomething that may confirm what you heard," he said eagerly as he slithered closer. He bent his head down so he could hear anything the little snake said.

"Well," Yumie started, acting as if remembering something that he shouldn't have heard. "There isss talk that the SSSnake Queen hasss many that sssupport her that are not of the Sssnake Huntersss tribe."

The cobra's head dipped a few times as he nodded. "Thisss isss true." As he responded, Yumie was surprised to see images of the human- and animal-kind who supported the Snake Queen run through the larger snake's thoughts as the Sentinel remembered when he had stood by his leader while she had met with members of other Hunter tribes.

"Oh, my! You have confirmed that her power doesss reach throughout Ritigabid!" Yumie exclaimed as he faked being excited by that prospect while trying to cover his elation over the valuable information he had just gotten.

The cobra drew back slightly to stare at the little snake in confusion. "How could they know thisss?"

"Really? You doubt that her power would not be feared by the other tribesss and they would sssusssspect there would be thossse in their ranksss who would be attracted to her?" Yumie added quickly as he tried to squelch the suspicion that had started to cloud the cobra's mind.

The larger snake pulled back a little more to look at him. His suspicions were now fed by other thoughts. "If you sssupported her, if you are happy about her great power, why did ssshe throw you out?"

Yumie dropped his head and shook it slightly. "I am afraid," he let his voice sound sorrowful and regretful, "that we had a misssunderstanding." *My memory is that ssshe tried to kill me, not sssimply throw me out!* he thought while he suppressed a shudder. He watched the bigger snake closely, glad that the cobra couldn't read his thoughts.

The cobra dropped his head closer to him again. The answer seemed to appease him. "I wasssn't there," he said after several moments. "But what you sssay could be true."

Yumie nodded at him, then waited. He scanned the larger snake's mind again. When he couldn't see anything of use, he realized that he needed to have the cobra think of certain things for him to see them in his thoughts. "Doesss her control include any Sssspiritsss?"

"Well," the cobra pulled back again. He eyed the little snake from a height as if to signal to him to stay in his lowly place. "That isss only for the onesss clossse to the queen to know!" He turned his back on the little snake as he started to leave the cavern. "I sssee you have no information for me. I will report to the queen that ssshe was correct and sssee what ssshe wantsss me to do with you."

Yumie wore an expression of consternation as he watched the cobra leave in case the other snake happened to look back at him. Inwardly, he was jubilant. As the cobra was thinking about the question about the Spirits, Yumie had picked up an image in his mind. He knew it was the true form of the Spirit that was in the Snake Queen's control, but he didn't know who it was. He didn't know all the Spirits or their true forms by sight, but once he saw them, he would be able to identify him.

As he sat waiting, he looked around the empty cavern. He saw that there was only one way out, but there was too much traffic in the main tunnel to be able to slip out unseen. As the wait extended, he became more and more nervous about his fate. He had useful knowledge to help save Ritigabid but didn't know how he could escape to use it. Increasingly fearful as time moved slowly forward, he slithered to the darkest corner of the cave and drew up into a small ball again. After frantically trying to think of any possible way to escape, when he knew there was none, he started to wonder if the All Power could hear the voice of a snake.

Chapter Thirty-eight

As they steadily approached the Snake Queen's haven, Kilala was still ecstatic that the unseen mode worked on somebody as large as a white tiger, especially since invisibility was essential for the rescue plan to work. As she glided alongside Nemr, her hand lightly touching his withers as he trotted over the desert sands of Snake Hunter territory, she also thought of why she had chosen only him. She knew that a rescue team that was too large would give them away, and she wasn't sure if she could make so many invisible. But she also knew that her Sentinel had received gifts of power from the Kuatrukai that she felt sure would help him in this dangerous mission.

As nervous as she was, she could still feel the tension in the white tiger's shoulders and neck as they reached their destination and entered into a large hole in the ground that opened into a wide, dark tunnel. Snakes were all around them but none of them reacted, which showed that they couldn't sense the pair of invaders at all.

When the tunnel led into a network of caverns, she had the big cat stop so she could look around. She couldn't leave Nemr so she could fly through the caves to find Yumie since leaving him would make him visible to the slithering horde around his paws. "Any ideas about how to find him?" she asked the white tiger.

He looked around, then shook his head. "I have never been in the Spirit of the Snake Hunters' haven. It looks like it is far more complicated than your haven. I wouldn't know the first place to look."

"It is much more extensive than my haven," she whispered as she wondered how they were going to find the little snake. She kept looking around, trying to see as much as she could with the little bit of light that was able to reach them from the tunnel entrance.

"Indeed," he growled as he shook his head. "I should've known snake-kind would make things more difficult." He turned his head to look up at her. "We don't even know that he is still alive."

She nodded to him. She had thought of that possibility but refused to let it keep her from trying. "But we have to find out one way or the other." Neither said a word as they both tried to think of a solution. Suddenly, she remembered something about Yumie's gift. "Can you contact him, like you would another Sentinel?"

"Why would you even think that would happen?" He looked up at her curiously.

"Remember the gift he got from the Kuatrukai?" The black-and-white-striped head nodded. "It is for communication. Communication of all kinds."

Nemr nodded again, but his eyes still registered disbelief. "Why don't you try? Since you are linked to all of cat-kind, wouldn't that mean you could connect with him?"

She smiled at him, then said, "Yes, that could be true. But I am still inexperienced with telepathy. I found out that I am more accurate with contacting who I want to when I can see them." She gestured around them with her free hand. "What if, with my penchant for mental shouting, it happens to reach them?" She pointed at the snakes slithering by them. "With your training and experience, you can focus the message to try to connect with him."

Nemr thought about it as he shook his head slightly. "I will try," he said quietly, "but I have my doubts."

As she waited to see what would happen, she heard an explosive, guttural, sibilant sound. She wasn't sure if it was an individual or a group or if it was a sound of misery or anger. She tensed up as she watched the snakes in the tunnel react immediately, writhing around them in frenzied activity. "Oh, this is not good," she muttered nervously. "What is going on?"

She snapped out of her thoughts when she felt an abrupt shudder move through Nemr. When he started to stride forward, she concentrated on staying alongside him to keep her hand on his withers. When she noticed that he was on a set course, she asked, "Are you in contact with him?"

"Yes," he answered. His ears pricked forward as he seemed to be listening to something.

When she saw that they were heading toward the origin of the noise, Kilala tensed more as her hearing sharpened. "Do you know what is going on?" she asked as his pace quickened urgently. He had to discard being careful about stepping on the snakes and simply pushed them aside with his large paws. Kilala looked behind them to see that the reptiles weren't hurt, but they did look very confused by what happened to them.

Abruptly, Nemr took a sharp left into a cavern. As Kilala took in what was there, she barely registered a king cobra and an anaconda flanking a sight that captured her full attention. Standing above them, nearly touching the cave ceiling, was a giant black snake that was coiled with the upper body upright and posed to strike at something in front of her. When they had moved around the large snakes, she could see Yumie coiled up but looking straight up at the huge black snake in defiance. He seemed to glow with a golden hue.

"Well," Nemr muttered as he stopped to take in the scene, "I'll be. He's a courageous little runt."

"He is," Kilala said with a smile, feeling proud of the little reptile. "I think he's found something to give him courage."

"Or someone," the white tiger added. She could see he was smiling, too.

"Well, let's go get him. As soon as you pick him up, he should go unseen as well."

Nemr, not wanting to test the reactions of the snakes to an unexpected event, such as their victim vanishing, moved to make sure he could run by Yumie, pick him up, and have a clear path to the exit. Kilala could feel his powerful muscles move fluidly underneath his thick, soft fur. She felt a building excitement as they circled the cavern, her Sentinel building up speed to run at the large snakes.

As they neared them, she could see the Snake Queen rise up higher. "Hurry, she's preparing to strike him," she shouted at Nemr.

"I see," he grunted, his mighty paws hitting the stone cavern floor even harder as he ramped up his speed.

Within seconds, he whipped past the large snakes, grabbed Yumie, and sped around the group as he headed for the exit. Kilala glanced behind them and saw that they had narrowly escaped the venom of the Snake Queen. Her head was down with mouth open, seeking for what was no longer there.

As they ran through the tunnels, they could hear the wrath of the Snake Queen as she screamed a horrible, screeching sound that threatened to freeze their blood and nerves in fear. The snake hordes were even more panicked than before as they rushed around the confined space of tunnels and caverns looking for an escape.

Nemr ran as fast as he could out of the Snake Queen's haven with Yumie in his mouth and Kilala flying alongside matching his speed to keep her hand on his shoulder. The sand flew from under his paws as he slalomed through the desert scrub heading for Cat Hunter territory, and Kilala knew she had been right to have him with her. He was moving faster than any big cat ever had.

Kilala looked around and saw that they were not alone in their escape. Hundreds of snakes of all kinds were also leaving the Snake Queen's haven very quickly. As the multitude of reptiles poured out into the desert, they fanned out in all directions.

Kilala kept looking over her shoulder to watch the action behind them. They were just entering their forestland, the boundary of their territory, when she saw the king cobra and the anaconda rush out of the tunnel. They were also running for their lives.

Turning to look forward as Nemr speed through the trees toward her haven, she breathed a deep sigh of relief. She looked down at the little green snake dangling from the white tiger's mouth. He was looking up at her with dark, lidless eyes. In them, she saw heartfelt gratitude. "Thank you, my cat lady and tiger friend," Yumie said quietly as he swayed back and forth with each stride of the big cat.

Kilala nodded at him. "We are glad you are okay," she said for both of them since Nemr couldn't reply. When she looked up, she was relieved to see her haven ahead.

Once they slipped through the protective boundary of haven and into her cave, they could see Teigra pacing the floor restlessly. When Kilala removed her hand from Nemr's shoulder, he and the little snake popped into view. "Oh, thank the Higher Power!" Teigra exclaimed in relief as she rushed to her mate. Nemr carefully placed Yumie on the table so she wouldn't accidently step on the reptile.

Chapter 39

As the two greeted each other, Kilala became seen and re-integrated with her physical self. Soon she was climbing out of her sleeping place to join them at the table. "Thank you, Nemr," she said as she bowed her head to the white tiger. "A very successful mission."

He bowed his head to her in response. "Yes, it was. I am glad the Greater Power was with us." Then he turned Yumie. "And I am glad you are well. Can you tell us anything from your time in the queen's haven?"

Kilala moved to sit on the chair as the little snake coiled up and raised his head to look at them. "I do have information that I feel can help," he said confidently.

"What did you tell them?" Nemr asked pointedly as he stared at the little snake with piercing blue eyes.

Yumie didn't look away from the big cat's intense scrutiny, nor did he move away. "I told them nothing." He looked to Kilala, then back at Nemr. "The gift imparted to me by the Kuatrukai enabled me to talk around their questionsss. At the same time, I was able to read their thoughtsss when I asked them questionsss. They had no idea I gained information from them even though they hadn't sssaid anything."

"What did you find out?" Kilala asked quickly.

"I saw the facesss of thossse within all the Hunter tribesss who sssupport her," he said as he looked from one to the other. "Sssspecifically, the onesss who had met with the Sssnake Queen in the presssence of her Sssentinelsss," he added quickly. "Alssso, I sssaw the face of the Ssspirit who isss working with her. But I do not know which Ssspirit it isss."

Kilala nodded as she thought. "So you saw the true form of the Spirit."

The little snake nodded to confirm. "I would need to sssee him in hisss physsssical form to identify him."

"This information will make revealing the traitors in our midst easier," she said happily as she sat back in her chair.

"Did you see any traitors in the Cat Hunter tribe?" Nemr growled his question to Yumie.

"Unfortunately, yesss. There are quite a few." The little snake nodded at him. When he saw the white tiger's and his mate's expressions of horror and betrayal, he added quickly, "It isss true in all the tribesss. Ssshe had done a good job of infiltrating the Hunter tribe sssysssstem. From the amount of sssupportersss, I am afraid ssshe isss poisssed to create an upheaval ssso great asss to crasssh the entire sssysssstem."

"I see," was all Kilala could say as her nameless fears became fact. As she felt a wave of helpless anxiety hit her, the words spoken to her about herself by the Spirit of the Bear Hunters, the Spirit of the Death Hunters, and her Sentinel swirled around in her mind. She felt the burden of responsibility weigh heavily on her shoulders. She was the one who was supposed to do something about this, that was a fact she knew in her heart, in her soul. Before the terror could completely envelope her and freeze her ability to act and think, she bowed her head and closed her eyes. "Higher Power," she whispered. Her words were softly spoken but intense, intent, and full of faith and trust. "Help me. Guide me." It was a simple, heartfelt prayer but she immediately felt an answer as the fear and weight of the situation was lifted from her.

Without warning, a vision, a clip from her dream, flashed before her mind's eye. She saw the three bright objects in her open hand. With a spark of discernment, she knew what they represented. They were tools, gifts, specifically for her to use during this crisis. They had been given to her directly from the Higher Power, undiminished by time like those imparted by the Kuatrukai. This ensured that she would be properly equipped. *Yes*, she thought as she smiled. With deliberate concentration, she closed her hand in the vision and accepted those additional tools from the Higher Power.

As those extra powers absorbed into her inner being, she had a general sense of things being added but wasn't sure what they were. After a few moments, she sat straight up and opened her eyes. She met the eyes of Yumie then Nemr and Teigra. She had a plan. She needed to start with the part that her Sentinels and her people must play. Looking back at the little snake, she asked. "Does your gift allow you to telepathically project the images you have seen of the traitors in our midst to the Sentinels?"

"I don't know," the little snake replied thoughtfully. "But sssince I haven't tried that yet, it may be posssssssible."

Kilala nodded at him then looked at her Sentinel. "See if you can receive those images." The black-and-white-striped head nodded at her as the bright blue eyes turned to look at the little snake.

Since each tribe had distinctive dress, jewelry, and other identifiable things, Kilala felt like the reptile should be able to filter out the images so that specific information could be given to each tribe. She got Yumie's attention. "Only project the images of those who appear to be part of the Cat Hunters tribe that are allied with the Snake Queen. If this works, we will try to contact the other tribes' Sentinels and let them know who in their tribes is helping her," she quickly instructed him.

Yumie nodded at her, then looked at Nemr. Kilala saw their locked gazes intensify, the determination to complete the task evident in their expressions of concentration. As she watched, she saw the white tiger's eyes widen in surprise, then narrow in rage. "I assume it worked?" she asked hopefully.

"Yes," he growled angrily. "It worked."

"Are any of the Cat Hunter Sentinels involved?" she asked quickly, dreading the answer.

The blue eyes of the white tiger met hers. "No, Companion," he said; his voice conveyed relief and thankfulness. "They are not."

She sighed deeply, then smiled. "I am glad and relieved to hear that."

"Me, as well," Teigra chimed in. "However, I am disturbed by those of human- and cat-kind that have given the Snake Queen their allegiance. Now what do we do with this information?"

Kilala glanced at her and then at her mate; she knew that he had shared what he had seen with her. "We need all the Sentinels to know who these traitors are. We need to contact the humans of our tribe that we can trust to help us rid our territory of these traitors."

"How are we to be rid of them?" Nemr asked quietly, his broad brow wrinkled in concern.

"Right now, I want them closely watched and, if possible, kept from any communications from the Snake Queen," Kilala said as she leaned forward. "Then, when we have coordinated a plan with the other tribes, we will move at the same time to entrap these traitors and imprison them. Once we have taken care of the Snake Queen, they will be put to trial and punished."

The white tiger and his mate nodded in agreement with her plan. "I understand," Nemr said as he bowed, then moved away to head for the cavern opening. "I will let the other Sentinels know who to locate. Once the traitors are found, we will place watches on all of them." Teigra bowed to Kilala. "I will inform the Shoku, and we will help our mates." Then she turned and followed Nemr out of the cave.

Kilala sat back in her chair as she turned her attention to the next part of the plan. Meeting the eyes of Yumie, she said, "I need to contact the Spirit of the Bear Hunters and then take you with us to see if we can find the tainted Spirit."

The little snake nodded, then asked, "How can we warn the Hunter tribe whossse Ssspirit isss tainted about the Sssnake Queen infiltratorsss? If he isss tainted, then hisss Sssentinels may be asss well."

Kilala instantly felt perplexed by that possible situation. After contemplating that scenario for a while, all she could do was shrug her shoulders and shake her head. "I have no idea. I hope that something will be revealed to us by the Higher Power when we need it." She was surprised when Yumie nodded in agreement. "I thought you didn't believe in the Higher Power?" she asked quickly.

The little, green reptile met her gaze steadily as he straightened his upper body up to stand taller. "When I wasss about to be killed in the Sssnake Queen'sss haven, I asssked the Higher Power to help me, and he did," he stated matter-of-factly.

She smiled at him broadly, happy that he had asked and had been helped. "And how did he do that?" she asked curiously. She had no doubt the Higher Power had helped him; she simply wondered how.

"Well," Yumie spoke quietly as he cocked his head thoughtfully, "he encouraged me to ssstand up to her, protected me againssst her telepathy, and he gave you the ability to ressscue me."

"I see," she said as she smiled and nodded. "I am glad you asked for his help."

"Me, too," the little snake said seriously. "I am convinced if I had not, I wouldn't be alive and able to help you now."

"Then I also thank the Higher Power for your safety," Kilala answered with heartfelt sincerity.

Yumie ducked his head at her in a slight bow. She could swear he seemed to be smiling. "What do we do now?" he asked.

"Let me translate and I will take you to the haven of the Bear Hunter Spirit. That way we can start our next phase of the plan."

"Okay!" the snake answered quickly.

Chapter Forty

She started to move toward her bed when she felt a prickling sensation. Someone had entered her haven. She turned around quickly to see Bemot pop into view. She was glad to know that the tweaks she had made to her security fence at least let her know when someone unseen came into her haven, even though it didn't keep them out.

His apparition bowed deeply to her. "I am sorry to invade like this, but I needed to know what was going on. Snake-kind is on the rampage. I don't know if it's an invasion, a wave of refugees, or what! There are all sorts of confusion going on in Ritigabid!"

Kilala thought of all the snakes running from their queen. Then she thought of the queen's plans and wondered if it could be a part of that. She shook her head in confusion. "I don't know what to tell you. But we were about to get you." She gestured to the snake on the table. Turning back, she walked over to it to sit down. The Bear Hunter Spirit glided to hover over it.

She gestured to Yumie again as she updated him with bullet points. "He was kidnapped by the Snake Queen. We just got back from rescuing him. He has information for us that is very useful. He has seen the images of the members of the Hunter tribes that are in allegiance with her. He has also seen the true form of the Spirit that is in alliance with her."

The shaggy head looked from her to the snake. "I see. You have been busy of late."

"And," she started as she decided to tell him the rest, "I had a chat with the Spirit of the Death Hunters." In the corner of her eyes, she saw Yumie startle into tense alertness at the news. As he started to look around the cave warily, Kilala was distracted by Bemot's reaction.

"A chat?!" The Spirit of the Bear Hunters jumped back in surprise at the news. He recovered quickly and glided forward to his previous position as he muttered, "You have been very busy." She could see he was looking at her with a new regard.

"He is not happy with what is going on," she said as she boiled down the conversation she had with the other Spirit. "And many of his tribe is following the Snake Queen."

"I see," the Bear Hunter Spirit looked pensive as he thought. "Do you think he could help us?"

"He wants to," she said quickly. "As much as he can."

Bemot looked her over again and smiled. "I knew there was something special about you. You even have the enemy wanting to help."

All Kilala could do was smile as she bowed her head a bit in embarrassment. After a few moments, she looked up and met his eyes. "We need to move quickly. Are any of your Sentinels with you?"

Bemot nodded. "Just outside your barrier. Why?"

"I'll let them in. Have them join us."

In a few minutes, the huge grizzly, Kuruk, came into the cave. He looked around suspiciously when he didn't see any of the Cat Hunter Sentinels. He looked at the two Spirits and the little snake. "What's going on?" he growled roughly.

"Do not worry, my friend," Bemot assured him. "These are unique times for us. We needed you here to accomplish a task."

"I am sorry my Sentinels are not here to greet you," Kilala said as she greeted the large bear. "They are currently on an important mission."

As Kuruk walked carefully across the carpeted floor, his large shaggy head nodded at her that he understood. After the bear reached them, he sat down on his haunches. "I am here," he said simply.

Kilala addressed the bear directly after Bemot nodded that she should fill him in. "The little snake has information about who amongst your tribe are under the Snake Queen's control." Kuruk switched his gaze from her to the snake. His dark eyes narrowed in suspicion at the reptile. "Don't worry," she added hastily. "What he tells you is the truth. He doesn't know any names but will telepathically send you images."

Kuruk looked at her in sudden surprise. "He can do that?" He glanced at Yumie, his Spirit, and then at her. He seemed very disturbed by the news. "Can all snake-kind do that?"

Kilala held up a hand to quiet the agitated bear. "No. Not all snake-kind can do that. He is special. He has received a gift from the Higher Power that enables him to help us in this way."

The bear's expression registered his greater surprise of this news as his muzzle dropped open. "You speak of the Higher Power!" He looked at Bemot. "Do Snake Hunters believe in the Higher Power?"

Bemot raised a hand and was about to answer when Yumie spoke up. "My friend, bear-kind." He bowed his head low to the bear. "My tribe doesss not ssspeak of a Higher Power in kindnessss. But I have come to believe in him."

"I know Cat Hunter Sentinels believe in the All Power," Kuruk said. "Does the rest of your tribe?" he asked quietly as he met Kilala's eyes.

"Not all. At least, not openly," Kilala said sadly. She dropped her gaze to the ground, ashamed that she had to admit this. "It is not taught to the children like cat-kind teach their young." She glanced back up at the bear to see his reaction. He seemed to accept her answer in stride.

Kuruk nodded once to her, then looked at Yumie. "Tell me what you need to share. I will see that the information spreads to all of the Bear Hunter tribe."

It wasn't but a few moments when the Sentinel stood up. "I have what I need, thank you, snake." He looked up at his Spirit. "I will start to attend to this. What do you want us to do once all the Sentinels know of these traitors?"

Bemot glanced at Kilala. They shared a look, then he answered, "Wait for my command. We need to coordinate our response with the other tribes."

"Yes, Bemot, I will await your command." Kuruk turned and lumbered out of the cave to head back to Bear Hunter territory.

"Now, what do we do?" Bemot asked Kilala. "Do you think the uproar happening right now is part of the Snake Queen's plans?"

"I am not sure," she answered as she reconsidered the possibilities of what was causing the tumult Bemot had reported earlier. "Whether or not it was her intent, she may use it to further her plans. In that case, we need to move quickly with our plans. We need to identify the traitorous Spirit."

Looking down at Yumie, she thought she might try to hold him and then translate, seeing if that would help her carry him so that she didn't have to call on her Sentinel again. She was reaching down to touch the snake when he called out, "Wait!"

"What?" she asked as her hand hovered over him.

"I know you trussst in the Ssspirit of the Bear Huntersss, and I have no reassson to doubt in him. But may we go to hisss haven and sssee hisss true form?" the little green snake asked quietly as he looked at Bemot and bowed.

Kilala began to protest, but Bemot raised a hand to stop her. "I understand. My only misgiving is that I do not look this young," he said quietly as he waved a hand over his translated form.

"I'm sorry, Bemot," Kilala said quickly. "I really hadn't planned to invade your haven."

"No, let's go. That can be our first stop." He looked sad at the prospect as he turned to leave her haven.

"Bemot, I am sorry," Kilala called out after him.

He hovered at the cave entrance and looked at her over his shoulder. "I hope that you don't hold what you see against me. Time has taken its toll, and it's a sad thing for a fair lady to see such an old man."

Kilala thought for a moment and answered him. "Don't worry. Your body may be worn, but your inner self is strong and virile. Isn't that all that matters?"

The Spirit of the Bear Hunters looked surprised. After a few moments of thought, a bright grin lit up his face.

"Thank you, Kilala, you made an old man happy today!" He turned again and then disappeared from sight.

Chapter 41

Kilala sat on the chair, then reached over to touch Yumie. After she translated, her hand sank into the snake's body as it did before. Despite the failure of that approach, she tried to scoop him up. Although she could lift him slightly from the surface of the table top, her hand slowly lifted through his body. She cringed, not only with the eerie sensation of her fingers passing through warm ooze, but also in sympathy when she saw the snake shudder violently when her hand passed through his body. When he gave her a pleading look for her not to do that again, she sighed. *Is there is no way to carry him while I am in the translated state?* she asked herself in frustration. Stubbornly, she kept trying to figure out some other way to do it.

Finally, she had to give up and could see no way around it; she had to contact Nemr. When she did, she was glad to find out that he was already done with the task of passing the information to the other Sentinels and to those of the Cat Hunter human-kind that could be trusted. He had assigned spies to watch the traitors and was on his way back. "We need to go on another trip," she said as he entered the cave. "Can Yumie ride on your back?"

"Of course," he said, then cocked his head as he looked from one to the other in confusion. "But why?"

"I need him to go with Bear Hunter Spirit and me to identify the traitorous Spirit."

"I see," Nemr replied as he sidled up to the table so that Yumie could slither onto his back. When the white tiger took a few steps, the snake started to slide off his thick pelt. "I really don't want to carry him in my mouth again," the big cat said quickly.

"I have an idea," Yumie offered, "if it isss okay with you." He slipped around Nemr's neck and then held his tail in his mouth. He looked like a green necklace. "Issth that okay?" he asked, his voice muffled by his tail.

The sensation of the scaly body lying around his neck caused the black-and-white-striped pelt to shudder slightly. It stopped before it caused the snake to lose his grip on his tail. "Yes," Nemr responded and started to trot out of the cavern.

Kilala called to them, "Wait for me! I need to touch you so we can be unseen!"

Flying quickly so she could glide near the Sentinel's shoulder, she lightly placed a hand on him as before. Switching to unseen mode, they all three disappeared.

Bemot was waiting outside his haven for them. "What took you all so long?" he asked curiously.

"I had problems with trying to carry the snake," Kilala said as way of explanation.

"So, you needed your Sentinel?" he asked as he nodded to the white tiger.

"Yes, it's how we rescued him from the Snake Queen's haven."

"That explains how you did that!" he exclaimed as he started to laugh and slapped a glowing silver knee. "I've been trying to figure out how you pulled that off!!" He continued to laugh as he led them into his haven.

It was much like Kilala had expected for the residence of a single male. There was a general air of disarray with clothes strewn everywhere. By the wall of the cave was a slightly elevated wooden frame in which a figure was swaddled in bear skins. Nemr took Yumie over to look at the person in repose. Kilala peeked over the bear skins to look at the aged face and smiled. She looked up at the translated form of the Bear Hunter Spirit and saw that he was looking anxious again as he watched her closely. "I don't know why you worried," she said to him. "You look distinguished. The silver hair is honorable."

"You are a sweet talker," Bemot said gruffly, hiding his relief at her reaction. Then he looked at the snake and growled in mock anger, "So, are you satisfied?"

Yumie let go of his tail to say, "It isss asss I thought. It isss not you I sssaw." He quickly grasped his tail again before he slipped off the white tiger's neck.

Bemot shook his head and looked at Kilala. "Now where?"

She looked at Yumie to ask him. "Which one should be the next one to view? Dog Hunter Spirit or Eagle Hunter Spirit?"

Nemr spoke up so the snake didn't have to let go of his tail again. "Either one. We have to visit both anyway. The one that is not the traitor, we need to warn him of who in their tribe are traitors."

Bemot and Kilala agreed with him. "Who is closer to here?"

Bemot answered, "Dog Hunter Territory. His haven is on the ground and easier to access. Eagle Hunter Haven is up in the mountains."

Kilala hovered in the Bear Hunter Spirit's cave, tapping her lips with a forefinger as she thought. "You know, we have two left. If Dog Hunter Spirit is not the one, then we know Eagle Hunter Spirit is. But how can we warn Eagle Hunter tribe of their traitorous Spirit?"

Bemot spoke up. "I feel we need to identify and verify who is what. Then once the Spirit who is not in league with the Snake Queen does what we are doing by identifying traitors within their tribe and coordinating with our tribes, we all will deal with the whole tribe of the Spirit who is influenced by the Snake Queen."

"But there will be innocents amongst the tribe of the traitor Spirit!" Kilala cried. "Shouldn't they be warned before their Spirit takes them into war?"

Bemot hovered near her to look straight in her eyes. "Do you think that the Spirit of another tribe can convince them their Spirit is a traitor?"

Kilala drew back as he made her look at the situation straight on. "No," she had to admit. "They wouldn't."

Bemot nodded at her in approval. "We will have to use any conflict as a way to reveal the truth."

"That's a hard way to learn," Kilala said softly. She hated for anyone to go through that to learn something that was the truth.

"But it is a way to learn," Bemot answered as he signaled that they needed to leave. "That is, if they are willing."

As Kilala followed him out of his haven with her hand still on the white tiger's withers, she thought about what he said. *And if they don't learn*, she thought, *then what?* She didn't want to think any more about that just yet. *I guess we'll cross that bridge when we come to it.*

With Nemr able to move quickly without needing rest, it didn't take them long to pass into Dog Hunter territory and arrive at their Spirit's haven. Being in unseen mode, they were able to go through his security fence and observe him. As it was, he was not in his translated state. He was playing with his Sentinels on a large flat plot of land outside his cave. As he tossed what looked like a bundle of rags, a group of wolves and large dogs chased after the bundle, then started to play tug of war with it.

Yumie glanced at the shirtless young man with dark hair and eyes and shook his head. He let go of his tail briefly to say, "No. It isss not him."

Kilala lingered a bit more watching the muscular male. She admired the way his muscles flexed as he threw out the bundle of rags whenever one of his Sentinels brought it back to him. She had never seen such a physique and was enthralled by him. She had to admit that his translated state looked like him, except he wore a shirt and cloak that hid his well-muscled form.

She felt eyes on her and looked around to see Bemot watching her with a bemused expression. "And now you see why he looks at you in such a way," he stated quietly.

She felt and saw the silver shine of her translated state start to turn pink. She quickly turned her back on the Dog Hunter Spirit. "How can you say that!" she blustered at Bemot. She was embarrassed that she had been caught and was so easily read by the other Spirit. "He hates me! Last time we all met, he was quite rude!"

Bemot shrugged shaggy shoulders and grinned. "Like you are to me right now!" he stated pointedly as he raised his bushy eyebrows at her.

Kilala pulled back, almost losing her touch on Nemr. "What are you implying?" she said in quieter voice.

"You are attracted to him," Bemot said reasonably. "And he to you. The gruffness and grouchiness are acts because you both cannot express your feelings."

He started to move toward the haven's fence. "In fact, sad to say, that's the way things need to be." He looked back at Kilala. "Our jobs are too important to be involved in a relationship."

Kilala glanced back at the Spirit of the Dog Hunters once more. She knew what Bemot had said was true. Before it hadn't bothered her, but now it did. Reluctantly, she turned away and followed Bemot out of the haven.

Outside the fence, Bemot turned to her. "We need to warn him of the traitors in his tribe." He studied her face intently, then added, "If I can borrow your Sentinel, I will send him in to ask for admittance." He stopped and then added, "I think I should go in. The tiger and snake won't need to be unseen while we're in there. I think since I'll have cat- and snake-kind with me, he'll be curious enough to hear me out."

Kilala was about to protest his plan because she wanted to see the Dog Hunter Spirit again and see how he would react to seeing her in his haven. Suddenly, her memories sparked a flashback, and the voice of the previous Cat Hunter Companion spoke to her, "Be aware of affairs of the heart." She closed her mouth and nodded mutely to him. She signaled Nemr and Yumie to go with him. "I will be waiting here. I will remain unseen," she said quietly.

Bemot smiled as he nodded to her. He became seen at the same time Kilala removed her hand from Nemr's shoulder. When all three popped into view at the same time, Kilala looked around the area, glad no one was around to witness it.

<u>Chapter Forty-two</u>

As she waited, Kilala still wished she had gone back into the haven to see the Dog Hunter Spirit again and gauge his reaction to seeing her. Then she thought about the warning from the previous Cat Hunter Spirit and Bemot's reaction. As she hovered around aimlessly, she shook her head in frustration as the full revelation and realization of the extent of her commitment to being a Spirit of a Hunter tribe sank in. Then she remembered that Bemot had pointed out that the Dog Spirit's reaction toward her was gruff because he couldn't admit his feelings because he, too, was bound by the same commitment. Shrugging her shoulders, she sighed heavily. "It is what it is," she whispered and then forced her thoughts onto something else.

Still in the unseen mode, she looked around at the area surrounding the Dog Spirit's haven. It was mostly flatlands with some scrub. So very different from the forestlands that took up most of her territory. She heard bird song and looked up to see a flock of birds flying overhead. Seeing them, she started to think about the Eagle Hunters.

With a heavy heart, she thought of how the Spirit of the Eagle Hunters had to be the Spirit that was under the Snake Queen's control. *How could that have happened?* she wondered as she tried to puzzle out how the Snake Queen could have gotten to him. *Is he a willing or unwilling accomplice to the reptile's plans?* she pondered further as her eyes followed several birds crisscrossing the skies.

Watching them, she thought of how all her life she had heard bird song and watched the majestic eagles and hawks fly effortlessly overhead as they commanded the blue expanse. Although they had land for them to perch, build nests, and hunt their own prey, their territory was primarily the skies. Birds were everywhere. Now she could see the danger of this tribe being under the Snake Queen's control.

They would be perfect spies. Eyes and ears for the Snake Queen! she thought in horror. Lifting a hand to her mouth, she continued to watch the skies. When she saw an eagle soar overhead, an image of a large bird swooping down to attack added to her consternation. *In battle, anyone against the Snake Queen would be in danger because of the eagles and hawks that would attack from the skies!*

The feeling of dread she had been carrying worsened even more, so much worse than she could have ever imagined. She wondered what they could do, what they could plan to combat this force. Her fretting revealed nothing of use. She couldn't think or even imagine how this could turn out in their favor. She could feel her thoughts darken and shied away from them. She shook her head to clear it and to try not to get stuck with the same thoughts that had no answers.

As she looked around at the surrounding grasslands and bushes, her eyes picked up bits of color here and there. As she made out what they were, she had to smile. They were flowers that were blooming. Even with all that was going on, the All Power still kept the trees in leaf, the grass growing, and the flowers blooming. Somehow, that thought made her feel better. It also reminded her that she needed to ask the Higher Power for what needed to be done.

Closing her eyes as she bowed her head, she prayed for guidance and wisdom. She asked for help to be able to remove the power the Snake Queen had over the Spirit of the Eagle Hunters. Again, in her mind's eye, she saw the three bright flashes in her hand from her dream. With that, she was reminded that she had all the tools to do what needed to be done. She may not ever know what they represented, but she needed to trust that the All Power would help her use whatever they were.

When Bemot, Nemr, and Yumie emerged from the Dog Hunter Spirit's haven, Kilala had a beginning of a plan put together.

"How did he take it?" Kilala asked as she glided down to touch the white tiger's shoulder to make him and the little snake unseen again. Bemot had activated his unseen mode as soon as he was clear of the security fence.

"It wasn't too hard to convince him of what we were telling him," Bemot said with a smile. "The very fact I showed up with cat-kind and snake-kind instead of my Sentinel alerted to him to the fact something very unusual and serious was going on."

"Is he putting a watch on those in his tribe that are under the Snake Queen's influence?"

Nemr nodded and said, "His Sentinel, the wolf, took the memories from the snake and was already contacting dog-kind with the message."

"Tahmores, the Spirit of the Dog Hunter tribe, is ready to help us," Bemot spoke next. "We just need to let him know what he and his tribe need to do and when to do it."

Tahmores, Kilala thought to herself, *what an interesting name.* She had heard Bemot say his name before, but now it had a greater significance to her since she could put a true face to the name. The image of him playing fetch with his Sentinels flashed in her mind again. Before she could shake it off, she caught Bemot watching her.

When the Spirit of the Bear Hunters saw her glance at him, he shook his shaggy head slowly. "It's always hard for the young," he said quietly. His voice was kind and understanding. "I remember those days," he said with a sigh.

"I'm sorry," Kilala whispered, thankful she hadn't blushed this time. "I try to keep my mind busy. The previous Companion did warn me about affairs of the heart."

"At least she was able to pass on that wisdom before she had to leave," Bemot said as he flashed a sadness-tinged smile. Suddenly, he clapped his hands and rubbed them together vigorously. "Now, what do we do next?"

She smiled at his enthusiasm, then gestured with an arm that they should leave Dog Hunter territory. As they traveled, she brought up the subject that the Spirit of the Eagle Hunters was the Spirit that was under the Snake Queen's control.

"Yeah," Bemot said. His face fell into a tragic expression. "I had thought of that once the little snake said it wasn't Tahmores. It's not good that she has control through him over the Eagle Hunter tribe," he said as he glanced up into the sky.

"I thought of that," she replied as she scanned the sky as well. She looked down at Bemot, then at Nemr. "Do you think we can do any good by trying to go to his haven?"

"Do you know where it is?" Bemot asked her pointedly as he met her eyes.

Kilala shook her head. She had no idea except in the mountains somewhere.

"It is up on the highest mountain peak," Nemr said. "It is inaccessible unless you have wings."

Kilala furrowed her brows in thought and then asked, "How does he get down from his haven in his physical form?"

Bemot answered this time, "He doesn't. When an Eagle Hunter Spirit is chosen, he is taken up to the peak by one of the largest eagles the All Power ever made. They are ten times larger than a man. And they would be the ones most feared if we came to a battle with them."

"Wow!" she said in amazement as she thought of how a life of total isolation, except for when he could leave in a translated state, could affect someone. "He must think he is above everyone."

"That's where his imperious attitude comes from," Bemot growled as he shook his head. "He's been a pain to deal with ever since I could remember."

"You would think that being a leader of a tribe that can see it all from above would grant him a greater understanding and knowledge of what is happening."

"Problem is," Bemot countered, "he chooses just to see everything at his level and forgets or belittles anything on the ground."

"I wonder how the Snake Queen got to him?" Kilala questioned out loud. She was still seeking details about what they had to come up against. "Do you think he's willingly under her power or not?"

Bemot shrugged shaggy shoulders in reply. "I don't know. I guess we can go ask."

Kilala flashed a quick smile at him. She had already been planning on doing that, or at least visiting the Eagle Spirit's haven. Since Bemot opened the door, she walked through. "I think that is a very good idea. Let's get to the border of Cat Hunter territory so Nemr can take Yumie back to my haven."

The Bear Hunter Spirit looked shocked for a moment. "Are you seriously considering going to his haven?"

She looked at him and shrugged her shoulders. "Why not? We can get to it and we can go in without his invitation. I want to see if there are any clues as to how we can get him to understand what is going on and see if we can change his position on things."

"Okay," Bemot said slowly and thoughtfully. "That would make sense. When do you think the Snake Queen will mobilize her forces?"

Kilala thought awhile and had to shake her head. "I do not know. But I do feel it will be very soon, and we need to do all we can to try to minimize the damage she could do."

Bemot nodded slowly. "Yes, I agree." He looked at her and asked, "Do you have a plan in mind?"

"I have pieces of one," she admitted. "But the more information we have can help strengthen it or poke holes in it."

"Okay. We'll head to Eagle Hunter territory next."

Chapter 43

In a rampaging rage, the Snake Queen forced her bulky serpentine body through the tunnels of her haven until she was outside. For several minutes, the sun's rays blinded her, something she had not seen with her natural eyes in decades. Once she was able to see, she scanned the desert outside her doorway for any movement. "Come back, you cowardsss!" she screamed as she hissed into the still desert air around her. "I command you all!!"

When she saw no one returning to her, she switched to using the powers as the Spirit of the Snake Hunters. Broadcasting her demand again, but this time telepathically, she reached out to all snake-kind. Again, she waited for a response. When things didn't happen quickly enough, she determined that someone had to be punished for her problems. Grunting with the effort, she pushed her massive body through the sand toward Cat Hunter territory.

When she hit the tree line marking the border between Snake Hunter and Cat Hunter territories, she used the power she acquired from the Death Hunters along with her telepathy to open Kilala's metaphysical protective barrier enough to allow herself in. As she crashed through brush and crushed small trees along with the less stout plant life, she didn't care how much noise she made as her thoughts were focused on her mission ahead.

As she crossed the rough terrain, she started to tire. It had been a long time since she had traveled any distance in her own physical body. But she couldn't use her translated form to exact the retaliation she wanted against the Spirit of the Cat Hunters. She spat out the extra venom that filled her mouth with the thought of what she planned.

Forcing her way forward despite her mounting discomfort and pain, she made her way to the mists that formed a barrier around Kilala's haven. There she was halted. She couldn't get around it, and she couldn't go through it. Frustrated, she began to slither back and forth in front of the barrier. As she paced, she hissed angrily, berating herself that in her haste to exact revenge she had forgotten that she hadn't been able to enter last time she had been there. Suddenly, she stopped pacing when she felt minute vibrations being telegraphed through the ground. She turned in the direction it was coming from to see a white tiger emerge from the forest.

She watched in satisfaction as the big cat stopped suddenly, surprised at seeing her. Then she saw that as he took in the situation, his eyes didn't widen in fear but stared at her hard and long. This upset her a bit; she expected some sign of fear. Before either she or the white tiger could say anything, a small voice spoke into the tense silence. "What are you doing here, mistresssss?"

The Snake Queen looked around in confusion. She knew that voice but couldn't see the little green snake. "Reveal yoursssself, you traitor!" she hissed back harshly. When she saw that the white tiger stayed where he was without cowering down or even looking frightened, it made her angrier. She felt she deserved more respect than that.

"That is a good question," the big cat growled lowly at her. "What are you doing here?"

"I have a right to be here!" she shouted at him. "I own all thessse territoriesss. I claim the whole of Ritigabid asss my domain. Everyone mussst look to me asss the Sssupreme ruler."

"Why is that?" the white tiger asked in a deeper growl as he crouched down and lowered his head. At the same time, he narrowed his blue eyes at her while his ears twitched around, then flattened against his head. Chusi could see that he was prepared to attack her.

"You dare to challenge me?!" the Snake Queen screamed as she coiled her massive body under her then elevated part of her front half to raise her head above the trees around them. "I can crusssh you." She leaned forward, her tongue flicking in and out faster. "You would make a tasssty sssnack!"

Suddenly, she felt the ground vibrate again. This time it was a low, constant rumble. She peered into the forest, knowing that it was caused by many footfalls. Slowly coming out of the bushes and forest undergrowth was a large group made up of human-, cat- and bear-kind. The humans carried hunting weapons, and the bears and cats were baring teeth and flexing claws.

Realizing what was happening, Chusi knew it was time to activate her endgame. Linking her mind to all her supporters, she gave the signal for them to rise up and fight. As she considered those gathered against her, she was determined to show her superiority. "You cannot harm me! I am the Ssspirit of the Sssnake Huntersss!" she screeched as she rose up even higher. She swiveled back and forth daring any of the humans or animals to try to attack her.

A rumble of protest rose from the people. When she heard several shouts at the same time, "That cannot be a Spirit. A human has to be a Spirit," she realized that her carefully concealed deception was out in the open. The shouts grew angrier as a mob of human-kind approached brandishing spears and arrows notched on bows. The Snake Queen simply stared down at them from her height and decided that she didn't care what they thought. She was more powerful than they were.

"You would fight me?!" she shouted in disbelief at the audacity of the little people. She started to pull back from them to wait until they got closer so she could strike. When she saw ripples through the crowd that was scattered throughout the forest, she watched carefully to see what was causing it. Whatever it was had distracted those that came against her. She was jubilant when she saw that it was her human- and snake-kind of the Snake Hunter tribe coming to her rescue.

Sudden sounds of battle could be heard throughout Cat, Bear, and Dog Hunter territories as those who supported the Snake Queen started to fight with their neighbors. As the battle intensified, she heard screeches high overhead and broke out in a piercing, sibilant laughter. Jubilant, she knew that all those little beings threatening her on the ground were in terrible trouble. The eagles were joining in the battle. She anticipated that the eagles and the other birds of prey would inflict injuries as they dove down from the sky, but the largest of the eagles would wreak the most horrible damage against her enemies. "Strike them down!" she called to her allies in the sky.

It quickly became apparent to the Snake Queen that the raptors couldn't deliver as much damage as she wanted since the fight was amongst trees and brush instead of open area like the desert of her home territory. "It ssstarted too sssoon," she grumbled as she blamed everyone else and didn't take to heart that it was her rash need for vengeance that produced this problem.

As the battle became louder and more involved, she couldn't tell who was winning and who was dying. She felt safe since those who were going to attack her had been distracted by their enemy slithering on the ground and those diving from the sky. But she wanted to know how close she was to victory and when she could finally take over the leadership of Ritigabid. Distracted by her efforts to view the fighting through the trees and low lying brush as she swerved from side to side, she visibly jumped when she heard a hollow whisper by her ear.

"I see you showed your true form." The Spirit of the Death Hunter spoke quietly with a slight echo to his words.

She whipped around to stare at the apparition with its skull head clothed in tatters of black shadow. "Ah, I sssee you've finally ssshowed up." She said haughtily. "Did your tribe join in the battle?"

The skull head gave a slight nod. "Those you direct are doing your bidding."

She liked the sound of that and didn't catch the subtleties of his carefully worded statement. "Ssso, you may ssstay with me and watch me win! That way you can declare me leader of Ritigabid when thisss isss done."

"We will see the outcome," the Spirit of the Death Hunters said matter-of-factly. "The battle is not yet won."

As the queen watched, she thought her minions were taking the upper hand, especially with the additional forces of the Death Hunter animal- and human-kind. She could smell blood, anger, and fear in the air, and it excited her. Suddenly, she was confused. *Where were the Spirits of the Cat Hunters and the Bear Hunters? Did they abandon their tribes?* She looked around for them but couldn't see nor sense them.

Suddenly, she heard the baying of dogs. She laughed in triumph as she thought the additions of her forces from the Dog Hunter tribes would bring a quick end to the fighting. Her euphoria was crushed when she saw that they were fighting on the side of the Cat and Bear Hunters. "What treachery isss thisss?!" she shouted to the heavens when she saw the tide of battle was turning against her.

"I would say the treachery has been done by you," said a haughty voice. She whipped her massive triangular head around and narrowed her slitted-pupil eyes. The apparition of the Eagle Hunter Spirit hovered nearby with Bear Hunter and Cat Hunter Spirits right behind him. "I couldn't believe what they were telling me," he said as he pointedly looked her up and down, taking in the huge, black serpent body. "Now I can't believe that I have been deceived for so long." He looked up to call to his Sentinels. They immediately stopped their attack and flew up to circle overhead.

With that, the battle started to taper off as everyone looked up from their fighting to see what had caused the change. During that time of confusion, the translated form of Spirit of the Dog Hunter tribe approached the group of hovering Spirits. "Did we make it in time?"

"Yes," Kilala smiled at him. "Your tribe has helped tremendously."

He simply smiled back at her and bowed his head. "I am glad."

"Was your tribe able to restrain the traitors in your midst?" Bemot asked him.

"Yes." He looked down at the ground. "Your warning gave us enough time to stop something that could've been even worse."

"Of that, I am glad," Bemot responded.

"Cut the back patting," the Snake Queen sneered at them. "I ssstill have the upper hand! Ssspirit of the Death Huntersss, you obey me! Kill all thossse who oppossse me!!"

Everyone on the ground close enough to hear her stood completely still in shock and fear. All eyes were on the Spirit of the Death Hunters. The Snake Queen threw back her head to laugh evilly in anticipation of the slaughter. The other Spirits hovered and watched. The silence, except for the huge snake laughing, stretched longer and longer. Suddenly, she stopped.

When nothing happened, she looked around in confusion. "Why are you not obeying me?!" she shouted at him as she moved to strike at him. He nimbly hovered away from her.

Suddenly, the apparition of the Death Hunter Spirit changed from a terror inducing horror to a bony-framed old man. His gentle brown eyes scanned the mass of human- and animal-kind that had gathered into the clearing and in the spaces between the trees so they could watch. With a kind voice pitched so that all present could hear, he said, "I do not kill needlessly. In fact, I do not kill. I simply help those who are deceased rest in peace. My human-kind buries any unattended humans so they can sleep in the depth of the earth. My animal-kind eats the dead animals so that the land will not be sickened." Then he turned his eyes to the Snake Queen. "I am not here for those that are living. We will help with the recently deceased. But I am here to make sure you join them."

With those words, the Snake Queen gasped in horror as she twisted around trying to find an escape. When she realized she was trapped against the mist barrier, surrounded by hostile animal- and human-kind, she froze in panic-stricken terror. She had no escape and no allies that she could see. Her head whipped around when she heard the Spirit of the Eagle Hunters speak.

"You have lived far longer than you needed to. A new Spirit of the Snake Hunters needs to be chosen. And that will be a human." He shook his head in disgust and turned away. "I am deeply ashamed. Summon me when this is over. I will be in my haven," he said quietly to the other Spirits.

Chapter Forty-four

As Kilala watched the Eagle Spirit leave with his proud head bent and narrow shoulders slumped in defeat, her heart went out to him. When he was out of sight, Kilala turned back to study the Snake Queen, wondering who should enact punishment. She heard Bemot speaking to her and the other Spirits. "We cannot kill one of our own. Even though she is not of human-kind, we cannot be the ones to enact judgment. The All Power will choose those who must carry it out."

As they looked down at the even larger crowd of human- and animal-kind, Kilala saw a sudden shifting around of the individuals. Coming to the forefront were the humans of the Snake Hunter's tribe. A tall, dark-haired, slender man with a snakeskin cloak acted as spokesperson for the tribe.

"Are we to understand that this snake has been our Spirit?"

"Yes," Kilala answered as the other Spirits hesitated.

"For how long?" he asked as he narrowed his eyes at the black snake.

"From what I have found out, for centuries," Kilala answered quietly.

A shocked ripple went throughout the group of Snake Hunter humans. The man angrily turned back to face the Spirits after trying to calm his people. "What has happened to our maidens that were chosen to be the Spirit of the Snake Hunters?"

Kilala really didn't want to answer that since the thought had sickened her ever since she had found out what was going on. She was spared when another voice spoke up.

"Dear sirs and madams." The Death Hunter Spirit floated a bit forward to address them. "It is with a heavy heart that I have to inform you that those who you entrusted to be trained as your Spirit were eaten."

Human- and animal-kind of the other Hunter tribes that were in the clearing and throughout the forest stood in rigid, shocked disbelief as the Snake Hunters instantly erupted with howls of shock and grief that echoed painfully in the thick silence. The women sobbed hysterically as the enraged men raised shaking fists at the snake and all the Spirits. "Why did you not stop her!! Why did no one tell us!!' was shouted repeatedly.

Bemot glided forward. The silvery shine to his translated form was dull, his shoulders slumped, and his head bowed as huge dark grey tears flowed down his cheeks and beard. "Do not blame the younger Spirits," he said. "They have not been around long enough to know anything that went beyond their own territories. The snake deceived the Eagle Hunter Spirit and me." He stretched out open hands in their direction, silently asking for their forgiveness. "I swear to the All Power, I had no idea this was going on until recently!" He gestured to Kilala. "Once she discovered the truth, I helped her. I know this does not repay all the damage that was done in ignorance."

At first, the mob seemed appeased until one of the men started to shout at him and stirred them back up. The humans from the other Hunter tribes started to circle them to stand in defense of their Spirits. It looked as if another battle was going to start when a small voice cut through the noise.

Kilala saw her Sentinel, Nemr, with bloody wounds on his shoulders and flanks as he worked his way through the crowd of human- and animal-kind. Once he stood in front of the Snake Hunter humans, he turned so they could see who he carried. She saw the little green snake move from around his neck to slither onto the black-and-white-striped back. There he carefully balanced himself to coil his body underneath him.

"My people," he said gently but with command. Kilala watched in amazement as the Snake Hunter humans quieted down and listened to him. "You are aware we take pride in our reputation for being deceitful." She saw how they nodded their heads in agreement. "Well," he cocked his head to look each one in the eye as he continued, "unfortunately, we had one of snake-kind that pulled off the greatessst deception of all. Ssshe ate the first Ssspirit of the Sssnake Huntersss and wasss able to sssomehow absssorb her power thusss ssstarting thessse many, many yearsss of sssubterfuge and deceit." He rose a bit higher as he balanced on the white tiger's shoulders. "How can we fault the Sssspiritsss of the other Hunter tribesss for not sssseeing sssomething we oursssselves like to boassst of?"

Kilala watched them closely to see their reaction. Although the little snake was able to quench the angry reaction, she hoped that they didn't start to admire the huge snake and keep her in some capacity as a leader.

The Snake Hunter tribesmen and women gathered together to confer amongst themselves. As the minutes flowed by, Kilala glanced at the other Spirits and at the big, black snake she knew as Chusi. As they waited, she had to ask a question.

"Was your name really Chusi?" she asked the big snake. The green, slit pupil eyes turned to stare at her, the tongue flicking in and out restlessly.

"No," she said after a few moments. "I took that name asss a memorial to the first Ssspirit of the Sssnake Hunterss."

"Why as a memorial?" Kilala asked in confusion. "You killed her."

The snake looked away, then swung back toward her. "It wasss an accident," she said quietly. "I wasss one of her attendantsss in her haven. Ssshe stepped on my tail in the dark one night. I reacted and bit her before I realizzzed what wasss happening."

Feeling even more confused, Kilala stared at her in dismay. "So what happened after that to bring us to this point?"

"Her power ssshrouded her corpssse, and I sssaw a chance to be more than reptile-kind." The big snake made a movement that looked like a careless shrug. "So I ate her and wasss able to absssorb the power."

Kilala shook her head slowly as she moved away. She knew the rest of the story and didn't need to hear the snake repeat how she lived an excessively long life and kept her power. She looked down at the people when there was a sudden silence to their deliberation. The spokesman came forward to address the Spirits.

"We have decided that she must die. Not for her deceit but because she has killed humans, our daughters, over and over again throughout the centuries. That will not be tolerated and will end."

Kilala moved away quickly as the Snake Queen began to writhe in terror at the pronouncement. When the huge reptile opened her mouth, preparing to fight for her life, it was wrapped tightly shut by the little green snake. Chusi reacted by violently shaking her head and scrubbing her face on the ground as she tried to dislodge him. With her distracted and vulnerable, several humans of the Snake Hunter tribe rushed forward to stab her over and over with their spears. When she kept writhing, they worked as one to impale her to the ground and left the spears in place.

When the huge snake thrashed violently as she tried to pull free from the spears, the three Spirits commanded their animal- and human-kind to move away to prevent them from getting hurt.

As the danger grew for the Snake Hunter humans, snake-kind came slithering out of the forest undergrowth where they had been waiting and watching to see what was going to happen. They were moving in to help their human-kind. They had also seen their chance to get rid of the leader who had commanded them unfairly and uncertainly for so long. With several strikes from the most venomous snakes, the Snake Queen laughed despite being muzzled.

Kilala watched in amazement as she saw that even after all the wounds and venom, the Snake Queen did not die. As she tried to figure out why, she heard a harsh whisper by her ear. "She has made herself tolerant to all snake venoms over the years. She knew there would be a time they would turn against her." She turned to glance at the Spirit of the Death Hunters and nodded her thanks for the solution to that mystery.

Suddenly, a huge, dark shape overshadowed them. Kilala looked up to see the largest eagle she had ever seen swoop down with huge talons extended. Each stroke of his mighty wings created swirling dirt-laden winds that drove all human- and animal-kind even farther away. When everyone was clear, he forcefully dug cruel, clawed toes into the huge serpent's flesh. With powerful upward strokes, he jerked her free of the spears, causing the ground underneath her to become quickly soaked with her blood as it gushed freely from her wounds. Despite her severe injuries and blood loss, the Snake Queen continued to writhe and strike at the eagle even though she was still muzzled by the little snake. The eagle ignored her struggles as he effortlessly lifted away from the ground to carry her high into the sky.

The mob broke up as they followed the eagle as he flew toward Snake Hunter territory. Everyone wanted to witness whatever was going to happen next. The Spirits followed and saw that as soon as the eagle was over the desert lands of the Snake Hunter territory, he climbed higher into the sky. When he leveled out, he simply released the snake.

Her elongated body whipped around powerlessly as she fell, and she screamed profanities at the eagle, all the Spirits, and her tribe. When she hit the ground with a wet thud, she was silenced forever. The Spirits flew down to check on her. After they all confirmed that she was dead, Kilala looked around for Yumie. She feared what had happened to him. As she started to look around the head of the body for any sign of him, the huge eagle landed near her.

Surprised, she looked up into the massive face of the eagle, with its yellow piercing eyes and cruelly hooked beak. Then she saw that on the back of the eagle, who was ten times the size of a man, rode an elderly man with piercing green eyes, nose like a hooked beak, and thin face. He was dressed in a robe made of feathers. She recognized the Spirit of the Eagle Hunters in his physical form.

"Oh, hello!" she greeted him. "I didn't see you on the eagle."

The man laughed a bit then said, "He's a big one." He patted the feathered shoulders of the huge bird.

"I thought Spirits couldn't kill another Spirit?" she asked mystified by what happened.

"Oh, I didn't kill her," he said simply as his eyes shone with hidden amusement.

"Well, you commanded the eagle to," she pointed out to him as she hovered near him.

"Oh, he didn't kill her either."

Kilala looked from him to the eagle then back again. "I don't understand."

"My dear," he said as he opened up one of his hands. The eagle reached back to gently remove something he held and then placed it on the ground. "Chusi had always told me that she wanted to achieve great heights. I gave her that gift. It was gravity that killed her."

"Oh," she uttered in shocked amazement at the logic. As she cocked her head to look at him sidelong, she added, "That is a very fine line."

"You're welcome," he said as the eagle spread his wings, readying for flight. "I hope that starts my road to salvation after all the years she had deceived me."

Kilala smiled, then waved as the eagle lifted off. When she looked down at the ground, curious as to what the eagle had placed there, she smiled more widely and waved more exuberantly as she shouted, "Thank you!"

The eagle banked as he turned so she could see the rider wave at her in reply. Then they flew quickly out of sight.

"I am glad to see you are okay," she said to the little green snake that was coiled on the ground under her hovering figure.

"Me, too," said Nemr, panting slightly. He had run as fast as he could to reach them. Kilala smiled at him in greeting and then looked beyond him as a huge mob of human- and animal-kind was coming behind him.

As she turned her attention back to the little snake, she asked, "What are your plans now? You can return to your people."

Yumie looked up at her, at Nemr, then at the human- and snake-kind that had started to gather around the huge body of the dead black snake. "That isss true," he said softly. Then he seemed lost in thought. Kilala could see he was indecisive about what to do next.

Kilala looked away from him as she saw movement coming toward her. She saw a few of the queen's Sentinels, the king cobra and the anaconda, along with the spokesman for the tribe approaching. She saw they had eyes on the little green snake and not her.

The human spoke first. "Little snake, you have helped our people." The large reptiles, coiled up on either side of him, nodded as they showed their agreement. "I understand the so-called Snake Queen banned you from our tribe." Yumie nodded at him. The spokesman continued. "I am here to welcome you back. You are a reptile small in size but stout of heart. I have also heard that you are gifted and can help our tribe recover from this disaster."

"I can do what I can to help," Yumie replied. He thought for a while, then continued, "You will need to choossse your Ssspirit of the Sssnake Huntersss very sssoon."

"There was already a choosing. A maiden was to go to the Spirit of the Snake Hunter's haven in a few days." He stopped as he wiped a shaking hand over his face and took a deep, shuddering breath. "Thankfully, the treachery was revealed before that happened. But who will mentor her?" the spokesman asked quickly. "How can we go from here as a Hunter tribe with a Spirit to lead?"

Kilala felt the other Spirits glide over to hover beside her as they listened to what was going on. They all knew for the balance of Ritigabid to return, the Snake Hunters must stay intact and have a Spirit as their leader.

Kilala had a sudden thought. "Yumie, what happened to her power when she died? Was it lost?"

He turned to directly look at her. As she locked eyes with him, she could see a slight glow in the dark, lidless eyes. "No, my cat lady. The Higher Power sssaw fit to bessstow it upon me until it could be transferred back to the rightful Ssspirit of the Sssnake Huntersss."

Everyone surrounding them reacted in amazement, disbelief, and concern. As Kilala looked over the crowd, she wasn't sure if they were reacting to the fact that a snake mentioned the Higher Power or if it was the fact that another reptile had the powers of a Spirit. The Snake Hunter spokesman held up his hand for silence. "You will be willing to relinquish this power? This is of truth and not deception?"

Yumie elevated the front of his body as much as he could to look at him and the other Snake Hunters. "I am but a little sssnake. I have no poissson. I have no desssire to be more than I ssshould be. Arrange the ceremony with your chosssen maiden and I sssswear to you that the power will be transssferred."

Before anything more could be said, a sudden rumble was felt under everyone's feet. As they looked at the desert horizon, a huge sand cloud could be seen coming their way.

"That can't be a sandstorm," the spokesman said as he looked at his tribe mates. They all shook their head in bewilderment. As the cloud came closer, they could see that it was created by the many paws of all kinds of prey animals that were running wildly toward the forest.

"What is going on?" the spokesman asked in bewilderment.

The anaconda spoke up. "I sent someone to release the prey that the Snake Queen had ordered to be trapped and held from all the Hunter territories."

The spokesman looked at him and then at his tribesmen in horror. "Did anyone know of this?" he demanded from them. They all shook their heads. Kilala could see they honestly knew nothing about this.

The dark-headed man turned to the hovering Spirits and bowed his head in shame. "I apologize on behalf of my tribe for this indiscretion. We had no idea this was going on."

Bemot answered, "It has been set right. All our territories will be satisfied as the lack will be no longer." He looked to the other Spirits to see if they agreed; Kilala nodded at him and saw that the Dog Hunter Spirit did as well.

The spokesman nodded, then smiled as he spread his hands to include everybody. "Let there be peace and rest in all the territories!"

"Agreed!" Bemot said, followed by Kilala and Tahmores.

"We will gather our tribe members now and go back to our homes," Tahmores added, his deep voice carrying over the large gathering of human- and animal-kind.

"Agreed," Bemot answered and started to move over the crowd, signaling his tribe to follow him. Tahmores did the same. Kilala was starting to follow their lead when Yumie spoke to her.

"Cat lady," he said as he looked straight up at her. "Thossse booksss you have in your haven." He stopped as he thought carefully about what he wanted to ask.

"Yes?" she answered as she moved to float closer to the ground.

"Isss there anything in thossse to help the new Ssspirit of the Sssnake Huntersss? I have the power but not all the knowledge to help her." The little snake looked at her earnestly through dark, lidless eyes.

"I believe there is information that can be useful," she said as she nodded her head. "When you are ready for it, let me know and I will send the books over."

"Thank you," he said with a nod. "And thank you all for helping free my tribe from a truly awful leader," he added as he looked to Kilala and Nemr. "Pleassse passss that on to the other Ssspiritsss and their tribesss."

Kilala smiled at him and then had the sudden thought of how Nemr was able to contact Yumie before they rescued him and how he was able to read her mind. "Does your gift extend to being able to contact anyone you want telepathically?"

"I don't know." The little green snake shook his head thoughtfully. "Essspecially at long distancesss." He looked around and then turned back to her to meet her eyes. "I don't think that it would be good to sssuggest that I may be able to do that. Or the other thingsss," he whispered so that only she could hear.

Kilala nodded. She could see what Yumie was saying in a cryptic fashion. She knew that such knowledge could cause great fear and concern considering what they had uncovered and resolved. She wondered about the full extent of his gift and keeping it hidden and for how long, but then she thought of the ability she had discovered to be unseen and have no boundaries. She knew she wouldn't abuse that ability. As she studied the little green snake, she truly felt that he wouldn't abuse his. She smiled and nodded again. "I must get my tribe back to our territory," she said as she moved off. "Goodbye for now. I hope we can stay in touch."

"Of courssse, my cat lady," she heard him say as she signaled to her tribe members to follow her back into their forest lands.

<u>*Epilogue*</u>

Back in her haven, she reintegrated with her body and slipped out of her sleeping area. She didn't bother to spend time stretching out the usual stiffness she experienced after each translation but started to gather herbs and other ingredients to treat her Sentinels' battle injuries. It wasn't long before they started to file into her cave with their various wounds. When they were all present, she was glad to see that she hadn't lost any of them, but there were a few that were badly damaged and would need a longer time to heal. She thanked the All Power that none of them had been poisoned by snake venom. As she worked, she wondered how the rest of her tribe had fared.

Once she felt she had done all she could, she asked Teigra to escort her home. She wanted to visit her grandmother and make sure all who were at the battle from her village were well. She would make sure to check on the rest of the tribe in the next few days. The white tigress agreed to take her when she saw her mate was well out of danger. Kilala grabbed her hooded cloak and traveled through the Kuatrukai with her hand on the big cat's black and white neck.

When she arrived at the medicine woman's hut, she stepped inside the doorway to see that her grandmother was busy making much the same concoctions she had just made. *Why did I not think to make extra to bring with me?* she berated herself. *It would have decreased grandmother's work load.* When she looked around, she saw that there was a young girl helping her. She smiled, glad that her grandmother already had a new apprentice. Before she took another step into the room, she asked quietly, "May I help?"

Both the old woman and the young girl jumped and turned quickly. Kilala pulled back the hood from her face, her fair hair with the dark stripe showing past the border of the head covering. She saw the little girl's eyes widen with recognition as the bowl in her hands dropped to the floor. When Mamm saw her, she paid no heed to the mess made by her apprentice. She flew to Kilala to hug her, her face bright with joyful surprise.

"Oh, my dear, my dear!" she said as she held onto Kilala. "I am so glad you are well!" She released her hug to stand back and hold her by the shoulders as she looked her over. "I feared for you when I found out what was going on!"

"Oh, I was safe," Kilala said as she smiled. "The Sentinels were there to protect me."

Mamm shook her head slightly, then whispered, "No, not the battle. Your father was there." She smiled widely as she continued. "He was so proud to see you as the Spirit of our tribe! He said that you were so lovely and powerful!"

Kilala smiled shyly but was confused by what Mamm had meant by her earlier statement. "What else do you know about what was going on?" she asked quietly.

"About you being in danger from the Snake Queen, how she tried to control you," Mamm whispered to her.

"How did you know all that was happening?" Kilala asked in a whisper. She was mystified how that information got to her. *No one else but the Sentinels should know of that,* she thought.

Mamm gestured behind her. "She kept me informed."

Kilala turned toward the doorway to see that Teigra had been watching them; her large black-and-white-striped head was just inside the hut. With a tiny squeak of fear, the little girl ran to a far corner of the hut. Mamm turned toward her apprentice. "There is nothing to be afraid of," she said as she approached her and then hugged her tightly.

Kilala turned from the pair to regard the white tigress. "So, you've been the source of information."

Teigra nodded, her blue eyes meeting Kilala's without wavering. "Anong and I shared the duty. Your grandmother is held in high esteem amongst cat-kind. It was a courtesy to tell her as you are her blood kin."

Kilala smiled as she stepped toward her to pet her head and rub her ears. "Well, at least I don't have to explain everything to her."

Teigra gave her a slight bow. "Call me when you are ready to go home." Then she pulled her head out of the doorway.

As soon as the white tigress was gone, a line of wounded human- and cat-kind came into the hut for remedies for their injuries. After she took off her cloak and slung it on the back of one of the chairs, Kilala helped her grandmother and her young apprentice take care of them. Her attentions surprised the wounded villagers that had watched her grow up and knew who she was now. Kilala smiled at them as she carefully tended them, willing to forgive those who had treated her badly before.

As the steady stream slowed to a trickle and then stopped, Kilala was thankful that most of the wounds had not been very serious, although she was saddened to discover that a few from her village had died. With no more patients, she started to tidy up the small hut, putting the many medicinal items back in their place.

"Thank you for your help," her grandmother said wearily as she started to brew some tea.

"It is my pleasure," Kilala said as she finished with her task. When she turned back around, her grandmother had already sat her exhausted apprentice at the table. Before she moved to join her, she politely asked the little girl, "May I sit down?"

The girl stared at her with wide, frightened eyes, then mutely nodded. Kilala smiled at her warmly, wondering why the apprentice still seemed frightened of her after hours of working together. When she sat down, she couldn't help but heave a deep sigh. The long day had wearied her to the bone.

Her grandmother placed a cup of tea in front of her and the girl. After she had sat down in a nearby chair, the old woman reached over to hold her hand resting on the table. Kilala gave her a tired smile as she squeezed her hand gently. "I am glad you are here," the older woman said quietly, smiling at her and then leaning back to sip her tea.

"I am glad I could help," Kilala replied quietly with a nod. As she sat quietly and sipped hot tea in the presence of the person who knew her best, the events of the last several days started to crash down on her. All the maybes and what-ifs of what could've happened at any turn and the thoughts of whether she could have done anything differently swirled in her mind and thoughts.

"Mamm," she started when they all had finished their tea, "I am so tired."

Her grandmother patted her hand, then looked at her apprentice. "Little one, we need more supplies from the forest. You know which plants to pick." She handed her a basket, then shooed her out the door.

She turned to look at Kilala. "She will pick all sorts of things we don't need, but it will be practice for her."

Kilala laughed at a memory from her childhood. The laughter and the pleasant memory felt good, causing the weight to lift a bit. "Yes, I remember I did that a few times. But you wouldn't admonish me. You would simply go through every plant and tell me what it was and whether it could be used for anything. Quite a learning experience."

Her grandmother refilled their cups with the fragrant tea and took a sip, then leaned back in her chair. "Everything is a learning experience, my dear," she said, her eyes shining from a wealth of experience and wisdom. "And it never stops," she added, then took another sip.

Kilala took a couple of sips from her cup, then held it as the warmth seeped into her hands, creating another kind of comfort in addition to the effects of the calming tea.

She knew her grandmother was watching her closely, reading her body language, as she always did when she was young. She had no words to relate. Her grandmother knew what had happened, and she didn't have the energy to add anything else. As tears started to flow down her face, she felt, she felt her grandmother's hand rest on her shoulder. She looked up and saw the older woman smile at her, pride and love shining in her eyes.

"You did well, my dear," she said quietly. "Do not spend time second-guessing things. That is a waste of time. Be thankful to the Higher Power that there has been victory for what is right."

Kilala felt the turmoil lift as she thought of her grandmother's words. "Yes," she nodded thoughtfully. "You are correct. Good has been victorious. Lies have been revealed, and the truth has overpowered them." *But I still have doubts about what lies ahead,* she thought.

She felt unfair to her friends as she thought of Bemot knowing the ability of the unseen state and Yumie and his gift of unknown power. As she considered the hidden abilities and gifts, she knew that they were given for the good of all, but she could also see how they could be used for evil. She looked into her cup of tea as she wondered if those who had them would eventually succumb to that evil. Then she considered that they could certainly remain true to the good intentions in using those gifts, but what of anyone they passed them on to or shared about their existence?

As the calming effects of the tea relaxed her, her mind settled on concrete facts. She knew she couldn't worry about what might happen, but she could assure that she would guard those secrets, even from her grandmother. Then she pondered the gift she received from the Kuatrukai and the three powers from her vision. *I wonder what they were and how they helped.* Then she felt it was wrong to analyze them. What was important was that they were given to her by the Higher Power to help her serve her people, not only for the crises now passed but also so that she could remain ever vigilant to work to keep the Land of Ritigabid in balance and the good victorious.

Suddenly, it registered that her grandmother had referred to a higher power. She placed the cup on the table and leaned forward. "Mamm, why did no one teach me of the Higher Power?"

Mamm smiled gently, and then her face fell into sad lines. "You were raised in a tribe that takes belief in a Higher Power very personally." She placed her cup carefully on the table, then dropped her hands into her lap. "Most everyone believes but doesn't want to impose their beliefs on others. We have found that in time, situations arise where the Higher Power reveals himself to each one. From there, that person walks with him in relationship, or they do not."

Kilala leaned back into the chair as she thought about what she learned. "But wouldn't it be easier for the young to be taught so they wouldn't have to go through something dire to find out about him? So they wouldn't have to learn the hard way?"

Mamm leaned back in her chair as she thought about what her granddaughter had said. She slowly sipped from her cup, then placed it back down on the table. Her gaze appeared distant, as if she looked through the walls to a faraway point. After several minutes, she focused on her granddaughter and nodded slightly. "A way for the young to hear of him so they can make their choice earlier than later in life." She nodded again. "That is a refreshing thought. The way things are now may not be the right way; it certainly is not perfect, but it is the way things are and have been for centuries."

Kilala listened to her grandmother carefully as she thought about her words. "Mamm, do you think that I could start to teach the young about the Higher Power?"

At first, Mamm frowned, but then her expression cleared into thoughtfulness. "There will be resistance from the elder ones. This kind of teaching in public may be construed as an invasion of privacy," she warned cautiously.

Kilala could see what her grandmother was worried about. Changing of old ways would be looked at with suspicion, even with it being for the good. She toyed with her cup of tea, watching how the movement caused the brown liquid to swirl slightly. "There is evil in this life," she started. She looked up to see her grandmother nod in agreement as she watched her. "We had several of our tribe that had been deceived by the Snake Queen." Again, the grey-haired head nodded. "If the next generation could be warned of that evil and given a way to resist it by knowledge of a higher power that is for good, couldn't that help keep what has just happened from happening again?"

The old medicine woman looked away for a moment to think about what Kilala had said. When she looked back to meet her eyes, Kilala saw a warning in her eyes. "This may be the time for this to begin," she said slowly, nodding thoughtfully. "But be cautious as you go about it. Make sure that you walk the path the Higher Power gives you. If you do it with a pure heart, it will find success. If you do this for your own reasons, it will end in disaster." She lifted the kettle and refilled her granddaughter's cup.

Kilala took her grandmother's wise words to heart as she met her gaze. "I understand." Then she took a deep breath and closed her eyes. After quieting her thoughts, she sensed that the deep dread she had felt since she became Spirit of the Cat Hunters had lifted but now was replaced by a sense of watchful warning.

Kilala thought about it after she opened her eyes and sipped her refreshed cup of tea. The books that the first Companion had written sprang into her thoughts. She had been reading a few of the volumes in order but had skimmed through all of them when she was searching for information about the Death Hunter tribe. She was surprised to find that much of what she had read remained in her memory. As she scanned back through what she remembered, she realized that along with recording the timeline of the formation of the Hunter tribes and the clues about someone who wanted to take control of the Land, there was a sense of something new that was to happen.

Kilala leaned forward as the contents of the white volume came to mind. She hadn't thought about it at the time she had flipped through it, but it was the only volume that hadn't been completed and it was also the only one that included something about a higher power. Words that were written popped in her thoughts.

She looked up and met her grandmother's questioning gaze. "Mamm, the very first Spirit of the Cat Hunters left a series of books. In the last one, she had written, 'There is power beyond us that is a mystery. But it is one that has endowed the Spirits of the Hunter tribes with their powers. Why it is not talked about aloud, for everyone must know it exists, baffles me. There must be a time that the knowledge of this entity comes out of the shadows and becomes known to all. When this will happen is beyond my scope to see, but it must happen for the good of all,'" she recited word for word.

The medicine woman took a thoughtful sip of her tea. As she held her cup to take another sip, she nodded at Kilala. "Sounds like very wise words from the past." She took another sip then added, "Does she give any thoughts on how this should be done?"

Kilala shook her head. "Right after that, the rest of the volume is blank," she had to admit.

Her grandmother nodded her head thoughtfully, then met her granddaughter's eyes. "Sounds as if it is left to be interpreted by the one this task falls upon." She took a slow sip from her cup, and then asked, "How will you proceed?"

Kilala sat back in her chair as she thought of being responsible for the dynamics of teaching her tribe something as important as the Higher Power, the entity she had just met. *How will I proceed?* she asked herself. *It is a big responsibility. It must be done carefully with truth being at the forefront. But how will I know what is truth?* Suddenly, she felt fearful dismay descend on her as she dealt with yet another unknown.

Then she snapped out of it; she had learned who she needed to go to during these uncertain times. She reached out to the All Power and asked him about teaching the young about him. Within a heartbeat, she felt a sense of acceptance of her plan flowing through her like a warm spring breeze. With that, she understood that she could accomplish this task in a correct fashion if she remained in contact with him and didn't deviate from what he taught her.

She opened her eyes and leaned back in her chair, relieved that she had a direction to go. She met her grandmother's gaze and smiled at her.

"I see you have your answer," the older woman said quietly. She nodded at her granddaughter approvingly.

"Yes, grandmother," Kilala said quietly. "The All Power will guide me. For the knowledge of him brings wisdom and truth."

"Very good." The older woman smiled and nodded. "You have wisely sought the source, and with that, he will make sure you will succeed."

Kilala nodded back firmly. "It is time for the young to know of an entity that is mightier than I, the Spirit of the Cat Hunters."

BOOKS BY P. CLAUSS

Cloud Riders series
Cloud Riders: The Underlands Revealed
Cloud Riders 2: The Overlands Visited
Cloud Riders 3: Mysteries Revealed

Time Keepers Chronicles series
Time Stealers: Time Keeper's Chronicles
Time Stealers: Hope Eternal
Time Stealers: Royal Stain

Path of Totality
Path of Totality: Author's Cut

Cat Hunters

Morsels from the Father's Table series
Volume 1
Volume 2: Thoughts of Salvation
Volume 3: Fears Anxieties, and Worries
Volume 4: Walking the Walk
Volume 5: The Collection
ABC Bible Journey for Adults (volume 6)
Morsels from the Father's Table: Holiday Edition:
(volume 7)- Contemplations of Holidays and Days of
Celebration
Songs from a Believing Heart

Children's books
Just Kid's Stories/Or Are They?: A Collection
SnarlNsnort and HissNpoots: Defending the Kingdom
of Cats

AUTHOR BIO

P. Clauss, writer of published poetry, Christian devotionals, Children's books, and Sci-Fi/Fantasy novels, is the wife of a wonderful husband, the mother of two amazing children, a servant to several cats, and a small animal veterinarian. She lives in the Dallas, Texas, area, has a weekly Christian blog on Facebook page P. Clauss, webpage authorpclass.com, is on social media, and has many more stories to tell...

www.ingramcontent.com/pod-product-compliance
Lightning Source LLC
Chambersburg PA
CBHW071450140726
47997CB00005B/1668